1970

book m   kept

EDINBURGH UNIVERSITY PUBLICATIONS

Language and Literature 14

Saint-John Perse in 1954

ARTHUR KNODEL

SAINT-JOHN PERSE

a study of his Poetry

at the University Press
EDINBURGH

© Arthur Knodel 1966
EDINBURGH UNIVERSITY PRESS
George Square, Edinburgh 8
North America
Aldine Publishing Company
320 West Adams Street, Chicago
Africa Oxford University Press
Australia Hodder & Stoughton Ltd
India P. C. Manaktala & Sons
Far East M. Graham Brash & Son

*Printed in Great Britain by
Robert Cunningham and Sons Ltd, Alva*

Contents

Acknowledgments

The Edinburgh University Press is grateful to the following publishers for permission to quote copyright material: to Faber & Faber Ltd for quotations from the Preface to *Anabasis* by T. S. Eliot; to Doubleday & Co. for quotations from *Dialogues and a Diary* by Igor Stravinsky and Robert Craft; to Editions Gallimard for the French poetry quotations of Saint-John Perse from *Œuvre poétique* I & II and *Oiseaux*; and likewise for the passages, translated into English in our text, from: *Poétique de St-J. Perse* by Roger Caillois; the *Correspondance* of Claudel, Jammes, & Frizeau; *Sous la lampe* by Léon-Paul Fargue; the *Correspondance* of Jammes & Fontaine; *Œuvres complètes de Valery Larbaud*, tome xe; *Poésie* by Saint-John Perse, and *Situations II* by J.-P. Sartre. The Press is especially indebted to Monsieur and Madame Leger for permission to reproduce the frontispiece and the poet's handwriting.

St John Perse

... Poésie, heure des grands, route d'exil
et d'alliance, levain des peuples forts et
lever d'astres chez les humbles ; poésie,
grandeur vraie, puissance stérile chez les
hommes, et, de tous les pouvoirs, le seul
peut-être qui ne corrompe point le cœur
de l'homme face aux hommes.

Final words of the speech given by Saint-John Perse
at the Inauguration of the International Congress
Florence 20th April 1965, on the occasion of
the seventh centenary of Dante.

Introduction

This is a book about Saint-John Perse and not about Alexis Leger.
Since these names belong to one and the same person, such a distinction may seem meaningless – all the more so because there is
far more of the autobiography of Alexis Leger in the poetry of
Saint-John Perse than the casual reader suspects. One can go even
further and say that the distinction between public figure and
private poet is meaningless for any true poet, for no matter how
'impersonal' his idiom, he is everywhere present in his poetry.
Indeed, the poetry that is signed 'Saint-John Perse' undoubtedly
tells us more about the essential Alexis Leger – the Leger that lies
beyond the realm of vital statistics – than any biographical notice
ever will. Yet the distinction between the public figure and the
poet will be seen to be legitimate and useful.

A satisfactory account of the diplomat and statesman Alexis
Leger could be written with almost no mention of the poet, for
Leger took great pains to keep his literary pursuits completely
apart from his diplomatic career. That career began officially in
1914, when Leger successfully passed the competitive Foreign
Service examination. Prior to that date a considerable number of
his poems had appeared in print, but though they were signed
'Saintléger Léger', their author remained practically unknown to
all but a few very close friends. Leger's diplomatic career came to
a dramatic close in May, 1940. During the long 1914-1940 period,
only two major pieces by him were published: *Anabase* and *Amitié*

du Prince, neither of which was widely circulated. Both, moreover, were signed 'St-J. Perse' – later expanded to 'Saint-John Perse'. The identity of the user of this strange bi-national pseudonym was known to a number of people, but since Leger unceremoniously brushed aside queries about literary pursuits and never made a public acknowledgment of the authorship of *Anabase* and *Amitié du Prince*, the anonymity of Leger-Perse remained largely intact during the 'diplomatic' years.

This careful compartmentalization of activities was not the rule at the Quai d'Orsay, where such men as Claudel, Giraudoux, and Morand openly pursued busy literary careers while at the same time performing their diplomatic functions. Leger, however, felt that he could be far more effective as a civil servant if he were unhampered by the demands that a public literary life inevitably entails. But this did not mean that he disdained literary activity. If, as some sources affirm, he spoke slightingly of literature to his superiors at the Quai d'Orsay, that was simply a way of stifling further inquiry. A few very close friends knew all along that Leger had never lost his interest in the writings of others and in his own writing. One of his close friends, Valery Larbaud, as late as 1934, made the following sketchy but revealing note in a diary[1]:

> Leger's uncompromising attitude is not only justified by his work, but is also based on a sound philosophy. It has, thus, nothing in common with the attitude of so many nonentities or failures who simply prove by their attitude that they were 'fated to be failures'. . . . And besides, the critical doctrine that comes through in his remarks is coherent, based on a hierarchy of human values, passions, and virtues. . . . Agreed with me when I spoke to him of the damage caused by the need, among writers not completely dedicated to their calling, of leading a life not their own, of living for public opinion – with the result that they deform their whole output just to achieve that end.

Clearly, there was no question of a renunciation of literature, and we now know that Leger's intention was to wait until he had retired from public life and then publish such of his writings as he deemed worth printing. The decision to maintain a watertight partition between his diplomatic and literary activities was undoubtedly a wise one, since Leger was to rise to a position of greater responsibility than any of his fellow writer-diplomats. In

1933 he was appointed Secrétaire Général des Affaires Etrangères – a position second in importance only to the Ministre des Affaires Etrangères himself. Leger was to hold that position until he was forced out of it by Paul Reynaud in 1940. The ministerial system of the Third Republic was such that a change in government usually meant a change of cabinet, and consequently, of the Minister of Foreign Affairs. There were, in fact, eight different Ministers of Foreign Affairs from 1933 to 1940. The Secrétaire Général had the crucial and thankless job of maintaining the continuity of the French foreign policy in spite of the extremely unstable internal situation that the constant change of governments reflected. It is difficult to imagine how such a demanding, indeed well nigh impossible, task could have been performed at all, had the Secrétaire Général also been obliged to deal with the complications of literary life in that most mercurial of all literary capitals, Paris.

From one point of view, however, Leger's decision was tragically unfortunate, for, had he published his works soon after their composition, we should today be in possession of five long poems, a play, and a political testament – all of which have disappeared. The sole manuscripts of these seven items were bound in a single volume, and that volume was confiscated by the Gestapo, who ransacked Leger's apartment immediately upon the arrival of the Nazi forces in Paris in June of 1940. The volume is presumably destroyed – an irreparable loss to French letters.

The military collapse of France was already under way when Reynaud dismissed his Secretary General of Foreign Affairs; and less than a month later Paris had been occupied by the Nazis. In the general *sauve qui peut* that followed, Leger was able to reach England, and shortly thereafter, the United States. The very next year, 1941, he decided that any further pretence at literary anonymity was pointless, for he declared in the very last line of the poem *Exil*, which he wrote during that year: 'Et c'est l'heure, ô Poète, de décliner ton nom, ta naissance, et ta race...'.[a] And even though he has continued to publish under the pseudonym of Saint-John Perse, that is chiefly a literary concession, for the issue of the magazine *Poetry* in which *Exil* first appeared, also contained the first authorized biographical account of the statesman-poet, rather than just of the statesman.

[a] And the time has come, O Poet, to declare your name, your birth, and your race...

Thus, if we reserve the name Alexis Leger for the diplomat, it can now be readily seen why the present book is not about him, but about Saint-John Perse. The biography of Alexis Leger is still to be written. The man who undertakes to write it will have a difficult, but surely fascinating, time; for Leger was involved in almost every important international crisis in Europe of *entre-les-deux-guerres*. Such a biography would be of the utmost importance for the understanding of that period. But it should now be obvious why this future biographer will not have to give the poems of Saint-John Perse more than marginal consideration. The converse, however, is not true. The critic who wishes to present Saint-John Perse's poems in intelligible terms will frequently have to refer to biographical data, including events in the life of the statesman. This will have to be done even where a determined effort is made to keep the poetry to the fore, as in the present study.

The published poems of Saint-John Perse already fill two large volumes. The beauty, richness, and profundity of this body of poetry were officially recognized in 1960 when its author was awarded the Nobel Prize for Literature. But the long 'silence' of Saint-John Perse, combined with the strangeness of his poetic idiom, has kept his audience rather limited. The situation is changing. More and more studies of his work are appearing. Some of these are ill-advised and hasty, others simply pedantic and irrelevant, but some are very good. France especially is at long last making up for its neglect of one of its great poets; an increasing number of critical and synoptic presentations are doing much to enlarge Perse's following in the French-speaking community.

Recognition of Perse's stature as a poet first really came outside of France, but such recognition was confined to a very small group of readers, most of them poets in their own right. The English-speaking world has known vaguely about Perse since 1931, when the first version of T. S. Eliot's translation of *Anabase* was published. Since that time, however, Perse has remained widely unread in Great Britain. In the United States, which has become Perse's second country in a very real sense, the situation is scarcely better. When the Nobel award was announced in 1960, only one bookstore in Washington, D.C., where Perse has been a resident a good part of the time since 1940, had a single work of his in stock! Such unawareness is all the more inexcusable when we consider that Perse is one of the very few French poets whose entire poetic output has been competently, and occasionally brilliantly, translated into English. It may be objected that translations of poetry are pretty poor stuff at best. That is true, but it is far less true of Perse than of most other poets – we shall point out later why this is so. Finally, some of the later poems celebrate the American continent with a sweep and grandeur that we usually associate only with certain native American poets. That fact alone would justify a study of Saint-John Perse intended, as this one is, primarily for English-speaking readers.

In seeking to fulfil that intention, however, we immediately run into an obstacle that cannot be very gracefully overcome. It will be necessary to quote Perse frequently, and sometimes at length. When the quotations are taken from his numerous prose pieces, the English translations of the passages can stand alone. More frequently, though, it will be necessary to cite the poetry, and in those instances the English translation will not do; the original French text must be quoted. But since Perse's vocabulary is unusually rich and his turns of phrase often very subtle, English translations of all passages quoted from the poems are included at the foot of each page, where they may be easily consulted.[2]

In any study of this kind a high frequency of quotations is unavoidable; in the present instance it will be even higher than usual because of a determined effort to let Saint-John Perse speak for himself whenever possible. Because his own declarations, both in the poems and critical pieces, are the surest safeguard against the gratuitous interpretations that his reputation as a 'difficult' and 'obscure' poet seems to have authorized. Perse is difficult because his vocabulary, figures of speech, and rhythmic devices do not yet have a familiar ring. He is difficult most of all, however, because the fund of knowledge and experience he draws upon is vast, varied, and unusual. And finally, at times he is difficult because the frequent allusions in his poems to events in his own life are purposely oblique and veiled.

Obscurity, however, is another matter. I would reserve the term for a quality that is inherent in the poem itself and that is hard to dispel by any exegetical procedure. Obscurity results when the poet is unsure of his own intentions in writing a poem, or when his technique as a craftsman is unequal to the task of expressing intentions that are quite clear to himself, or, finally, obscurity arises when the poet regards meaning and intention as irrelevant and makes obscurity a necessary condition of the poetic art. This latter case is classically exemplified by Saint-John Perse's friend and fellow-poet, Paul Valéry, and it is natural to ask whether Perse (who was writing *Anabase* about the same time that Valéry was composing *La Jeune Parque*) does not share the Valéryan view. I do not think he does, but in order to justify this statement, we must recall the exact terms of Valéry's view, which has become so widespread and fashionable.

It was some thirty years ago that Valéry formulated what may be called the 'Humpty-Dumpty' view of poetry. 'My verses',[3] he wrote, 'have the meaning attributed to them. The one I give them suits only myself and does not contradict anyone else. It is an error contrary to the nature of poetry, and one which may even be fatal to it, to claim that for each poem there is a corresponding true meaning, unique and conformable to, or identical with, some thought of the author's.'

I call this the Humpty-Dumpty view because it puts every reader in the position of Lewis Carroll's character, so far as the meaning of a poem is concerned: a poem means simply what any reader wants it to mean. This view denies the possibility of effective human communication and ignores the *sine qua non* of an art that takes words as its raw materials: every verbal act, other than the most rudimentary exclamation, takes for granted the validity of an exchange-medium that is the life-blood of a speech-community. The problems arising from this *donnée* are many and difficult; and the statesman, the scientist, the businessman, and the teacher, quite as much as the poet and novelist, are constantly wrestling with the paradoxes and ambiguities arising from it. Valéry, however, simply compounds confusion by ignoring the *donnée*.

In the same unfortunate essay he goes on to say: 'Once a work is finished and presented, whether in verse or prose, its author can propose or affirm nothing about it that would have any more weight or would explain it more exactly than what anyone else might say. . . . If a painter does a portrait of *Socrates* and a passer-by recognizes *Plato*, all the creator's explanations, protests, and excuses will not change this immediate recognition.'[4]

To begin with, by shifting from the verbal to the plastic arts, Valéry confuses things still further. A poem does not have the continuous objective existence of a painting or statue or any other physical object. A poem comes into being only when its printed or recited text is plunged into the impalpable exchange-medium of the speech-community, to which we referred above. But even when we disregard this illegitimate shift from the verbal to the plastic, Valéry's comparison still leads into a curious impasse. If the creator actually sought to portray Socrates and no one recognizes the portrait as Socrates, he has failed as a craftsman. Or, if some isolated individual can see only Plato in the likeness, that will prove very little other than, perhaps, that the individual has faulty vision.

No one seriously reflecting on the cognitive situation here involved would for a moment maintain that, having taken the artist's intent into account, the whole problem of artistic communication has thereby been solved. But what I *am* maintaining is that in literature – the art of words – very little of real value can be said when the author's own meanings are regarded as no more relevant or irrelevant than the meanings anyone else attributes to his work. Valéry is, I think, the first eminent writer on record to be so ostensibly indifferent to the comprehension of his own intentions in his work. The countless writers who, through the centuries, have stormed and raged and declared, 'That is *not* what I mean! How can you be so blind!' etc., have been, according to Valéry's view, not simply ill-mannered, but unconscionably stupid.

This is indeed a curious impasse for so fervent an admirer of Poe's 'The Philosophy of Composition' to have been led into, for Poe's basic assumption is that the desired effect of a poem on a reader is so completely predictable that the whole process of composing a poem may be reduced to a lucid and systematic search for elements that will satisfy conditions determined exclusively by that desired effect. Saint-John Perse, who has never been a victim of this Poe-esque delusion, has likewise never espoused the Humpty-Dumpty view of poetry. When a Swedish reader sent him a letter asking about the meaning and intention of the long poem *Amers* (*Seamarks*), Perse did not reply that the poem meant whatever the inquirer thought it meant. Instead, he wrote a letter stating exactly what he had set out to do in *Amers*, even indicating section by section how he had sought to elaborate his meanings. Thus, if *Amers* or any other poem by Perse is obscure, it is not because of an indifference to meaning or because of any uncertainty of intention.

That is why I feel justified in adopting as a guiding principle in this study the eminently un-Valéryan view that the critic's first job is to discover what the poet's own intentions were in writing his works. That is only a part of the critic's function, but it is a first and indispensable part. In seeking to fulfil it, I shall not, of course, always hit the mark; but I shall not hesitate to follow the many explicit leads that Saint-John Perse has generously supplied to his readers.

I

The Antillean Poems

Eloges

When a reader is confronted with a strange and disconcerting text, it is always reassuring to find passages that remind him, by their tone or actual wording, of some writer he is already familiar with. Just as often as not, such recognition hinders rather than helps in grasping the originality and true meaning of a text. Pushed one step farther, the search for 'recognizable' passages becomes the dreary game of source-and-influence hunting. Saint-John Perse, alas, will not be spared any more in this respect than any other major writer. The strangeness of his idiom and the extreme scarcity of any obvious borrowings will combine to add zest to the game. The rarer the quarry, the greater the sport.

Well, so far as I am able to determine, the only unequivocal borrowings in the poems of Saint-John Perse are from a writer generally ignored in literary circles, for the simple reason that he was not a literary man but a natural scientist. He is the Reverend Father Düss, a botanist-priest who compiled manuals on Antillean flora that are among the standard works in their field. In one of these manuals we learn that the *Aniba bracteata* has an 'ovoid olive-shaped fruit, blackish brown when mature, set in a warty cupule truncated at the top'. In the fourth poem of the series entitled 'Eloges' there is mention of the 'fruit noir de l'Anibe dans sa cupule verruqueuse et tronquée'.[a] Farther along in the same poem there is mention of 'les abutilons, ces fleurs jaunes-tachées-

[a] black fruit of the Aniba in its warty and truncated cupule

de-noir-pourpre-à-la-base que l'on emploie dans la diarhhée des
bêtes à cornes'.[a] The *Abutilon hirtum* is described by Father Düss
as follows: 'Broad flowers, orange-yellow; petals bearing a large
black spot at the base ... from the Greek privative prefix *a* ('not'),
bous ('ox'), *tilos* ('diarrhoea'), because these plants are a remedy
for diarrhoea in horned arnimals.' Several other such direct borrowings occur in the 'Eloges' series and in 'Pour fêter une enfance',[1] while all of the plants mentioned in these and earlier poems
are to be found in Father Düss's manuals, along with the descriptive technical terms from botany that occur in these and in later
poems as well.

Perse himself has indicated how he came under the influence of
Father Düss. In 1910 a hair-raisingly inaccurate text of the 'Eloges'
poems appeared in the *Nouvelle Revue française*. André Gide, who
was responsible for their publication, had not been able to correct the proofs. So upset was Gide that he insisted on publishing
the accurate text of the poems, along with a few others, in book-
form and at his own expense. This was the 1911 edition of *Eloges*
(the book as distinct from the series in it that bears the same title).
Perse expressed his thanks by having a tree back in his native
Guadeloupe dedicated to Gide. The tree was a particularly beautiful cabbage-palm (*Oreodoxa*), popularly known in French as
palmiste. In a letter to Gide, Perse wrote concerning the *palmiste*:
'a scientist whom I met when I was a boy, Father Düss, because
he was Catholic, sometimes purposely made the error of calling
it *psalmiste*.'[2] One wonders whether Father Düss ever suspected
how effective he was in initiating his young friend to botany. His
lessons have, in fact, never been forgotten. And his influence was
not confined to the purely scientific aspect of botany, for Father
Düss had the solid classical background of the educated French
priest, and he was fascinated by the popular names of the plants
he catalogued, as a glance at his manuals makes immediately evident. Surely Father Düss helped sharpen young Alexis's awareness of language and thereby helped him to sense the poetic
potential latent in scientific description, which Perse was to exploit so remarkably throughout his poetry.

The love of the scientifically exact term explains in a large
measure Perse's whole vast and recondite vocabulary. Alongside

---

[a] the abutilons, those yellow-flowers-with-purplish-black-spots-at-the-base
that are used against the diarrhoea of horned animals

the purely scientific terms there are the technical terms from the trades, specialized crafts, and professions. On first contact, Perse's poetic vocabulary may seem discouragingly complex. Yet almost all the strange words occurring in his poetry may be found in the large standard French dictionaries, and consequently in the unabridged Webster, where the English translations are concerned. For most of the words, the handy *Petit Larousse*, or an English equivalent, will suffice. Perse never plays with words, never creates a synthetic vocabulary the way, for example, Joyce or Henri Michaux does. Instead, Perse draws on the vast reservoir of technical terms that is already at his disposal. When we examine the actual poems, we shall see how he exploits these terms for poetic ends. Father Düss's influence was unquestionably real.

So much for *direct* influences. There are also some faint echoes of other writers, exclusively literary ones, here and there in various poems. These will be noted in passing, but they are too faint and scattered to be of any great interest. We do know, however, who Perse's literary associates were, and it is not hard to trace the course of a number of his literary friendships. Certain attitudes and tastes he clearly shared with some of these associates; but it is futile and, most often, simply impossible to say who influenced whom. It is, none the less, worth while situating Saint-John Perse in his proper literary setting. Doing this will, if anything, increase our wonderment at the originality of his work and in no way diminish the illusion of literary spontaneous generation that it presents.

Valery Larbaud, writing in 1925, reviewed the poetic scene in France at that time and concluded that 'only the works of Claudel, Valéry, Jammes, Fargue, and St.-John Perse endure today and will continue to endure'.[3] If we add Larbaud's own name to that list, it may be taken as the roster of the chief literary figures with whom Leger associated. The first on the scene was Francis Jammes, who befriended the Leger family upon their moving to Pau from the French Antilles in 1899. Jammes, whose own family had Antillean connections, remained to the end of his life a faithful friend of the Legers and was instrumental in guiding young Alexis towards a diplomatic career. On the literary level, however, the commerce between the good gray poet of Orthez and the future Secrétaire Général des Affaires Etrangères was not great. Leger recalls that Jammes, on reading *Anabase*, wrote that his young friend had better reread Boileau for the sake of clarity and Veuillot for moral edification.... But it was through Jammes that he came to meet Paul Claudel in 1905, the period when Claudel was composing his *Cinq Grandes Odes*. In December, 1906, Leger was to meet Jacques Rivière at the home of Gabriel Frizeau, the highly literate vintner who was a friend of both Jammes and Claudel. One can see the future 'team' of the *Nouvelle Revue française* already taking shape. It was in that periodical that Leger's poetry was first published in 1909 ('Images à Crusoé' in the August issue). On reading these poems, the wealthy young *littérateur*, Valery Larbaud, sought out Leger at his home in Pau in 1911, and shortly thereafter Larbaud's friend, Léon-Paul Fargue, appeared upon the scene. At about the same time, though independent of any literary concerns, Leger became acquainted with Paul Valéry. Finally, also in 1911, he was to meet the two other important members of the N.R.F. team, Rivière's friend Alain Fournier, and the patron saint of the enterprise, André Gide.

Though Leger was to see Gide several times after this first meeting, his connections with Gide were to remain largely epistolary. Gide's letters, as is well known, played a crucial role in the revitalizing of French literature. Leger himself has said that, 'through them a loose network of literary affinities was established that produced one day in 1909, almost without the participants' realizing it, the varied and scattered elements of a singular *Pléiade* involving no binding agreements, no commitments, and having no charter or manifesto – a *Pléiade*, once more devoted to a "Defence and Illustration of the French Language".'[4] With the publication of 'Images à Crusoé' in 1909, Leger, without *his* realizing it, was enrolled as a charter member of this varied and uncoercive *Pléiade*, whose only rule, unwritten, was that there should be no charter. But he was soon to begin his studies for the Foreign Service in earnest, and from 1914 to 1940 Leger remained a kind of silent partner to the group, undoubtedly its most far-roving and taciturn member. But his loyalty never swerved. To realize this one has only to enumerate the names of those writers he has warmly eulogized: chronologically, they are Rivière, Gide, Larbaud, Claudel, Fargue.

It must be re-emphasized, however, that this *Pléiade* was indeed exempt from all commitments, charters, and manifestos. Other than a deep love of literature, the only common denominator among the 'members' was an essentially negative one. Each in his way was against the most flagrant evils of the fashionable best-selling literature of the time – evils neatly summed up in the opening words of Leger's tribute to Gide: 'Literary France in 1909. Academism, Parisianism, opportunism . . . '. For all of the N.R.F. *Pléiade*, literature was a serious, almost a sacred, pursuit – too serious to permit compromise with the demands of commercial success. The disinterestedness of the writer was a necessary, though far from sufficient, condition for the validity of the work produced. In pursuit of this disinterestedness none outshone Saint-John Perse. Not until his diplomatic career was over did he ever really write for publication, and the best-seller kind of success has always been a matter of supreme indifference to him.

Saint-John Perse is, moreover, the last survivor of the *Pléiade*,[5] and the great body of his writing was produced at a period when the others had already published their most significant work. He is, thus, by force of circumstance, strangely outside the French literary currents of the last forty years. This situation is undoubtedly to his liking, for timelessness, rather than timeliness, has always been one of his chief preoccupations in poetry. And consequently, coming to grips with the poetry itself is far more illuminating than any detailed consideration of Perse's literary friendships.

The poems of Saint-John Perse fall quite naturally into three simple, chronologically determined groups. First there is the Antillean group, which includes all the poems written between 1904 and 1914. They proceed directly from Leger's Antillean childhood in and around Guadeloupe and comprise 'Images à Crusoé', 'Pour fêter une enfance', 'Eloges' – all of which appear, along with a few later poems, in the volume with the overall title of *Eloges*. The second group belongs to the diplomatic years, 1914-1940. Only two major works of this group remain to us, the other five being those that were presumably destroyed in manuscript by the Nazis in 1940. But the two surviving texts are extremely important ones: *Anabase* and *Amitié du Prince*. The third, and by far the most extensive group, includes all the poems written since 1940. We shall refer to them as the 'American series'. The main items in it are *Exil, Poème à l'Etrangère, Pluies, Neiges, Vents, Amers, Chronique,* and *Oiseaux.*

The order of composition of the poems in each group does not necessarily follow the order in which the texts of the poems appear in the 1960 Gallimard edition, which must be taken as definitive. Only in the 'American series' do the two orders nearly coincide. The poems belonging to the two earlier periods are regrouped according to subject matter. The fact that such a reshuffling is feasible is interesting. It shows, first, how persistent the style of Saint-John Perse has been through the years. For example, the five poems that are grouped together under the collective title of 'La Gloire des Rois' belong to all three of the periods we are using as the basis of our discussion. Yet these five poems present no fundamental disharmony or feeling of anachronism. Second, the disregard for purely chronological ordering is another indication of the poet's concern with timelessness. In our discussion, however, we shall try to re-establish the purely chronological order of composition, insofar as that is possible, in an effort to dispel a number of prevalent misconceptions.

The earliest poems of Saint-John Perse we possess are those entitled 'Images à Crusoé'. They were composed in 1904, when Alexis Leger was seventeen years of age. If this makes them qualify as juvenilia, one can only say that to find juvenilia of comparable quality one must go back to Rimbaud. These poems, in spite of occasional awkwardness in their narrative framework, are almost completely successful – so successful, in fact, that when they were discovered by Rainer Maria Rilke, he took the trouble to translate them into German. They are a cry of pure nostalgia for the islands Leger had to leave behind when he was eleven years old. The poet imagines Robinson Crusoe, back in England, in a grimy seaport, aging and longing for his desert island. The melancholy tolling of the abbey bells makes him weep for the sound of breakers in the moonlight, for the whistlings of the farther shores, the 'musiques étranges qui naissent et s'assourdissent sous l'aile close de la nuit, / pareilles aux cercles enchaînés que sont les ondes d'une conque'.[a] The hideous city-wall that obstructs his view makes him think all the more of the fresh smells and pungent tastes of his desert island, each detailed with characteristic specificity: 'le suint amer des plantes à siliques, l'âcre insinuation des mangliers charnus et l'acide bonheur d'une subs-

---

[a] strange music that is born and muffled under the folded wing of the night, / like the linked circles that are a conch-shell's waves

tance noire dans les gousses'.[a] Then the whole city is described
and contrasted with the islands, giving us the first and most eloquent expression of Perse's deep dislike of large cities. Though
the port-town of the poem is ostensibly in England, it is really
a transposition of Bordeaux, where young Leger had begun his
studies in 1904. A striking figure sums up his nausea: ' – La Ville
par le fleuve coule à la mer comme un abcès...'[b] A far cry from
the Island, where the sea and the sky reign supreme; where everything is salty, viscous, and heavy 'comme la vie des plasmes'[c];
where birds and fishes, giant flowers and trees proliferate. The cry
that concludes the preceding section of the poem is reiterated:
'Joie! ô joie déliée dans les hauteurs du ciel!'[d] Then comes Friday,
who once moved the 'ruissellement bleu'[e] of his limbs in the light,
but who is now depraved and shabby – shabby as Crusoe's parrot,
who is the subject of the next section. The home-made goatskin
parasol and the improvised bow are likewise shabby and disinte-
grating. The brief section about the seed brought from the Island
sums it all up: 'Dans un pot tu l'as enfouie, la graine pourpre
demeurée à ton habit de chèvre. / Elle n'a point germé.'[f] The last
section, entitled 'Le Livre', is the only part of the poem that suffers
from being patently literary. The book is the Bible; and Crusoe,
who lets his finger wander among the prophecies, longs for death,
that second departure for some remote and silent shore. It is the
only part of the series that does not have the ring of first-hand
experience. But, taken in its entirety, this series is a remarkable
achievement, and the poet Saint-John Perse, who was not *invented*
until the 1920's, is already present on every page.

Each section of the poem is divided into 'verses' of very unequal lengths extending, somewhat capriciously, from a single
word to a whole paragraph. On the printed page these poems
look typographically like some of Rimbaud's *Illuminations*. There
is no suggestion whatever of their being, as some critics maintain,
regular verse-forms that have been dislocated, expanded, or other-

[a] the bitter ooze of siliqua-bearing plants, the acrid insinuations of fleshy
mangroves, and the acid delight of a black substance in the pods
[b] – The City, by way of the river, drains into the sea like an abscess...
[c] as the life of plasms
[d] Joy, o joy turned loose in the heights of the sky!
[e] blue streaming
[f] You planted it in a flowerpot, the dark red seed that stuck to your goatskin jacket. / It has never sprouted.

wise modified. The subordination of prosody to imagery that is
so characteristic of Perse is already here, and there is a rightness
in the varied rhythms of these poems that bespeaks achievement,
not experimentation. The same is true of the sureness of the
vocabulary. But it is in the imagery that mastery is most evident.
On the very first page, those strains of strange music 'qui naissent
et s'assourdissent sous l'aile close de la nuit'[a] present a complex
image involving auditory, visual, and even tactile elements. The
basic phenomenon described is auditory – the nocturnal sounds
that are heard but immediately muffled. But visual and tactile sensations are contained in the metaphor of night's folded wing,
which makes us think immediately of a bird tucking its head into
its soft plumage. In the French, the whole thing is reinforced by
the recurrent sibilant sounds, both voiced and unvoiced. But this
seventeen-year-old poet elaborates his image even further – a dangerous procedure, one may think, of the kind to which young
poets are all too prone. But not here. The strange sounds are said
to be 'pareilles aux cercles enchaînés que sont les ondes d'une
conque, à l'amplification de clameurs sous la mer...'.[b] The interpenetration of sea and land, the seamless continuity could hardly
be more economically conveyed than in this total synesthetic complex. Other synesthetic metaphors are terser, but no less effective:
'Mais les chauves-souris découpent le soir mol à petits cris.'[c]
.... ' – Mais un craquement fissure l'ombre chantante: c'est
ton arc, à son clou, qui éclate.'[d]

The young poet is also already exploiting etymologies, thus
prefiguring the later Saint-John Perse: 'l'aube verte s'élucide au
sein des eaux mystérieuses'. In standard parlance, a mystery or a
difficult problem is elucidated; but here it is the green dawn that
is elucidated – that is, grows bright – for that is the literal meaning of the Latin root. And already there is the transposing of a
word from its ordinary context into an unusual one. The metro-
politan evening descends 'sur les statues de pierre blette'. *Blet* is
used exclusively in ordinary speech to indicate bruised or over-
ripe fruit. Here the effluvia of the filthy city have eaten away the

---

[a] that are born and muted under the folded wing of the night
[b] like the linked circles that are a conch-shell's waves, like the amplification
of noises undersea...
[c] But the bats cut the soft evening up with little cries.
[d] – But a snapping fissures the singing darkness: it is your bow, on its
nail, that has burst.

very stone of the statues. The adjective carries an effective metaphor with it. Here, too, we already find painstaking precision of
detail. Speaking of the parrot, the poet says to Crusoe: 'Tu regardes l'œil rond sous le pollen gâté de la paupière; tu regardes le
deuxième cercle comme un anneau de sève morte.'[a] The vegetable
metaphor exactly conveys the look of a sickly parrot's eyes – the
granular deposits like yellow pollen and the sclerotized circle of
the iris like a ring of hardened sap on the rim of a cut twig.

There are also strikingly premonitory phrases in 'Images à
Crusoé'. The long rains marching against the town ('un soir de
longues pluies en marche vers la ville') will become the key-
metaphor of *Pluies*, composed some forty years later. And almost
immediately following that phrase is the notation about 'un exil
lumineux'. In 1941, on the empty sun-drenched stretches of Long
Beach Island, the refugee Alexis Leger was to compose *Exil*.
Indeed, the whole of 'Images à Crusoé' is already a poem of exile,
the exile suffered by a boy who had to leave behind a shimmering tropical paradise and acclimatize himself to the provincial
French towns of southwest France. This same theme, stripped
of every vestige of literary device, is developed even more
poignantly in 'Pour fêter une enfance', composed in 1908. But,
between the composition of these first two major poems, young
Leger wrote a poem in alexandrines entitled 'Des Villes sur trois
modes'.

That poem was never reprinted in any subsequent collection
of Perse's works. It appeared in the July-August 1908 issue of
an ephemeral review, *Pan*, published in Montpellier. It is, thus,
the first known poem by Saint-John Perse to have appeared in
print. But if we trust the 1906 date that is placed at the end of the
poem – and I see no reason to question it – its composition *followed*
that of 'Images à Crusoé' by two years. Its subsequent rejection
by Leger seems to indicate that he regards the poem as something
of an aberration. As a matter of fact, the poem is not on a par
with 'Images à Crusoé' or 'Pour fêter une enfance', but it is still
a very interesting poem and deserves examination.

It is divided into three roughly equal parts corresponding to
the 'trois modes' of the title. The alexandrines are in no way
classical; they do not obey the conventions of medial caesura,

[a] You look at his round eye under the mouldy pollen of the lid; you look
at the second circle that is like a ring of dead sap.

alternation of masculine and feminine rhymes, avoidance of sin-
gulars rhyming with plurals, etc. The rhyme-scheme, moreover,
is quite irregular. The flamboyant vocabulary and riotous colours
are reminiscent of Hugo. The poem, throughout, is constantly
bursting the seams of its alexandrine strait-jacket.

The whole thing is declaimed by a pirate-captain, and each of
the three sections is given a Latin epigraph taken ironically from
one of the Church Fathers. The first section apostrophizes sleepy
provincial towns so steeped in boredom that they are not even
worth plundering. These towns, where the anvils and factories
are silent, these towns 'où les fruits ont pourri aux larmiers / Où
s'épuise le temps comme un broutement d'âne'[a] – these towns are
'indignes d'un pillage'.[b] The pirate-captain merely mocks them
with his buccaneer's laughter. Surely these towns have about them
something of the Pyrenean spa, for there is explicit mention of
'l'heure qui surprit les Femmes aux piscines'.[c] A different sort of
city is the one where there is wealth to be plundered, art-works
to be desecrated and pilfered, officials to be kidnapped and ran-
somed. The buccaneer-chief says that 'sur la toile plate, / Pour
vos jeunes désirs, je tracerai de haut / La grand'ville comme une
bête sur le dos'.[d] The young pirates are urged to sail their frigates
up the estuary. (The image of Bordeaux lurks in the background.)
The third and last kind of town described is a distant port 'où le
soleil brutal / Fait jaillir de son lit une mer de métal'.[e] We are
back in the Antilles, along the Spanish Main, for the deep sky is
'étayé de volcans'[f] and the paunchy carracks sway in basins of
'eau lucide où naviguent les squales'.[g] Here in the ports of leisure,
lechery, and violence is where the booty will be squandered.
These are the ports where the pirates pay off mestiza whores in
gold-nuggets; and here is where 'des enfants en rires ivoirins /
Susciteront le vice agile dans leurs reins'.[h] One suspects that the
poet's sexual awakening came some time between the composition

---

[a] where fruits rot in the rain-spouts, / Where time is nibbled away like
the dry weeds a donkey grazes

[b] unworthy of being pillaged

[c] the hour that caught the Women in their swimming-pools

[d] on the flat canvas, / To slake your youthful desires, I'll sketch / The Big
City, like a beast sprawled on its back.

[e] where the brutal sun / Makes the metallic sea leap out of its bed

[f] propped up by volcanoes

[g] lucent water where the squalus glides

[h] children with ivoried laughter / Will arouse agile vice in their loins.

of 'Images à Crusoé' and 'Des Villes sur trois modes', though there may be something of adolescent sexual boasting here. In any case, there is an undeniable quality of lusty derring-do about this poem.

If one removes the alexandrine strait-jacket, the pirate artifice, and the literary allusions (the epigraphs, a reference to Werther and a traditional character of the *commedia dell'arte*) what is left is a poem very much like 'Images à Crusoé' and worthy of being put alongside it. The torpid emptiness of a provincial town is beautifully caught in the mention of the goatherd who plays his ocarina for the sick child behind the blinds – a thin music punctuated by the goats themselves, who 'debout pour les rosiers des grilles, / Avec un sabot net sont retombées, sonores'.[a] This is the sort of concrete detail that will make up the very substance of the later 'Eloges'. And the 'Tumulte des parfums dans l'éternel balan, / O gloire sur les eaux, lumineuses cadences!'[b] could easily fit into one of the *éloges* that celebrate the sea. The vocabulary, too, is thoroughly characteristic: the technical plant and animal names (*silènes, squale*), the nautical terms (*frégates, balan, caraques*), the capitalized generic terms (*Rançonneurs et Pirates, les Scribes vains, le Fossoyeur et l'Accoucheuse, les Banquiers, les Poètes*). About the only terms that will disappear subsequently are the 'tough-talk' (*tafias, garces, jurons d'Eglise*) necessitated by the pirate setting.

Both the tough-talk and the pirate setting disappear once and for all with the composition of 'Pour fêter une enfance', the next in order of Perse's poems. This poem is probably destined to become Perse's most anthologized and popular one. It is as forthright as its title – so direct, in fact, that one hesitates to comment on it. Yet a few indications may enhance enjoyment of the piece. The mere fact of childhood is here celebrated: ' – Sinon l'enfance, qu'y avait-il alors qu'il n'y a plus?'[c] But, as always in Perse, the presentation is never abstract or general, but particularized. In this instance it is the poet's own childhood that supplies the particular 'illustration'. Perse was born on an islet in a roadstead of Guadeloupe in 1887 and spent the first eleven years of his life in

[a] standing on their hind legs to reach the climbing rose, / Came down on all fours with a sharp hoof, resoundingly.

[b] Tumult of perfumes in the eternal rolling of the ship, / O glory upon the waters, luminous cadences!

[c] Other than childhood, what was there in those days that is not here today?

the islands. Except for his schooling in the dismal town of Pointe-à-Pitre, most of these years were spent on two family properties: a coffee plantation, 'La Joséphine', on the western slope of Basse-Terre near the large volcano called La Soufrière, and a sugar plantation in the coastal lowlands looking out towards the Iles des Saintes and Marie-Galante. Boat and horseback were the standard modes of transport, and Alexis Leger was taught horsemanship and navigation at a very early age. He was given his own horse and his own boat when he was eight. Water and riotous vegetation were the two dominant elements in the setting of this life, and 'Pour fêter une enfance' catches the wonder of this water-and-vegetation childhood as completely as it is caught in certain sections of *Huckleberry Finn*, that other celebration of a boyhood steeped in greenery and water.

Once more the reader has only to keep in mind that everything described in the poem is authentic. It is pure autobiography. Jean Paulhan, in his curious article entitled 'Enigmes de Perse', declares that Perse almost never uses the first-person pronoun.[6] In 'Pour fêter...' alone, *je* occurs over twenty times. Paulhan's error, however, is understandable and revealing, because Perse achieves a de-emphasis of the poet's ego that keeps the reader from taking notice of the narrative *I*. In 'Pour fêter...' the *I* blends with the very texture of the poem, much as a protectively-marked insect blends with its background. Young Alexis tells us a great deal about himself, but that is incidental. What interests him, and what he wants the reader to be interested in, is the wonder of his surroundings. Often the specific details of time and place are simply skipped over, much as a child will leave out all orientational details when he recounts something that has deeply moved or delighted him – frequently to the puzzlement of his listener. Perse, of course, does not leave us puzzled in this way. When he writes: 'Les bouquets au jardin sentaient le cimetière de famille. Et une très petite sœur était morte: j'avais eu, qui sent bon, son cercueil d'acajou entre les glaces de trois chambres,'[a] we need not know that the baby-sister died in 1895 at La Joséphine, the coffee-plantation, to appreciate what went on and why the event stuck in the poet's memory.

---

[a] The shrubs in the garden smelled of the family cemetery. And a very little sister had died: I had had, which smelled good, her mahogany coffin between the mirrors of three bedrooms.

On occasion, however, a little more specific data can help to enrich a passage. Consider, for example, the fascinating episode described in the following lines:

'Le sorcier noir sentenciait à l'office: "Le monde est comme une pirogue, qui, tournant et tournant, ne sait plus si le vent voulait rire ou pleurer..."

Et aussitôt mes yeux tâchaient à peindre

un monde balancé entre des eaux brillantes, connaissaient le mât lisse des fûts, la hune sous les feuilles, et les guis et les vergues, les haubans de liane,

où trop longues, les fleurs

s'achevaient en des cris de perruches.'[a]

The haranguing black man, perhaps a voodoo priest, is overheard by young Alexis. So much is clear. But what about the fantasy that the sorcerer's comparison sets in motion in the child's mind? It turns out not to be fantasy at all. MacLeish reports that one of Leger's vivid memories is of a cyclone 'which left a large American boat in the middle of the island where it soon became a basket of flowers'.[7]

Such improbable details as this floral-piece boat have caused some critics to accuse Perse of leg-pulling and mystification. Maurice Saillet even went so far as to say that Perse invented words, especially names of non-existent animals.[8] Saillet's choice of examples could hardly have been less felicitous. He singled out the Anhinga and the Annaô. Any large dictionary would have enlightened him about the anhinga-bird, which is the snake-bird familiar to tourists in Florida and which is mentioned in Perse's *Vents*. The Annaô-bird mentioned in the third section of 'Pour fêter...' cannot be found in any dictionary. But to assume that it is therefore a fictitious creature mentioned simply to baffle readers is to betray a fundamental misunderstanding of Perse's whole poetic outlook. The opposite assumption is clearly the safe one, namely, that no term used in this poetry, no matter how outlandish it appears, is ever gratuitous, fanciful, or made-up. The mystery of the Annaô was cleared up in a letter from Leger to

[a] The black sorcerer harangued in the pantry: 'The world is like a dugout canoe which, turning and turning, can no longer tell whether the wind would laugh or cry...' / And straightway my eyes tried to picture / a world poised between shimmering waters, would recognize the smooth mast of the tree trunks, the crow's-nest under the leaves, and the booms and the yards and the shrouds of lianas, / where too-long flowers / ended in parrot cries.

Roger Caillois.[9] It turns out that 'Annaô' is the local name for the Lesser Antillean grackle, *Quiscalus lugubris*. The bird's call, which is mentioned in 'Pour fêter...', is peculiarly mournful, hence the qualifier *lugubris*. 'Annaô', in fact, is one of the very few words in Perse's extraordinary lexicon that cannot be found in any standard manual. One other is the patois term *pieds-gris*, which occurs in the first printed version of 'Pour fêter...'[10] but which was, significantly, replaced by the perfectly familiar word for mosquito (*moustique*) in the book-version of the poem.

Another truth-is-stranger-than-fiction reference is the mention of the tin and ebony halls that were lit up 'à l'heure où l'on joignait nos mains devant l'idole à robe de gala'.[a]

'Once,' MacLeish tells us, 'when Léger's parents were in Europe, his nurse, a Hindu and secretly a priestess of Shiva, took him to a Shiva temple, painted him black, stood him in a niche over the worshippers and then carried him from house to house among the workers of the plantation to touch the foreheads of all who were ill – Hindu, Malay, Chinese, Japanese, men of every blood.'[11] And this explains, too, why the various servants and plantation-hands are seldom described as black, but more often as yellow or 'couleur de papaye et d'ennui'.[b]

Once more we are made aware that the 'raw materials' of this poetry are all real. Indeed, most of them have been witnessed or experienced at first hand by the poet. There is no fantasy and very little 'fabulation' in Perse. Even the most shadowy figure in these poems moves in a world of flesh and blood that is rooted in concrete experience. It is this aspect of his work that has earned Perse the label of 'realist' in some quarters. The term is unfortunate, for the way Perse apprehends reality has nothing in common with the manner of those novelists for whom the term 'realist' was originally invented.

Returning to 'Pour fêter...', we find that it bears an English epigraph: 'King Light's Settlements'. I suspect this *is* a fictitious place-name – though it would not surprise me if it turned out otherwise. It sounds like some imaginary British colony – after all, Trinidad and Barbados and other English colonies were not far off. But I think that it really designates Guadeloupe, which is

[a] at the hour when they folded our hands before the idol decked out in gala dress

[b] colour of papaya and boredom

presented throughout the poem as a realm truly ruled over by King Light: 'et la lumière alors, en de plus purs exploits féconde, inaugurait le blanc royaume où j'ai mené peut-être un corps sans ombre...'[a]........ 'Et tout n'était que règnes et confins de lueurs. Et l'ombre et la lumière alors étaient plus près d'être une même chose...'[b] In this and all subsequent poems, brilliant sunlight is the expression of supreme joy.

In fact, 'Pour fêter...', even more than 'Images à Crusoé', contains the germs of themes and of whole strains of imagery that will be developed extensively in subsequent works. There is the fleeting mention of the poet's father, who will furnish the model for the plantation-owner of 'Ecrit sur la porte', to be written the next year, 1908. Here in 'Pour fêter...' the poet recalls the arrival of 'des hommes sains, vêtus de belle toile et casqués de sureau (comme mon père, qui fut noble et décent)'.[c] The father died the very year 'Pour fêter...' was composed, leaving his twenty-year-old son Alexis to look after the family. We also meet the poet's mother for the first time, beautiful and pale, tall and weary. Perse's veneration for her will never cease. Many years later, in 1944, when she is blocked in occupied France and he is in self-imposed exile, he will devote a whole poem to her – *Neiges*, which is one of his loveliest and most poignant. Here, though, she is still young, and is seconded by a dignified elderly woman, the poet's grandmother, the 'aïeule jaunissante' who consoled the child when he suffered from fever.

The family is the principle of order that underlies the whole world of King Light's Settlements. There, things were calm and ordered. All was in its rightful place and achieved maximum self-realization because of being in place. The concern with hierarchy that is expressed in various ways in later poems certainly has its origins here. Young Leger already realized when he wrote 'Pour fêter...' that the paternalistic hierarchy he revered was no longer viable, for the seismic disasters in the Antilles had already ruined the economy of Martinique and Guadeloupe and forced many plantation families, including Leger's, to leave the Caribbean. In

[a] and the light in those days, fecund in purer exploits, inaugurated the white realm where my body perhaps moved without making a shadow...

[b] And everything was but shimmering reigns and frontiers of light. And shadow and light in those days were more nearly the same thing...

[c] sound men, dressed in fine linen and wearing pith helmets (like my father, who was noble and seemly)

sjp c

a wider sense, too, Leger realized that the whole colonial system
of which the plantation-complex was a part, was doomed by the
onrush of history. But the memory of the plantation-complex,
where even the largest undertakings were still of human proportions, and where the relation of all activities to the primordial
necessities of life was constantly evident, will never cease to haunt
Leger. The image of the family-run plantation crops up in the
later poems as a contrast to the terrifying inhumanity of the various present-day social structures, largely imposed by runaway
scientific technology – against which Saint-John Perse will ultimately inveigh. In these early poems, however, the paternalistic hierarchy is still simply one element in the marvellous lost
paradise of childhood. The tone is one of praise, of a praise
that is at once reverent and ecstatic. The phrase, 'O! j'ai lieu
de louer!'[a] recurs like a refrain, and the title adopted for the
whole collection in which 'Pour fêter...' will be incorporated is
Eloges.

Among Leger's contemporaries, the writer who was to carry
the idea of poetry as praise to its ultimate limit was Claudel, and
it is possible that Claudel had something to do with the poetic
'awakening' of young Alexis. It should be noted, however, that
'Images à Crusoé', which 'Pour fêter...' really continues, was
written in 1904, a year *before* Leger met Claudel for the first time.
It is probable, though, that Leger had read some of the early
Claudel poetic dramas (*Tête d'Or, La Ville*), and perhaps the prose
sketches of *Connaissance de l'Est*, before that meeting. But there is
little in those works that has much in common with Perse's early
poetry. We do know, however, that shortly before composing
'Pour fêter...' – in December, 1906, to be precise – Leger heard
Claudel's long ode, 'Les Muses', for the first time.[12] There is, as
a matter of fact, an occasional faint similarity between the two
poems. In his ode, Claudel addresses one of the Muses who, as a
servant of God, approves His creation and transposes it into song
– a work in which the poet, of course, collaborates.

'Ainsi quand tu parles, ô poète, dans une énumération dé-
lectable
    Proférant de chaque chose le nom.'[b]

---

[a] O! I have reason to praise!
[b] Thus it is when you speak, O poet, in a delectable enumeration, / Of
each thing, proferring the name.

And further on:

'Toi, considérant toutes choses!

Pour voir ce qu'elle répondra tu t'amuses à appeler l'une
après l'autre par son nom.'[a]

In 'Pour fêter...' we find: 'Appelant toute chose, je récitai qu'elle
était grande, appellant toute bête, qu'elle était belle et bonne.'[b] (11)
The whole poem is indeed a 'delectable enumeration', but it is
dangerous to take such tenuous evidence as proof that Claudel's
ode directly affected the poem. I suspect that what was far more
influential than any specific passage in Claudel's work was the
example he set by imperiously rejecting classical prosody and
standard French poetic forms. And then, the older man's condemnation of the hot-house aspect of *fin de siècle* symbolism must
surely have struck a sympathetic chord in the young Antillean
exile. But from the very outset, Perse's poetic idiom and major
themes are strikingly different from Claudel's. And the differences
were to become greater, as we shall see.

In any case, a poem that bears the same date of composition as
'Pour fêter...' is as radically un-Claudelian as one could imagine.
It is the fascinating tribal litany entitled 'Récitation à l'éloge d'une
Reine'. The poem is recited by the leader of a chorus of young
men, and the queen they are honouring is a placid, monolithic
figure in whom reside the fortunes of a primitive tribal group
somewhere in the Antilles. The geographical locus is indicated
by plant references such as the rocou (from which the Carib
Indians obtained the red annatto which makes them 'redskins')
or the familiar West Indian sapodilla. The poem is divided into
five short sections, each concluding with the refrain, ' – Mais qui
saurait par où faire entrée dans Son cœur?'[c] The young man reciting the poem addresses his queen as 'Haut asile des graisses
vers qui cheminent les désirs / d'un peuple de guerriers muets
avaleurs de salive'.[d] He is requesting that the queen permit the
young men to bathe naked before her. But she sits, unmoving
and unmoved, her body painted with annatto. The young choric

[a] You, considering all things! / Just to see how they will answer, you play
at calling each of them, one by one, by name.
[b] Naming each thing, I pronounced that it was great, naming each beast
that it was beautiful and good.
[c] – But who would know by what breach to enter Her heart?
[d] High sanctuary of unguent flesh towards which journey the desires of
a warrior people, mute swallowers of saliva

leader speaks with religious awe of her pubic hair, her limbs, her
infecund womb, and of the 'proud rite' of her menses that follow
the rhythm of the Moon. She it is who must eventually deliver
these young men in rut from the itch that burns them and that,
in the poem, is conveyed by references to various irritant plants.
The mixture of awe and intense sexuality, expressed exclusively
in a primitive kind of anatomical and botanical imagery, makes
this a poem without precedent in the French tradition. It does
not seem to have provoked much comment when it was first published in 1910, nor has it been particularly noticed since. Yet it is,
in its modest way, as authentic an eruption of primitivism in
French poetry as the 'Sacre du Printemps' was in music some
years later. In the development of Perse's own work it is the first
completely impersonal poem we possess. The contrast with the
overtly autobiographical 'Pour fêter...' is marked, and it is this
impersonal note that will be developed in later poems, coming
to a climax in the two major items that have survived from the
'diplomatic period': *Anabase* and *Amitié du Prince*.

The stripping away of autobiographical references is also evident in a few of the eighteen short poems that make up the series
entitled 'Eloges', composed in 1908. The first and fourth of the
'Eloges' (1960 numeration) are completely devoid of explicit autobiography and take a place alongside the 'Récitation à l'éloge
d'une Reine' for violence and sexuality. In the first one, someone
designated simply as 'le Songeur aux joues sales'[a] is drawn from
his dream 'tout rayé de violences, de ruses et d'éclats'[b] towards
the smell of meat being barbecued and of sauces being thickened.
There is a peculiar rawness in this little poem, which presents to
us sensations almost completely separated from the experiencer –
sensations-in-themselves, so to speak. The same is true of number
iv, which is surely one of the most striking poems in the series.
Its subject is the awakening of sexual desire, and the series of
elliptical images used to convey it are of the same order as those
of the 'Récitation'. The plants, insects, and animals of the Antilles
are again the raw materials of the imagery. A sleeper awakens
suddenly, still dreaming of the 'fruit noir de l'Anibe dans sa cupule
verruqueuse et tronquée'.[c] The exact scientific source of this des-

---

[a] the dirty-cheeked Dreamer
[b] streaked with violence, wiles, and radiance
[c] black fruit of the Aniba in its warty and truncated cupule

cription has already been pointed out.[13] The Aniba, in its form, is like a very much enlarged acorn, and its resemblance to the male glans (etymologically, L. acorn) is obvious. The sexual force of the poem is then reinforced by an accumulation of other images without any explanatory transitional material. We are told that crabs have devoured a whole tree-ful of soft fruit – the reference here being to the migratory land-crabs one finds in the tropics. Another tree has its trunk all scarred where the flowers grew along it. Another tree rains down coloured flies when it is touched. A line of ants scurries back and forth. And there is the provocative laughter of women alone in the diarrhoea-arresting abutilons, which are described in Father Düss's imperturbably scientific language. Then all this is followed by the simple notation: 'Et le sexe sent bon'. The remaining few lines revert to the pullulating insects and another vegetable image – an oar that puts forth buds in the hands of the rower. Then we are told that the best way to catch a shark is with a live dog on a gaff. Finally, there is a return to the Aniba, supplemented by a reference to flowers in packets under the leaf-axils. Technically, this juxtaposing of images without 'modulating' devices is exactly that of the greater part of *Anabase*, the much later and better-known poem.

Most of the 'Eloges', however, are a continuation of the autobiographical 'Pour fêter...'. In number iii the silent man 'qui rit sous l'aile calme du sourcil'[a] is reminiscent of the noble and seemly father, though here there is nothing explicit to indicate the relationship. The same is true of the man who is presented in a poem belonging to the same year and written in the same idiom as 'Eloges' – namely, the text subsequently chosen by Saint-John Perse as the liminary piece for his collected work, entitled appropriately, 'Ecrit sur la porte'. The man who speaks is a pith-helmeted plantation-owner whose pride is a beautiful daughter who runs the household and is not put off by the earthy smells of plants and sweat and animals. Had it been possible for that life to continue, it might have been for Alexis Leger, as for the man in the poem, enough 'pour n'envier pas les voiles des voiliers'.[b] When this plantation-owner arrives at his white-painted house, he is seen 'faisant grâce à son cheval de l'étreinte des genoux'.[c]

[a] who laughs under the calm wing of the eyebrow
[b] to keep one from envying the sails of the sailboats
[c] freeing his horse from the pressure of his knees

Young Alexis devotes the brief second éloge entirely to his own horse: 'j'ai pressé des lunes à ses flancs sous mes genoux d'enfant...'.[a] The child is carried by the horse the way man is carried along by the mysterious forces of life:

> 'J'ai aimé un cheval – qui était-ce ? – et parfois (car une bête sait mieux quelles forces nous vantent)
> il levait à ses dieux une tête d'airain: soufflante, sillonnée d'un pétiole de veines.'[b]

The application of the technical botanical term 'petiole' to an animal is wholly characteristic.

The greater number of these 'Eloges' (numbers v to ix and xv to xviii) are devoted to those aspects of the poet's childhood directly connected with the sea or the plantation-houses. They are the ones closest in diction and feeling to 'Pour fêter...'. Again and again the phrase, 'Enfance, mon amour', is repeated. And the actual progress of the day is presented as stages in a child's growth. First there is the dawn, 'l'enfance adorable du jour'[c] in number v, then 'l'enfance aggressive du jour'[d] in number vi, and then, as the sun moves higher, ' – Ce navire est à nous et mon enfance n'a sa fin'[e] (viii). And finally, 'Enfance, mon amour, j'ai bien aimé le soir aussi: c'est l'heure de sortir'[f] (xv).

This particular set of poems, in a way that had only been hinted at in French poetry before Saint-John Perse, conveys a sense of sheer well-being, of *volupté* quite apart from sexual satisfaction. Metaphor after metaphor, underscored by rhythms that never quite repeat themselves in spite of their sameness, celebrate a oneness with the world of water, sunlight, and warm winds:

> 'Il fait si calme et puis si tiède,
> Il fait si continuel aussi,
> qu'il est étrange d'être là, mêlé des mains à la facilité du jour...'[g] (v)

[a] and I pressed moons on his flanks with my child's knees
[b] I loved a horse – who was he? – and sometimes (for a beast knows better what forces applaud us) / he lifted toward his gods a head of bronze: blowing, and furrowed with a petiole of veins.
[c] the adorable childhood of the day
[d] the aggressive childhood of the day
[e] – This boat is ours and my childhood is still not over.
[f] Childhood, my love, I have loved the evening too: the hour for going out.
[g] It seems so calm and then so warm, / and so continuous too, / that it seems strange to be here, gently kneaded into / the facility of day...

What strikes one about the original French texts of these poems is their *rightness*. It is in this particular set of 'éloges' that one comes to the full realization of what Valery Larbaud was talking about when, back in 1911,[14] he wrote a review of the entire *Eloges* collection:

> Every one of these poems was long in gestation, soaked up quantities of air and light, of memories and of all life, second by second, until it was filled to overflowing; every strophe and every sound, after being repeatedly tested, took its place in the natural rhythm of breathing and became perfectly adapted to the human mouth....
>
> One cannot say that their expression and form are 'so clever' or that they charm us with the wit they contain. They are simply *right....* As with a satisfying scientific demonstration, one can only say, 'That's it'.

It is curious how the quality of these poems seems to have escaped most other critics at the time of their publication. For one thing, they have about them the seriousness of a child, and a tone of wonder is constantly sustained in them. Such a combination is what was farthest from the 'Parisianism' of 1909-14. And yet, and yet... how could almost everyone have overlooked imagery so marvellous and carried along by so suave a music as – '...et la présence de la voile, grande âme malaisée, la voile étrange, là, et chaleureuse révélée, comme la présence d'une joue... O / bouf-fées!... Vraiment j'habite la gorge d'un Dieu'[a] (ix)? The metaphors are so apt that one hardly notices how many of them are telescoped into so few lines. The sail is personified, becomes a great restless soul in its promptness to respond to the slightest change in the wind. But the soul is given a body, suggested by the synecdoche of the warm cheek, a close human presence. The figure also suggests those childish heads that one finds at the four corners of old maps, blowing the four winds with puffed-out cheeks, for the next words are simply 'O / bouffées!' – which are really puffs of wind, rather than gusts. They are warm sea-breezes, the breath from the throat of some god, all expressed in a radical ellipse: the sensation of well-being is so complete that the boy is not merely surrounded by the blown breath of the god, he feels

[a] ... and the presence of the sail, great restless soul, the sail, strange, there, and warm revealed, like the presence of a cheek... O / gusts!... Truly I inhabit the throat of a god.

as if he is in the god's very throat. Rhythmically the passage is made up of two lines approximately the length of an alexandrine, with a re-echoing of é-sounds, even in the end-rhymes:

'*et* la pr*é*sence de la voile, grande âme malais*ée*

la voile *é*trange, là, *et* chaleureuse r*évé*l*ée*'

– plus two roughly decasyllabic lines:

'comme la pr*é*sence d'une joue... O bouff*ée*s!

Vraiment j'habite la gorge d'un Dieu.'

The last decasyllabic line, avoiding the é-rhymes, seems to 'open out'.

Such analyses do not usually contribute much to our enjoyment of a poem; at best they help to explain why we have enjoyed it in the first place. Bad poetry, though, cannot stand up under this sort of dissection. But these poems do. And any of the 'sea-and-plantation' *éloges* may be subjected to this test and come out unharmed.

In some of the other 'Eloges' we learn that Perse's hatred of towns, first expressed in 'Images à Crusoé', actually pre-dated his arrival in Europe. But at least the port-town of Pointe-à-Pitre (described by Perse as 'un bidonville affreux, affreux' – 'a hideous, hideous shantytown') had colour. It is in this reeking town that young Alexis was sent to school in 1896: 'Et l'enfant qui revient de l'école des Pères, affectueux longeant l'affection des Murs qui sentent le pain chaud'[a] (xiv). And here, in several of the 'Eloges', the fetid and garish Pointe-à-Pitre of the 1890's comes to life, seen through the eyes of a sensitive young schoolboy longing for the forests and beaches, for the plantation worksheds and, most of all, for the family boat. But the very intensity of light, heat, and filth gives a certain beauty to this town 'jaune de rancune'[b] (xi). Again the imagery is precise and saturated, though it is here somewhat external and 'pictural' in the manner of some of the pieces in Claudel's *Connaissance de l'Est*:

'La chienne rose traîne, à la barbe du pauvre, toute une viande de mamelles. Et la marchande de bonbons

se bat

contre les guêpes dont le vol est pareil aux morsures du jour sur le dos de la mer. Un enfant voit cela,

[a] And the child, coming home from parochial school, affectionate, loitering in the affection of the Walls smelling of hot bread
[b] yellow with rancour

si beau

qu'il ne peut plus fermer ses doigts... Mais le coco que l'on a bu et lancé là, tête aveugle qui clame affranchie de l'épaule, détourne du dalot

la splendeur des eaux pourpres lamées de graisses et d'urines, où trame le savon comme de la toile d'araignée.'[a] (xiii)

Back in 'Pour fêter...' there is a passing mention of the constant threat of seismic disturbances that hung over the islands. The purple and yellow cloud that hangs over the 'golden volcano' – that is, La Soufrière – brings the serving-women out of their quarters, because it means eruption and earth-tremors ('Pour fêter...' iii). But it is in the populated centres that the seismic disturbances wreak the greatest havoc. One thinks immediately of the destruction of the whole town of Saint-Pierre by the eruption of Mont Pelé in 1902. The Leger family had left the islands before that terrifying disaster, but they were very directly affected by the great earthquake of 1897, which virtually destroyed the economy of Guadeloupe. Here in the 'Eloges' are recorded vivid memories of the soldered zinc boxes that were piled up in the covered market-place of Pointe-à-Pitre – hastily improvised coffins for disaster victims. And again the sky is watched: 'le ciel pommelé annonce pour ce soir / un autre tremblement de terre'[b] (xii).

Finally, there is an isolated short poem that was published separately in 1910 and incorporated into the 'Eloges' series in the 1911 book, only to be taken out of that series in later editions. In later editions it is entitled 'Histoire du Régent'. In form it is like the 'Eloges' we have just been considering, but in its impersonality it reminds one of the 'Récitation à l'éloge d'une Reine', and its violence recalls 'Des Villes sur trois modes'. The setting, though, is not Antillean. There is a 'prophète qui courait derrière les palissades, sur une chamelle borgne...',[c] suggesting North Africa or Asia. And its condensed picture of a barbarian conqueror burning the heaped-up dead on pyres and the Kings lying down 'nus

[a] The pink bitch drags, under the beggar's very nose, a whole belly of dugs. And the candy-girl / fights off / the wasps whose flight is like the bites of day on the back of the sea. A child sees it all, / so beautiful, / that he can no longer close his fingers... But the coconut that's been drained and tossed there, a blind clamouring head wrenched from its shoulder, / diverts from the gutter / the splendour of dark red waters fretted with grease and urine, where soap spins out a spidery filament.

[b] the dappled sky presaging for this evening / another earthquake.

[c] prophet speeding on a one-eyed camel behind the high fences

dans l'odeur de la mort',[a] rather than recalling any poem yet discussed, foreshadows the poems of the diplomatic period, especially *Anabase*.

But before we pass on to the poems of that period, it is well to consider the overall picture presented by the Antillean poems. Surely one of their striking features is the maturity of their idiom. There is almost no experimenting, no pastiche of other poets, no groping or fumbling for a style. We are already in the presence of a finished product. In reality we possess no juvenilia by Alexis Leger, in spite of the fact that 'Images à Crusoé 'was written when he was seventeen years old. This does not, of course, mean that there was no experimenting, fumbling or imitative writing. It simply means that Saint-John Perse had a very sure critical sense at an age when most writers have no critical sense at all. The phenomenon is all the more remarkable in that the Persean idiom is something without precedent in the French literary tradition. The danger of seeking affinities with Claudel has already been pointed out. The truest literary filiation is, rather, with a poet who (somewhat unbelievably) also inspired Claudel: namely, Rimbaud, and in particular the Rimbaud of *Les Illuminations*. But the apocalyptic, narcotic-visionary quality of these Rimbaud pieces, and the sullen revolt that smoulders throughout Rimbaud's work, are totally absent from Perse's Antillean poems. Young Alexis Leger actually lived the boyhood of which Rimbaud, in his landlocked Charleville, dreamed when he wrote 'Le Bateau ivre'. By some miracle, the boy Leger possessed a talent that enabled him to transmit this lived experience into authentic and finished poems. And it is worth noting in passing that, remarkable as 'Le Bateau ivre' may be, it exhibits far more mimesis, padding, and verbalism than anything in Perse's Antillean poems.

The resemblance to Rimbaud is strongest where poetic technique is concerned. The violent ellipses, the imperious short-circuiting of diction and imagery that one finds in *Les Illuminations* may well have furnished Leger with a model for his own increasingly condensed and stenographic mode of writing. But what separates the two poets completely is their psychological attitude in the face of reality. Rimbaud's poetry is a poetry of surly refusal and revolt, as was the conduct of his whole life. Perse's basic attitude is one of acceptance. At the level of childhood, this accep-

[a] naked in the odour of death

tance takes the form of an embrace of the natural world, an extraordinary connivance with stones and plants, with insects and animals, along with a spontaneous reverence for the family-centred plantation life. The childhood that is celebrated was marvellously self-sufficient: an enchanted solitude without loneliness, beautifully summed up in the last poem of the 'Eloges' series:

'A présent laissez-moi, je vais seul.

Je sortirai, car j'ai affaire; un insecte m'attend pour traiter. Je me fais joie

du gros œil à facettes: anguleux, imprévu, comme le fruit du cyprès.

Ou bien j'ai une alliance avec les pierres veinées-bleu: et vous me laissez également,

assis, dans l'amitié de mes genoux.'[a] (xviii)

[a] And now let me be, I'm going out alone. / I'll go out, for I've something to do: an insect is waiting to treat with me. I can't wait to see / his big, faceted eye: angular, unexpected, like the fruit of the cypress. / Or else I'm in league with the blue-veined stones: so, just let me be, / seated, in the friendship of my knees.

2

The Diplomatic Years

Anabase and *Amitié du Prince*

In 1916 the Quai d'Orsay sent Alexis Leger to China. Thereafter
he rapidly became something of a legend back home. In 1920, for
example, Francis Jammes, in the course of a letter to Arthur
Fontaine, wrote: 'As for another Alexis [i.e., Leger], I've finally
had outrageously fantastic news about him through his sister. As
soon as he enters the picture, everything becomes extravagant.
Not a single letter from him other than the one in which he re-
commended Mr. Li to you. Well, this time it's the whole Chinese
rigmarole. Bell-rimmed hats, pigtails, pagodas, mandarins, spies,
stolen letters, castor oil, and I don't know what all. The whole
family is so delighted to learn authoritatively – "the scepticism of
certain emissaries he had sent to France notwithstanding" – that
it was only too true that his letters had been fed to the sperm-
whales, that they – his family, swallowed his latest missive and
all its ridiculous explanations with the dispatch of Mr. Li down-
ing a bird's nest. He ended by saying: "Above all, please see that
no one doubts my friendship because of my silence." He'll be
able to write memoirs that Thibaudet will have to put alongside
Mérimée's.'[1]

The busy young diplomat may have stretched a point or two to
excuse his negligence as a correspondent; but Jammes, the most
stay-at-home of men, seems to forget that the wildest things did
happen in those early years of the Chinese Revolution. We know
that *Anabase* was composed in China. *Amitié du Prince*, published

in 1924, was probably composed shortly after 1921, the year of Leger's departure from China.[2] Thus, both these major works are the outgrowth of Leger's Asiatic years, and a few dates and un-legendary facts about that period should be of some help in under-standing both of the poems.

First, it should be noted that Leger's decision to pursue a diplo-matic career was anything but hasty. He began his preparation for the Foreign Service Examination in earnest in 1911, taking trips to Spain, England, and Germany for that purpose. He passed the examination brilliantly, and on the first try, in 1914. Had he waited one more year, he would have been unable to take the examin-ation because of the age-limit stipulation. After a brief stint in the press services of the Affaires Etrangères in Paris and then, because of the oncoming Germans, in Bordeaux, he was sent to China. That, as we have said, was in 1916. There was trouble in the French concession at Tientsin, and Leger was originally sent out on a temporary basis to help relieve pressures arising from that trouble. Instead, he almost immediately took up residence in Pei-ping and stayed on until 1921, steadily rising in the diplomatic ranks. In 1917 he observed at close quarters the abortive attempt to restore the Manchu dynasty. During part of his stay in Peiping, Leger had a disused Taoist temple at his disposal, about a day's journey on horseback from the city. He was particularly fond of this retreat, as it looked out on the caravan-routes leading to the northwest. It is in that setting that he is said to have composed *Anabase*. Subsequently he was able to follow the caravan routes into the Gobi Desert. He would like to have gone on to Touen Huang, where his friend Paul Pelliot, along with Sir Aurel Stein, had made such sensational finds, but the unsettled military con-ditions in western China prevented him from doing this, and like-wise from reaching Tibet. During one of his recreation leaves, Leger sailed the Sumatra-Borneo region in a small yacht. And finally, on his way home via America, in 1921, he took advantage of the travel-interlude to explore the inland Sea of Japan, and then to explore the isles of the South Pacific, again in a small yacht.

No sooner was Leger back in Paris than he was called to Wash-ington, D.C., for the 1921 International Conference on the Limi-tation of Armaments. It was there that he first met Aristide Briand, and from that moment on, Leger's rise in the French Foreign

Office was steady and rapid, culminating in his seven-year occu-
pancy of the post of Secretary General of Foreign Affairs from
1933 to 1940. Thus, from 1921 on, Paris, where he never did feel
entirely at home, was to be Leger's official place of residence. The
meeting with Briand was so decisive that it is quite legitimate to
speak of two periods in Leger's diplomatic career: the pre-Briand
era of 1914-1921, and the post-Briand era of 1922-1940.

During both periods the poet Saint-John Perse was not idle.
Bad correspondent that he may have been, his friends of the N.R.F.
team managed to keep track of him even during the Asiatic years.
When he reappeared in Paris, he was naturally the object of great
curiosity, and the 'team' wanted to see what he had written and
to publish it forthwith. But by this time Leger had decided to
keep his literary and diplomatic pursuits absolutely separate. This
he succeeded in doing to a remarkable degree, but pressures were
such that an absolutely water-tight partition could not be established. There were, fortunately, a few leaks.

There was, for example, the visit at which Fargue and Larbaud
were present, shortly after Leger's return to Paris. A concerted
effort was made to get Leger to reveal what he had written. He
produced an attaché case, opened it, and revealed a sheaf of manuscripts. Leger recalls the incident vividly, because Larbaud, peer-
ing in at the manuscripts, said in English, 'A whole bunch of
them!'[3] This would seem to indicate that a good part of the
'book' of manuscripts confiscated, and presumably destroyed, by
the Nazis in 1940 had been written before 1921. At any rate, Leger
authorized Larbaud to pick out one manuscript at random for
eventual publication. Out of the grab-bag came *Anabase*, which
was thus saved from oblivion. The Opening and Closing Songs
of *Anabase* were then published without a signature in the April,
1922, issue of the *Nouvelle Revue française* and the November, 1922,
issue of *Intentions*, respectively. That same year Leger wrote a
short poem in tribute to Larbaud that was also published in *Intentions*, likewise without signature. It was not until the main body
of *Anabase* – the ten cantos for which the Opening and Closing
Songs form parentheses, so to speak – appeared in the April, 1924,
issue of the *Nouvelle Revue française* that the now-famous pseudonym appeared, but only in the truncated form St-J. Perse, which
likewise appeared on the title page of the first complete text of
Anabase published in book-form in 1924. The same abbreviated

pseudonym appeared on another poem published in 1924. This was *Amitié du Prince*, which appeared in the sumptuous new international review *Commerce*.

Leger had, in fact, become a silent partner of the editorial staff of *Commerce*, which was financed by the princess Bassiano. This extraordinarily enlightened patroness, who was to launch *Botteghe Oscure* after World War II, was the half-sister of Mrs. Katherine Biddle née Chapin, the wife of Francis Biddle, future Attorney General of the United States. Thus began a connection that, some sixteen years later, was to be of great importance in the life of the refugee, Alexis Leger. The title of the review *Commerce* was actually suggested by Leger,[4] and in *Anabase*, which appeared just before the review was launched, the nomad chieftain declares: 'j'arrêtais sur les marchés déserts ce pur commerce de mon âme' (Canto I).[a] Unfortunately, after the publication of *Amitié du Prince*, only one other poem by the mysterious St-J. Perse was to appear, namely, the brief 'Chanson' (later to be called 'Chanson du présomptif' and incorporated with *Amitié du Prince* in *La Gloire des Rois*). It was first printed in the winter, 1924, issue of *Commerce*. After that, the long silence set in,[5] to be broken only eighteen years later, with the publication of *Exil*, still signed with the abbreviated St-J. Perse. Fortunately, the two big items salvaged from the diplomatic years are of major importance. Both require detailed commentary, though for somewhat different reasons.

Before we approach *Anabase* and *Amitié du Prince*, however, a word must be said about the 'Poème' for Valery Larbaud. It was a 'command performance' for an homage-to-Larbaud issue of *Intentions*, undoubtedly written shortly before the issue was published in November 1922. It was, therefore, composed after *Anabase* and, most probably, after *Amitié du Prince*. Because of the marginal character of the 'Poème', however, we mention it before tackling the two major items. Perse has not permitted its inclusion in any of the collected editions of his work, undoubtedly because of the occasional nature of the piece, which is as much in the style of Larbaud's A. O. Barnabooth as it is of St-J. Perse. The poem is exclusively for Valery Larbaud and contains private allusions that students of Larbaud may someday explain to us ('des pence pour Haendel', 'la fille de Lady J...', the twice-cited English sequence 'Roses, rosemaries, marigold leaves and daisies...').[6] The

---

[a] I established in the desolate markets the pure commerce of my soul.

poem depicts a proto-Barnabooth, somewhat bored, but fittingly ensconced in a luxurious British colonial hotel, thinking about departure. Here and there a sumptuous line suggests Perse's grand manner: 'un peu avant le gong du soir et la saison d'un souffle dans les toiles, quand le soleil fait son miel du corps des femmes dans les chambres.'[a] But this is clearly not the carefully distilled concentrate of *Anabase*.

This latter poem, of all Perse's work, is the most widely known and commented upon – a fact that is partially explained by its having been promptly translated, and frequently by poets of great talent, into several foreign languages: Russian (1926), German (1929), English (1930 – the T. S. Eliot version), Spanish (1931), Rumanian (1931) and later into several other languages. From the outset *Anabase* has exercised great fascination, yet it remains one of the most austere and baffling of Perse's works. The commentaries on it have been so numerous and contradictory that, instead of passing them in review, I shall simply state my own interpretation, indicating where I have borrowed from earlier exegeses. Here more than anywhere else it is important to let Perse speak for himself. He has, unfortunately, said much less about *Anabase* than about some of his other poems, and the little he did say came late and at second remove. But that little cannot be neglected.

In the fall of 1960, immediately after announcement of the Nobel award, Perse granted an interview to the journalist, Pierre Mazars. During the course of that interview, the poet is quoted as saying: '*Anabase* has as its object the poem of the loneliness of action. Action among men quite as much as the action of the human spirit upon itself. I sought to bring together the synthesis – not the passive, but the active synthesis – of human resourcefulness. But one does not treat psychological themes by using abstract means. It was necessary to "illustrate": it is the poem most filled with concreteness; and some persons have seen orientalism in it.'[7]

This quotation was undoubtedly reported from notes that had to be taken down very hastily, for the inelegance and fuzziness it exhibits are most un-Persean. But even though we see in a glass darkly, what does come through is of great interest. There is insistence on the main theme being that of the loneliness of action.

[a] shortly before the evening gong and the season of gusts in the canvas, when the sun draws its honey from the bodies of women in the chambers

Or rather, since Perse wanted to 'illustrate' the theme concretely, the loneliness of the man of action. That man of action is both the protagonist and the reciter of *Anabase*. He is the military, political, and psychological leader of a nomadic people, and we shall refer to him simply as the Leader. As such, he serves as the focal image of the *ressource humaine* – that reservoir of human potentialities that Perse seeks to present in the poem. The Leader remains nameless and even faceless. The more one becomes familiar with the poem, the more does the Leader become an astonishingly live presence. Yet we know him *only from within*. He reveals to us his inmost thoughts and urges, yet he is most reticent about his biography. We know nothing of his appearance, his manners or habits, let alone his ancestry and origins.

The military expedition (*anabasis*) that is the burden of the Leader's tale takes place in unspecified regions of the Asiatic continent.[8] It is entirely probable that the poet's travels in China and Mongolia, as well as his association with such Asiatic specialists as Pelliot, may have given him the basic idea for the external framework of his poem – whence the statement that 'some persons have seen orientalism in it'. But the Asiatic setting is quite incidental to the main business of the poem. The desert-wastes that are so powerfully evoked could be duplicated in North Africa or even in various parts of the New World. And, more important, there is nothing specifically Asiatic about the various peoples referred to in the poem. The choice of Asia as the setting for the poem does, however, have one very real advantage. Asia, more than any of the other continents, has been the place where, in spite of immense geographical barriers, the tides of conquest and migration have repeatedly flowed and ebbed. Within its vastnesses, Occident and Orient, Arctic and Tropic, have met, clashed, intermingled, and drifted apart from time immemorial in the most prolonged exhibition known to us of the working out of *la ressource humaine*.

The poem's chronological setting is as vague as its geographical one. Since there is a reference to 'great Seleucid histories', we may suppose that its action takes place some time after the Alexandrian conquest of Western Asia. But the time-limit at the near end is much vaguer. All one can say is that it pre-dates the era of mechanization, for the Leader moves among peoples who have writing, metallurgy, some sort of banking, and a complex social organization, but they are as yet untouched by mechanization. The omission of the mechanized phase of human history is, I feel, intentional and significant. In the Mazars interview, Perse is further quoted as saying, 'People say I travelled in the desert for scholarly and archaeological reasons. What really attracted me out there was simply a mode of life on the natural and animal level, which is in touch with things eternal, as is always the case in the desert.' It is this preoccupation that underlies *Anabase*: a concern with elemental and eternal human needs. These, the machine tends more and more to obscure and disguise, just as the physical extremes encountered in desert places tend to accentuate them. It is this same concern that accounts for the aspect of *Anabase* that has been so neatly caught in Morand's phrase: 'une sorte de jansénisme du pittoresque'.[9]

This astringent tone is established from the very outset, and if one can, so to speak, hear the melody of the Opening Song, the rest of the poem becomes much easier to follow. That is why we shall here subject the Opening Song to a rather pitiless explication. Like all the rest of the poem, it is divided into verse-paragraphs that we shall refer to as 'strophes'. Here in the Song there are only three strophes. The first and third begin with a statement concerning the birth of a colt: 'Il naissait un poulain sous les feuilles de bronze',[a] the tense of the verb becoming 'naquit' in the second instance. At the outset, the birth is still in process; by the beginning of the last strophe the colt has been successfully foaled. We are concerned with horse-nomads, and the successful foaling of a colt at the very outset of the poem augurs well for the nomad tribe, and the Leader will not be long in resolving on further cavalcades.

He tells us that 'Un homme mit des baies amères dans nos mains. Etranger. Qui passait.'[b] The mention in the first strophe is taken up again in the third, where the partitive 'des' becomes 'ces' – '*these* berries' that are now contemplated by the Leader, who goes on to say 'et l'Etranger à ses façons par les chemins de toute la terre'.[c] So we know that the Leader has tasted and found bitter these berries put in his hands by a wanderer over the roads of the world. The fruit has been brought from a land through

[a] Under the bronze leaves a colt was foaled.
[b] A man laid bitter berries in our hands. Stranger. Who was passing by.
[c] and the Stranger is about his ways on the roads of all the earth.

which he has passed and about which he has spoken, for the
Leader says: 'Et voici qu'il est bruit d'autres provinces à mon
gré...'.[a] The second strophe, in fact, has already revealed something about these far-off provinces: 'Car le Soleil entre au Lion
et l'Etranger a mis son doigt dans la bouche des morts. Etranger.
Qui riait. Et nous parle d'une herbe.'[b] It is high summer, late in
July, for the sun is entering the sign of Leo. In the northern
hemisphere this may be a time of drought and pestilence. (The
suggestion of pestilence is reinforced when we learn that Alexis
Leger, while he was in charge of the administration of the section
of Peiping reserved for the various diplomatic corps, had to take
measures against an epidemic of plague.) The distant province
are, thus, vulnerable; and, even more important, they are grasslands. The Stranger laughs provocatively. And in the lines that
follow, we learn that the Leader's own people seem to have
reached a plateau of material well-being that is beginning to weigh
on the restless spirit of the Leader.

This well-being is curiously embodied in the ambiguous figure
of the Leader's daughter, who appears at the end of the first
strophe under the tallest tree of the year, and at the end of the
third, 'sous la plus belle robe de l'année'.[c] The ambiguity arises
in the intermediate reference at the end of the second strophe:
'Mon âme, grande fille, vous aviez vos façons qui ne sont pas les
nôtres.'[d] Is there an actual daughter with whom the Leader momentarily and figuratively identifies the passive, sensual side of his
being, to which he opposes his real *self*, the self which has restless
ways that must always eventually triumph? The ellipse here, as
in a number of other places in *Anabase*, is extreme to the point of
obscurity. What *is* clear, however, is that the Leader's real self
rejoices in the trumpet-call and freedom of movement: 'que la
trompette m'est délice et la plume savante au scandale de l'aile!'[e]

Throughout the Opening Song, and intermittently throughout
the body of the whole poem, we find isolated nouns, set off by a

---

[a] And here now is news of other provinces to my liking...
[b] For the Sun enters the sign of the Lion and the Stranger has put his
finger in the mouth of the Dead. Stranger. Who laughed. And tells us of a
grass.
[c] robed in the loveliest robe of the year
[d] 'My soul, great girl, you had your ways which are not ours.'
[e] how the trumpet rejoices my heart and how adept is the feather to the
scandal of the wing!

period in order to draw attention to them. Such setting-off usually means that the words will occur later on in contexts that will make their meaning clear and add to their significance. The Stranger ('Etranger. Qui passait.'), for example, will reappear at the end of Canto v and also in Canto ix. He has been present all along, the symbol of the mysterious force that drives the Leader and his people on. Or again, in the last strophe of the Opening Song, there are 'Bitume et roses, don du chant! Tonnerre et flûtes dans les chambres!'[a] These substantive phrases reinforce the already-stated suggestions of ease and well-being. But they go even farther. Later in the poem (Canto v) there is another reference to bitumen. It is connected with the dead, for it was used in embalming corpses as far back as the early Egyptian dynasties. And roses, cultivated as opposed to wild, have funereal overtones in *Anabase* (Cantos vi and x). The well-being verges, thus, on boredom and stagnation. The vaguely ominous thunder mingles with the fluting and song. The ease and indolence are becoming stifling. But all this is very obliquely suggested by a combination of 'cross-referencing' and thematic development of imagery. It is one of several devices that helps convert a highly condensed narrative into a poem of vast proportions and resonance.

The main lines of that narrative are quite simple. The first five cantos are an account of the actual work of constructing and organizing a great port-city on an estuary. But even while the construction-work proceeds, there are signs of restlessness in the Leader. These signs become explicit in the sixth and seventh cantos, leading finally to the *anabasis* proper (Gr. ἀνάβασις – a going up and into), which is described in the last three cantos. The elliptical technique already evident in the Opening Song is carried on throughout the body of the poem, and while vividness and intensity are achieved thereby, the suppression of transitional materials is sometimes so great, and the symbolic detail so heavily weighted, that it is not always easy to say just what is going on within each canto. T. S. Eliot clearly sensed this when he translated *Anabase* into English, and in the well-known preface to his first English version he gives a series of 'canto-headings' which he borrows from Lucien Fabre – one of the earliest and best commentators on *Anabase*. Though I am in general agreement with most of Fabre's indications, there are a few places where I think

[a] Bitumen and roses, gift of song! Thunder and fluting in the chambers!

he has gone seriously astray, and a few others where a shift in emphasis seems called for. Here, then, are my own 'canto-headings':

I. Establishment of a new order in a coastal region
II. Chthonic ritual
III. Reaffirmation of the principle of action
IV. Founding of the city
V. Nocturne: solitude of the Leader
VI. Propaganda and recruiting
VII. The eve of departure
VIII. Migration to the Western Lands
IX. Reception by the women of the new country
X. Celebration, census, and the pursuits of leisure

It is my hope that the interested reader might 'extrapolate' the exegesis given for the Opening Song, and that further explication would be superfluous.[10] It may, however, be of some use to consider a few points in each canto that are either particularly disconcerting or that are considerably illuminated by passages in other writings by Perse.

In Canto I, for example, after the Leader has auspiciously launched his epic, he tells how he and his people were driven on by a collective dream that is difficult to recall, and even more difficult to comprehend, 'Aux ides pures du matin...'[a]. The ides being the mid-point, or very nearly, of Roman months, the time of day indicated would be shortly before high noon. The compelling dream is older than the Leader and even than the history of his people: 'songe, notre aînesse' are his words, rendered by an unavoidable makeshift, 'our dream, older than ourselves'. 'Aînesse' actually means primogeniture and here stresses the fact of priority. This arresting association of dream with primogeniture occurs once again, almost forty years after the composition of *Anabase*, in a tribute Perse devoted to the memory of Rabindranath Tagore. He speaks of Tagore thus: 'Poète, il a su porter haut l'aînesse de son rêve sans se laisser distraire de l'homme de son temps', which may be approximately rendered, 'As a poet, he managed to bear high the prior claims of his dream without letting himself be turned away from the men of his own time.'[11] The nomad Leader, too, bears aloft the primacy of his people's dream, which he translates into action by means of an idea 'pure as salt'. Throughout the poem, salt will be the symbol of the pure stimulus to action, of a deep-seated desire beyond immediate physical needs.

The Leader fully realizes that his main role is not that of the

[a] At the pure ides of day...

military tactician or even of the builder. His mission and his strength lie in his ability to keep alive the psychological motivation to act. His function is pervasive and powerful, like that of the Sun he has privately invoked: ('Et le soleil n'est point nommé, mais sa puissance est parmi nous.')[a] In many primitive religions, naming a thing robs it of its potency, and the covert force that is the basis of the Leader's relationship with his followers is conveyed in an even more striking image when the Leader says that his soul is 'parmi vous / invisible et fréquente ainsi qu'un feu d'épines en plein vent',[b] i.e., like a fire that burns with so pure a flame that it is almost invisible in the light of day.

In this opening canto we also come across the first of a number of homologous enumerations that occur in *Anabase* and subsequent poems. In fact, these lists have been seized upon as the 'trademark' of Perse's poetic technique. It is indeed a device that he uses extensively, but it is neither altogether new nor any more important than some other aspects of his technique. These Persean enumerations, which must surely make the English-speaking reader think of Whitman, have been excellently characterized by Roger Caillois. He says of them, in part:

> The poet calls upon the totality of the world in order to
> establish, among the infinite variety of phenomena it offers,
> fragile and tenuous homologies. The unsuspected justifica-
> tion of them appears slowly and gradually as the accumula-
> tion of data reveals ever a little more and, finally, completely
> reveals the common denominator, latent throughout, which
> explains the prodigious concourse.[12]

The common denominator of the relatively short series of this First Canto is given in the last item of the enumeration: 'ô chercheurs, ô trouveurs de raisons pour s'en aller ailleurs.'[c] Once more, the Leader knows that what he must appeal to is the deep, inexplicable urge of pure restlessness, beyond all conscious reasons.

The Second Canto presents a sudden change in tone and tempo. It is brief, brooding, and mysterious. The royal linen is spread out on the aromatic bushes of the high slopes in order to dry. The silence is made more oppressive by the insistent chirp of crickets.

---

[a] (And the Sun is not named, but his power is amongst us.)
[b] among you / invisible and insistent as a fire of thorns in the gale,
[c] O seekers, O finders of reasons to be up and be gone

The comments of the Leader as he and his party step over the gowns of the Queen and her daughter are fraught with sexual overtones. And the troubling surge of sexuality is also a reminder of mortality. For the first time in the narrative the Dead are mentioned, enigmatically and uneasily. But a sudden gust of wind, presaging a storm, disperses both the royal linen and the sultriness, and along with them, the oppressive sexuality. The air is cleared for action.

The inner struggle between action and contemplation is the source of tension in Canto III. In the midst of the parleyings with ambassadors and foreign kings, in the midst of all the business of administration, the Leader is constantly being distracted by the fascination he finds in contemplating the ways of his own soul. He must be on guard against his own persuasiveness, for 'Mon âme est pleine de mensonge, comme la mer agile et forte sous la vocation de l'éloquence!'[a] As on the aromatic hillside of Canto II: 'L'odeur puissante m'environne. Et le doute s'élève sur la réalité des choses.'[b] Contemplation that leads to nothing but further contemplation is not merely sterile, it is dangerous, one might almost say narcotic. That is why the Leader follows the lines just quoted with a declaration that is central to the whole poem: 'Mais si un homme tient pour agréable sa tristesse, qu'on le produise dans le jour! et mon avis est qu'on le tue, sinon / il y aura une sédition.'[c] The Leader has just won a victory over his own soul's sedition. He goes on to belittle the Dead, whose presence was suddenly felt in the preceding canto. Finally, the hoisting of the horse's skull on a lance presages further cavalcades, further action.

The Fourth Canto is one of the easiest to follow and one of the most striking. The building of the harbour-city and the flourishing trade that comes to it are set forth in a flood of vivid imagery. The face of the land has changed; the city has been dedicated 'sous les labiales d'un nom pur'.[d] It is characteristic that we should be given such a precise detail about the city's name and yet never

[a] My soul is full of deceit like the agile strong sea under the vocation of eloquence!
[b] The strong smells encompass me. And doubt is cast on the reality of things.
[c] But if a man shall cherish his sorrow – let him be brought to light! and I say, let him be slain, otherwise / there will be an uprising.
[d] under the labials of a clear sounding name

learn what that name is. This device creates a curious concreteness without specificity that characterizes the whole of *Anabase* and much of the subsequent poetry of Perse.

There is in this same canto, however, a sentence – one of three that is set off by parentheses – that may seem very baffling on first reading. It comes after the Leader says impatiently that this is not the moment to tell of alliances concluded with peoples on the other shores. As if to indicate glancingly the state of some of these peoples, he adds: '(Un enfant triste comme la mort des singes – sœur aînée d'une grande beauté – nous offrait une caille dans un soulier de satin rose.)'[a] Knowingly or unknowingly, the child is soliciting for his beautiful elder sister. The gesture is common in depressed, poverty-stricken communities throughout the world. These nearby peoples inhabit, as a later canto tells us (Canto VI), 'pays épuisés où les coutumes sont à reprendre'.[b] At the very end of Canto IV there is another suggestion of 'pays épuisés': 'Et un homme s'avança à l'entrée du Désert – profession de son père: marchand de flacons.'[c] Eliot has translated 'flacons' by 'scent-bottles'. But that does not agree with Perse's own declaration that the boy's father deals in the most basic of items for desert areas: a container for liquids.[13] When life can 'get by' without almost everything else, it can hardly survive in desert areas without some container for liquids. Life, once again, is reduced to its barest necessities.

The shouting and tumult of the festivities that climax Canto IV are followed by the silent withdrawal of Canto V, which is a nocturne of great beauty. Canto V is actually the crux of the psychological aspect of the whole poem, the most overt expression of the loneliness of the man of action. The Leader cannot help feeling contempt for those who follow him, and yet he is bound to them in a curiously tender way: 'Je vous hais tous avec douceur...'.[d] Contemplating the starry hosts on a clear desert night, he cannot help longing to join these Confederated Kings of Heaven, to wander alone among the pamphleteering Princes of the sky: 'Que j'aille seul avec les souffles de la nuit, parmi les Princes pamphlé-

---

[a] (A child sorrowful as the death of apes – with an elder sister of great beauty – offered us a quail in a slipper of rose-coloured satin.)

[b] exhausted countries where the ways of life are to be made over

[c] And a man strode forth at the threshold of the desert – profession of his father: dealer in flasks.

[d] I hate you all, gently...

taires, parmi les chutes de Biélides!...'[a] The Leader, like most nomads, is understandably concerned with the stars, but his knowledge of astronomy, in the case of the Bielids, does seem a bit disconcerting. The Bielids are a meteor-shower that occurs in late November. Though it is certainly not a recent phenomenon, its name *is*, for it is derived from that of the German astronomer, Wilhelm von Biela (1782-1856).

Far more in harmony with the prevailing tone of the poem is the metaphor drawn from falconry, which we find a few lines further on. 'Ame jointe en silence au bitume des Mortes! Cousues d'aiguilles nos paupières! louée l'attente sous nos cils!'[b] One notes first that the bitumen, which occurs in the Opening Song, is here once again connected with the dead. Second, one notes that the dead are *women* ('Mortes') – a fact that is lost in Eliot's translation where, undoubtedly for reasons of euphony, 'Mortes' simply becomes 'the Dead'. But the most striking reference is the one to falconry. Before the practice of hooding became generalized, it was customary to sew together the eyelids of prized falcons with a single thread, thus facilitating the training of the bird in going after only desirable quarry. This cruel procedure is known as 'seeling', from the Old French *siller* or *ciller*. The Leader's impulses, held in check and plunged in darkness, like those of the seeled falcon, are forced inward. And in this inner darkness there is communion with the Dead Women, the fecund past.

Darkness and night pervade this whole canto. The dreams dreamed while we are asleep are here characterized by the Leader as 'pures pestilences de la nuit',[c] a principle of demoralization that is exactly the reverse of the collective Dream invoked in Canto I. Just as the Leader, in Canto III, would take measures against those who delight in their sadness, here he declares even more explicitly 'je m'élèverai dans mes pensées contre l'activité du songe'.[d]

The canto ends with dawn breaking. And at this hour of the dissipation of dreams, the Stranger of the Opening Song suddenly reappears. Clearly, it is time to be moving on. It is time to stir up passions and recruit men for a new cavalcade.

[a] Let me go alone with the night winds, among the pamphleteering Princes, among the Bielid showers!...
[b] Soul united in silence to the bitumen of the female Dead! our eyelids sewn with needles! praised be the waiting under our eyelids!
[c] pure pestilences of the night
[d] in my thought I will protest against the activity of dream!

Thus, in Canto vi, the horsemen on the capes broadcast word of the new expedition in the making. They speak of farther shores, of 'lois données sur d'autres rives, et les alliances par les femmes au sein des peuples dissolus; de grands pays vendus à la criée sous l'inflation solaire'.[a] These lands recall those far provinces, prostrate under the July heat, referred to by the Stranger in the Opening Song – the curious phrase, 'inflation solaire' suggests the connection. The identical phrase occurs in one of Perse's most recent poems. Speaking of birds in general in his essay-poem *Oiseaux* (1962), Perse describes the bird as 'Migrateur, et hanté d'inflation solaire...'.[b] The shell of air around the earth expands where the sun strikes most directly, and the migratory birds pursue this shifting summer. Here in *Anabase*, however, the context adds the suggestion of economic inflation. These lands, parched under the merciless sun, are economically vulnerable. And the words occurring a line or so later: 'les provinces mises à prix dans l'odeur solennelle des roses'[c] suggests death once again, and the pestilence mentioned in the Opening Song. It is likewise in this Sixth Canto that the second homologous series occurs, much longer than the first, this time telescoping into one riotous tangle all the possible happenings of a great military expedition.

The call has gone out, and then there is the waiting for the response, the slow awakening to the lure of the vast spaces and the search for the ultimate sources of the primeval Dream. The marvellous desert imagery of Canto vii conveys all this and, with a last withdrawal for communion with the Dead, concludes the preparations for the actual anabasis, the march up and into the interior.

The grass-provinces spoken of by the Stranger are at an indeterminate place far to the west, and the trek there is long, harsh, and killing. It is a trek to some ultimate frontier, not merely geographic: 'beaucoup de choses entreprises sur les ténèbres de l'esprit – beaucoup de choses à loisir sur les frontières de l'esprit –'.[d] The dissensions that arise in the ranks as the going gets harder

---

[a] laws enacted upon other shores, alliances by marriage in the midst of dissolute peoples, great territories auctioned off beneath the inflation of the sun
[b] Migratory, haunted by the inflation of the sun...
[c] the provinces priced for sale in the solemn odour of roses
[d] many things undertaken on the darkness of the spirit – infinity of things at leisure on the frontiers of the spirit –

have to be controlled by the Leader, whose only weapon now is the ultimate psychological one. And at a crucial moment, at a halt by a desert crossroads, a lightning bolt flashes down, making manifest the will of the gods: 'et l'éclair famélique m'assigne ces provinces en Ouest'.[a] Beyond are the grasslands of greater leisure. The expedition presses on toward them. Summing up, the Leader declares brutally, 'Un grand principe de violence commandait à nos mœurs'.[b]

The anabasis has been an exclusively male venture; so, when the Western Lands are finally sighted, their nubility is symbolized by the female delegation that comes out to meet the conquerors. Like a choric leader, one member of the delegation makes a welcoming prophecy. The actual invasion of the Western Lands turns out to be less a battle than an embrace. The conquerors fecundate the country, and from this springs a new order.

The last Canto, number Ten, consecrates this new order. It is made up chiefly of the third and most dizzying homologous series of the poem. In this series the whole organization of a highly complex culture-unit is brought to life with all its strangeness, brutality, refinement, all its complex and interweaving crosscurrents. First there are the ritual acts, followed by a staggering list of public works and private transactions, each suggested by a telling concrete detail. The rhetorical device at the base of all these homologous series is the synecdoche. By way of example, consider the final phrase of one section of the series under discussion: 'et la fumée des hommes en tous lieux...'.[c] What better way of suggesting the teeming activities of a flourishing community?

In the last portion of the series, which enumerates a bewildering array of vocations, avocations, and idle pastimes, there occurs a curious reference that brings home once more how deeply rooted in concrete fact this poetry is. In the crowd there is 'celui qui mange ... des vers de palmes'.[d] This unlikely delicacy, it turns out, was eaten by the poet himself. In 1911, when André Gide had the 'Eloge' poems published in book-form at his own expense, Leger thanked Gide in a charming letter. He explained that he would

[a] and the starved lightning allots me these provinces in the West.
[b] A great principle of violence dictated our fashions.
[c] and the firesmoke of man everywhere...
[d] he who eats ... the maggots of the palmtree

request that a particularly lovely tree back in his native Guadeloupe be named after Gide. The tree in question was a specimen
of Oreodoxa, the cabbage-palm, which Léger went on to describe at length. Among other things, he wrote: 'And have the
Botanists further told you that it is this tall palmtree, the hand-
somest of its race, that is doomed to death by having its heart
cut out, that is, the leaves, still white and tender, that are curled
at the centre of the crown, which are eaten, chopped up in an
extraordinarily good salad? And then, two months later, one has
a fine harvest of "cabbage-palm worms", fat larvae of a beetle
(calandra palmarum) that lays its eggs in the tree-pith. You eat
them alive or slightly roasted, always in a salad, with lemon-juice,
pepper, and salt. It's very good...'[14]

Such is the strange variety of the forms taken by *la ressource
humaine*. And this Tenth Canto is the ultimate celebration of that
reservoir of human potentialities. They are literally inexhaustible,
and the whole homologous series is one vast synecdoche – the
merest sampling of infinite human possibilities. Not even the
Western Lands will give them ample play. The Leader's last words
are 'et ma pensée n'est point distraite du navigateur'.[a]

The Closing Song that follows is a serene coda in a major key.
After strenuous effort there come these interludes of complete fulfilment. Even the gentle hatred the Leader has felt for his followers is gone now. Let those who have never experienced such a
day as this die in peace: 'Et paix à ceux, s'ils vont mourir, qui
n'ont point vu ce jour.'[b]

The Song ends with the famous line wherein the diplomat
Alexis Léger, future statesman and leader of men, speaks of his
alter ego, Saint-John Perse. 'Mais de mon frère le poète on a eu
des nouvelles. Il a écrit encore une chose très douce. Et quelques-
uns en eurent connaissance...'[c]

Among the few who had knowledge thereof at a fairly early
date was T. S. Eliot. As we know, he was so impressed with the
poem that he took the trouble to translate it into English. Yet
even Eliot had misgivings about the poem's piling up of ellipses
and radical suppression of transitional material. 'I was not con-

[a] and my thought is not heedless of the navigator.
[b] And peace to those, if they die, who have not seen this day.
[c] But there is word from my brother the poet. Once more he has written
a song of great sweetness. And some there are who have seen it."

vinced of Mr. Perse's imaginative order,' he admits, 'until I had
read the poem five or six times.' That admission should be reassuring to those of us who are still baffled by certain sequences
in the poem. The 'stenographic technique' that first appears in
certain of the 'Eloges'[15] is here carried to an extreme. There are,
in fact, other poems by Perse that one may prefer to *Anabase*,
even though it still remains the best known of his works. Yet the
extraordinary *tone* of the poem, which we mentioned at the outset,
is so compelling that a sensitive reader reads on without unduly
resisting the hard passages. It is a tone of solemnity and ease that
had not been struck before in French poetry in so sustained a
fashion. Perhaps it is essentially a poem for other poets. Von
Hofmannsthal and Eliot and MacLeish were among its early admirers, and so was Rainer Maria Rilke.[16] The list of names is im-
pressive, but it does not keep me from giving my preference to
the other major poem surviving from Perse's diplomatic period,
Amitié du Prince.

Like *Anabase*, *Amitié du Prince* is a poem about anonymous
potentates and movements through vast regions. Because of these
similarities in the actual content of the poems, and also because
Amitié du Prince was composed either during or immediately after
Perse's stay in China,[17] critics have rather summarily decided that
the setting of the latter poem is also Asiatic. Nothing in the text
clearly indicates the Asiatic mainland, or any other clearly defined
region, for that matter. All we know is that the Sage who recounts
the poem (it is rather as if the Stranger of *Anabase* broke his
silence) is on his way to visit a Prince whose domain is a region
of reddish lands: 'un pays de terres pourpres'. Fleeting references
to the mimosa, to the ipomea root, to an unspecified stimulant
leaf, to marshlands and camphor woods are really of little help,
since these items could form part of the physical environment of
several widely separated areas on the face of the earth. Perse
has said that he himself visualizes the poem in a landscape something like certain parts of Ethiopia or of Borneo which had impressed him. Thus, the exact geographical setting is here even
less important than the purposely vague Asiatic setting of
Anabase.

The structure of *Amitié du Prince* is, however, quite different
from *Anabase*. Here there are only four cantos, each concluding
with the refrain: ' – C'est du Roi que je parle, ornement de nos

veilles, honneur du sage sans honneur.'[a] The term 'prince' in the poem's title is, thus, used in the generic sense to designate any noble of the blood royal, here, the king himself. The whole poem is really an apostrophe addressed to the Prince by a shadowy figure, a man of letters, a 'sage sans honneur', who is nevertheless honoured by the Prince. In the first canto the Sage reports what the people along his route say of their King, 'et la louange n'était point maigre'.[b] In the second canto the report is continued and amplified until a very complex image of the Prince is created. The third canto is an exchange of letters; first there is the Prince's welcoming letter to the Sage, and then the text of the Sage's reply. Finally, the last canto recounts the arrival of the Sage and his caravan at the royal residence. *Anabase* is exclusively mono-phonic; *Amitié*, on the other hand, has two voices. Its tone, more-over, is that of relaxed conversation and meditation. There is none of the epic tension of *Anabase*. The Prince seems to have gone one step beyond the Leader of *Anabase*: the Prince's worldly conquests are over; his migrations are now inward, beyond the known frontiers of the human spirit. And though he says in his letter to the Sage, 'et j'ai moi-même affaire ailleurs',[c] the prevailing tone of the poem indicates that this Prince is essentially sedentary, the embodiment of order and well-being rather than of restless-ness and conquest.

The terms used to describe the Prince recall those that are applied to the Stranger in *Anabase*. In the earlier poem it is said:

' – Et l'Etranger tout habillé

   de ses pensées nouvelles se fait encore des partisans dans les voies du silence: son œil est plein d'une salive,

      il n'y a plus en lui substance d'homme.'[d]

In *Amitié* the Prince is constantly referred to as 'lean'; the open-ing words of the poem read: 'Et toi plus maigre qu'il ne sied au tranchant de l'esprit, homme aux narines minces parmi nous, ô Très-Maigre! ô Subtil! Prince vêtu de tes sentences ainsi qu'un

---

[a] – It is of the King that I speak, ornament of our vigils, honour of the sage without honour.

[b] and the praise was not meagre

[c] and I too have concerns elsewhere

[d] – And the Stranger clothed / in his new thoughts, acquires still more partisans in the ways of silence: his eye is full of a sort of saliva, / there is no more substance of man in him.

arbre sous bandelettes.'[a] He has his 'Bouche close à jamais sur la feuille de l'âme!'[b] and he is referred to as 'prince taciturne'. Indeed, the roles of the Stranger and the Leader in *Anabase* seem reversed in *Amitié du Prince*, for in the letter which the Prince sends to his visitor he says:

> '...La guerre, le négoce, les règlements de dettes religieuses sont d'ordinaire la cause des déplacements lointains: toi tu te plais aux longs déplacements sans cause. Je connais ce tourment de l'esprit. Je t'enseignerai la source de ton mal. Hâte-toi.'[c]

It is as if the Leader of *Anabase*, having overcome his wanderlust, becomes the adviser to the Stranger.

In *Amitié*, as in the earlier poem, the technique of concreteness without specificity is used with great effectiveness. We know the Leader of *Anabase* only from within; here we know the Prince only from without. Except in the brief letter of welcome to the visiting Sage, we see him only through the eyes of his admiring subjects and of the Sage himself. His physical appearance is made very plain: generally lean, with even leaner nostrils. His royal headgear carries an aigrette that is reflected in his welcoming smile: 'Et par dessus la foule des lettrés, l'aigrette d'un sourire me guide jusqu'à lui.'[d] His eyes are deep-set, 'les cils hantés d'ombrages immortels et la barbe poudrée d'un pollen de sagesse'.[e] His movements are seemly and graceful; and his clothes, at least for the welcoming of his visitor, are sumptuous robes of gold.

We also know a good deal about his solitary ways. He avoids the mad Queen, his wife. He sings princely songs for his own pleasure at night. He sleeps little, is ascetic in his tastes, spurns the opulence of the royal couch, 'sur des nattes maigres fréquentant nos filles les plus minces'.[f] But if he is 'dur pour soi-même',[g]

[a] And you, leaner than is befitting, on the keen edge of the spirit, man of the thin nostrils among us, o Very-Lean! o Subtle one! Prince attired in your sayings like a tree wrapped in narrow bands

[b] Mouth forever closed on the leaf of the soul!

[c] ... War and trading, religious debts to discharge, these are mostly the reason for distant displacements: but you take pleasure in long displacements without reason. I know this torment of the spirit. I shall teach you the source of your ill. Make haste.

[d] And above the throng of scholars, the aigrette of a smile guides me to him.

[e] eyelashes haunted by immortal shadows and beard powdered with a pollen of wisdom

[f] on meagre mats frequenting our thinnest girls

[g] stern with himself

he is tolerant of others and at ease among his subjects. When the visiting Sage arrives, the Prince is gaming on the threshold, indulging in witty exchanges, all of which is interrupted with the utmost simplicity to welcome the visitor. The visit is an annual one, and the visitor a man of a race different from the Prince's: 'Mais d'une race à l'autre la route est longue.'[a] The purpose of these annual visits is for the two men to exchange views on matters of the mind and spirit, 'choses probantes et peu sûres'.[b] And the Prince adds: 'Et nous nous réjouirons des convoitises de l'esprit...'.[c]

This Prince, like the Leader of *Anabase*, has learned to judge and manipulate the non-material forces that motivate mankind, and that is why his kingdom is well-ordered, flourishing, and content. The lands of white earth, where wander the men 'de basse civilisation' – recalling the 'pays épuisés où les coutumes sont à reprendre' of *Anabase* – are far away. Here, 'le pays est gouverné... La lampe brille sous Son toit'.[d] Those are the last words of the poem, except for the final repetition of the brief refrain. Immediately preceding these lines is a verse-paragraph that fixes once and for all the image of civilized contentment. It is the passage beginning 'Et la nuit vient avant que nous n'ayons coutume de ces lieux'[e]; it is to my mind one of the high points, not merely of Perse's poetry, but of all French poetry. This passage is the coda of a magnificent poem, the texture of which is seamless.

The vocabulary of *Amitié du Prince* is the simplest of any of the longer poems of Saint-John Perse. As usual, certain key words are reiterated in constantly varying grammatical contexts: *maigre, sécheresse, mince, sage, simple, secret*; and yet the overall impression is one of the most complete 'luxe, calme, et volupté'. The purity of the language and the stateliness of the rhythms are such that one is not aware of the extreme complexity of some of the figures of speech – a complexity which comes rudely to the fore, however, when the sonorities and rhythms of the original French disappear. Consider, for example, the parallelisms and ellipses, the reciprocal enrichment of imagery in such a passage as the following, where the visiting Sage quotes what he has heard concerning the Prince from his subjects. So great is their admiration

[a] But from one race to another the road is long.
[b] things probative and unsure
[c] And we shall rejoice in the avidity of the spirit...
[d] the country is governed... The lamp shines under His roof.
[e] And the night comes before we are used to these places.

that, even when they speak about the Prince far from his presence, they seem to be addressing him directly.

'...Nourri des souffles de la terre, environné des signes les plus fastes et devisant de telles prémisses, de tels schismes, ô Prince sous l'aigrette, comme la tige en fleurs à la cime de l'herbe (et l'oiseau qui s'y berce et s'enfuit y laisse un tel balancement... et te voici toi-même, ô Prince par l'absurde, comme une grande fille folle sous la grâce à se bercer soi-même au souffle de sa naissance...),

'docile aux souffles de la terre, ô Prince sous l'aigrette et le signe invisible du songe, ô Prince sous la huppe, comme l'oiseau chantant le signe de sa naissance, [...]'[a]

The whole passage is constructed around the simple words *souffle* and *aigrette*. Through the various changes rung on them, not only does the Prince take shape as a physical presence, we learn as well what forces shape his conduct and destiny. The breaths of earth – gusts that bring rain, wind that carries pollen and seeds and the smell of vegetation – nourish this Prince. He is one with the land. But he is likewise animated by another *souffle*, the breath of life bestowed on him by his royal parents, the 'souffle de sa naissance' – a circumstance that is no less real for being the result of blind chance ('ô Prince par l'absurde'). The double comparison is suggested by the aigrette which the Prince wears on his head-dress, an upright plume forming a crest ('ô Prince sous la huppe') that is set quivering by the slightest movement. It curves like the tip of tall grass in bloom, and it sways as such grass-tips do when the bird that has alighted on them flies off. But the aigrette itself is from a wing, is bird, and it figuratively 'sings' of the high station it symbolizes, the sign of the Prince's high birth ('le signe de sa naissance'). The sign is also, like the memory of the bird that has flown from the grass-top, the invisible sign of the dream ('le signe invisible du songe'). This Prince, like the leader of *Anabase*, respects the priority of the Dream. But all this dignity is divested of

---

[a] '. . . Nourished by the breaths of earth, surrounded by the most auspicious omens, conversing about such premises and such schisms, O Prince under the aigrette, like the flowering stem on the tops of the grass (and the bird that rocks there and flies off leaves such a swaying . . . and lo, you yourself, O Prince, absurdly, like a tall girl swaying with wild grace in the breath of her own high birth . . .), / obedient to the breaths of the earth, O Prince under the aigrette and the invisible sign of the dream, O Prince under the crest, like the bird singing the sign of his birth, . . .'

SJP E

ponderousness by an almost girlish eargerness that is part of the Prince's heredity. The tall beautiful girl to whom he is compared is said to be 'folle', surely in the sense of the term in the expression *avoine folle* (wild oats). Which brings us back to the figure of the dancing grass-tops and the quivering aigrette. The whole passage illustrates very concretely what Perse means when he speaks of poetry, and especially of his own, as 'a very allusive and mysterious play of hidden analogies or correspondences, and even of multiple associations, at the extreme verge of what consciousness can grasp'.[18] And it also illustrates, in the way it exploits the meanings of French words and underscores the interplay of imagery with sonorities peculiar to the French language, how intimately this poetry is wedded to that language.

Amitié du Prince, even more than *Anabase*, is 'conditioned' by a moral attitude that is essentially aristocratic, arising from a sense of hierarchy that is inseparable from a sense of reciprocal esteem. The sense of hierarchy is already evident in some of the Antillean poems, as we have seen. Each human being has his function, and his contentment resides in fulfilling it. But if this hierarchy is tyrannously imposed, then its justification is utterly destroyed. Without a hierarchy of functions there is no order nor durable social intercourse; but the hierarchy is valid only when it is based on the mutual respect of one human being for the potential abilities of others. A parenthetical declaration occurring in a letter from Perse to MacLeish is most apposite here: 'And isn't politeness still the best formula for liberty?'[19] The whole of *Amitié du Prince* is based on a polite exchange of letters proceeding from the mutual esteem existing between the Sage and his Princely host. The Prince is a king by virtue of his birth, but that circumstance is regarded as 'absurd'; he really rules by virtue of his superior abilities, his superior insight and self-denial.

Finally, the Prince is much more the diplomat and much less the military leader than his counterpart in *Anabase*. No reference is made to his feats of arms; instead, we are told that 'he keeps vigil' ('il veille'), 'Et c'est là sa fonction. Et il n'en a point d'autre parmi nous.'[a] He is not the conqueror, but 'le Guérisseur et l'Assesseur et l'Enchanteur aux sources de l'esprit!'[b] In short, he is the philosopher-king.

[a] And that is his function. And he has no other among us.
[b] the Healer and the Assessor and the Enchanter at the springs of the mind!

Finally, we must comment briefly on the short poem that was published for the first time in the winter of 1924 and which, by its content and tone, obviously belongs to the poems of the 'pre-Briand' period. In the 'Chanson du Présomptif' we are again concerned with a prince.[20] This young heir-apparent finds the accrued grandeur of his lineage, 'la maison chargée d'honneurs', stifling. He expresses a restlessness like that of the Leader in *Anabase*. Curiously, though, the poem's last line is an only slightly different version of a line in *Amitié du Prince*. In that poem the visiting Sage, speaking of the hour of fulfilment and utter relaxation after he has been welcomed by the Prince, says, 'Tous les chemins silencieux du monde sont ouverts'.[a] Enriching the figure, the heir-apparent concludes, '... tous les chemins du monde nous mange dans la main'.[b] Alexis Leger, during his 'Chinese years', could have said the same thing.

[a] All the silent paths of the world are open.
[b] ... all the paths of the world eat out of our hand.

3

The Earlier Exile Poems

Exil . Poème à l'Etrangère . Pluies . Neiges

In a letter of tribute written shortly after the death of Jacques Rivière in 1925, Perse stated flatly, 'My name does not belong to letters'.[1] We know this was not really a rejection of literature, but simply a special form of self-defence. In practical terms, however, it meant that from 1925 until 1942 no new text was published over the signature 'St-J. Perse'. And since Leger was at the very heart of the turmoil of those troublous years, there must have been less and less time to devote to writing. We also know that when he arrived in the United States in 1940 after the Fall of France, the writing of poetry was far from his mind. In 1941 ,the Librarian of Congress, Archibald MacLeish, persuaded Leger to take a modest post at the Library as a means of subsistence. Mac-Leish writes of that period, 'Certainly when he came to Washington poetry was the last thing in his mind. When, cautiously, I spoke to him at that time of the opportunity for his own work which the Library could offer, I was told, almost harshly, that there could be no thought, no possibility, of poetry again.'[2] After all, Leger had witnessed the undoing of his life's work as a diplomat and statesman. The Nazis had occupied more than half of France, and the rest was ruled by the Vichy government, which had promptly deprived Leger of his French nationality and confiscated his private property. The persons closest to him, including the remaining members of his immediate family, had to stay behind in captive France. Leger had acquaintances in America, but scarcely any really close friends. To make his outlook even bleaker, America had not yet become an active participant in the war; and, of course, as a refugee, Alexis Leger had to register as an alien. Mere subsistence, for a man as proud as Leger, became an acute problem. He was determined not to accept financial help from any foreign government, and it was not until MacLeish made quite clear to him that the funds for the salaries of Fellows of the Library of Congress did not come from governmental sources, but from a fund contributed by private citizens, that Leger finally consented to be a Fellow with the title of Consultant in French Literature. In that capacity, he did advisory work and bibliographical compilation.[3]

The spring of 1941 was a dark moment for France and for most of the rest of Europe, and Leger's state of mind seems to have been particularly distressed at that time. Feeling the need for complete isolation, he accepted the offer of Francis and Katherine Biddle to spend some time at a beach-house of theirs on Long Beach Island. It was there that an extraordinary thing happened. MacLeish speaks of it thus:

> But all this is explained, for those who have ears to hear, in *Exil*. 'Que voulez-vous encore de moi, ô souffle originel? Et vous, que pensez-vous encore tirer de ma lèvre vivante...'
> There is a small, naked house on the long New Jersey beaches, facing east across the whole Atlantic, where, if I do not misread this poem, Perse faced not only his exile from his country, but the demand upon him – the ancient and often silenced demand – of that one companion of his journey whom, of all companions he could not leave behind.[4]

The 'primal breath', the forces of poetic creativity, had been held back for years. Now the pressures of public life were no longer present to check them. But extreme depression hardly seemed a propitious state for the resurgence of these forces, and Leger himself was taken by surprise. He is the Foreigner, the 'Etranger' of *Exil*, of whom it is said, 'Et la naissance de son chant ne lui est pas moins étrangère'.[a] The wellspring that was unsealed during those days on Long Beach Island has not ceased flowing. A steady stream of poems, certainly among the most remarkable of modern times, continues to pour forth. We have referred to them collectively as Perse's 'American series'.

[a] And the birth of his song is no less foreign to him.

Exil was published in 1942 some eight or nine months after its composition. Thereafter, major pieces followed in steady succession. By date of composition, they came in the following order: *Exil* (1941), *Poème à l'Etrangère* (1942), *Pluies* (1943), *Neiges* (1944), *Vents* (1945). All these are poems of considerable length, and all are directly connected in one way or another with the theme of exile. In *Vents*, however (which runs to over a hundred pages in ordinary editions), there is a dramatic about-face at the point where exile is about to become a panicky flight, a forsaking of human allegiance. From then on, the poet accepts his responsibility as a member of the human community; and thereafter he writes poems that are expressions of fulfilment and affirmation: *Amers* (1948-1956), *Chronique* (1959), *Oiseaux* (1962). These last three poems are, so to speak, earnests of a vow of solidarity with mankind; we shall refer to them as the 'Votive Poems'.

Marginal to the Exile and the Votive poems is a short piece entitled 'Berceuse', first published in 1945. Like *Amitiè du Prince*, it was later subsumed under the title of *La Gloire des Rois*. In tone and subject-matter it is closer to the poems of the diplomatic period than to any of the post-1941 poems. It is likewise the only poem by Perse in 'regular' metre, apart from the uncollected 'Des Villes sur trois modes'. 'Berceuse' is a lullaby made up of eleven five-line stanzas of unrhymed octosyllables. It is a piercingly sad lullaby, a funeral lament for the first-born of a very regal household. To the desolation of the whole kingdom, this first-born was a female child, and now her death, natural or otherwise, is mourned. The poem is very Chinese in feeling. The theme itself fits in with the well-known male dominance of Imperial China. The crickets in cages and the orioles make one think of the Far East.[5] The insistence on 'tant de flûtes aux cuisines',[a] and 'les flûtes mortes aux cuisines'[b] recall the 'Tonnerre et flûtes dans les chambres!'[c] of the Opening Song of *Anabase* – that most Asiatic of Perse's poems. Further echoes from *Anabase* may be heard in 'Et l'eau de neige de mes outres'[d] and the 'salles blanches comme semoule',[e] as well as in the impersonal tone of the whole poem. Yet, for an impersonal poem, it achieves a strangely pervasive

[a] so many flutes in the kitchens
[b] the flutes silenced in the kitchens
[c] Thunder and fluting in the chambers!
[d] And the snow-water in skins
[e] halls white as semolina

poignancy. One wonders, though, whether it was not a poem left over from the diplomatic period, for it has little 'family resemblance' to any of the poems of the American series.

We have already touched upon the circumstances of composition of *Exil*, the first poem of that American series. *Exil*, in fact, remains largely incomprehensible if one ignores those circumstances. The poem is a complex ode in seven cantos. The first and shortest canto states a number of motifs that are developed in the rest of the poem, somewhat the way motifs are stated in the Opening Song of *Anabase*. The beach-house lent by the Biddles (which has since been washed away by a storm) is immediately referred to. 'Mon hôte, laissez-moi votre maison de verre dans les sables...'[a] The barren beach on which it was situated is fixed in a striking phrase: 'un lieu flagrant et nul comme l'ossuaire des saisons.'[b] In the background is the violence that was loosed on the world at that moment. 'Et, sur toutes grèves de ce monde, l'esprit du dieu fumant déserte sa couche d'amiante.'[c] The fiery god is abroad, no longer contained in his asbestos bed. Then, in the last line of this brief canto, lightning appears. The rest of the poem makes quite clear that this lightning is revelatory; in an almost literal sense, Perse's renewal of contact with the forces of creativity comes to him in a flash. As one frequently finds in Perse, the first occurrence of a crucial image is somewhat cryptic, not yet having accumulated a context: 'Les spasmes de l'éclair sont pour le ravissement des Princes en Tauride.'[d] But something of a context is already suggested by the reference to the Princes in Tauris.

In the ancient Greek world, Tauris, the present-day Crimea, was a very remote strand – at least as remote as New Jersey is today from the shores of France. It was to this far country that, according to the Euripidean version, Iphigenia was spirited at the time Agamemnon sought to sacrifice her. On the lonely Tauridean beach, Iphigenia's brother Orestes comes, along with another Argive prince, Pylades, to rescue her. In a famous scene of the Euripidean tragedy, Orestes, still pursued by the Furies, has a feverish dialogue with phantom-monsters on the lonely beach. He is finally freed of these phantoms and, with Pylades' help, is

[a] Leave me, dear host, your house of glass upon the sands...
[b] a place flagrant and null as the boneyard of the seasons
[c] And, on all the shores of the world, the spirit of the god in smoke abandons his amianthine bed.
[d] The spasms of the lightning are for the delight of the Princes in Tauris.

able to rescue Iphigenia. In *Exil*, the lightning first appears to delight these princes far from home. For the exiled prince, Alexis Leger, there was also a meeting on the lonely beach: 'Je vous connais, ô monstre!',[a] and lightning will provide the language with which to tame this monster.

The second canto expresses Perse's own astonishment at finding himself once more, in the extremest circumstances, endowed with the gift of song. Here we are told how this particular poem came into being and what its subject-matter is. In the interview granted to Pierre Mazars, to which we have already alluded,[6] Perse is reported as replying to an inquiry about the meaning of *Exil*, 'it is a poem born of nothing, a poem composed from nothing'. The interviewer does not seem to have recognized that Perse was simply quoting a line from the second canto of the poem itself: '...un grand poème né de rien, un grand poème fait de rien.' The phrase, I think, simply means that the poem took shape around no positive or pre-conceived theme. In the opening lines of this canto the poet has rejected the writing of war-poems, *vers de circonstance* of the sort that Aragon, Eluard, Supervielle, and a host of other important poets wrote during the 1939-1945 period. 'D'autres saisissent dans les temples la corne peinte des autels.'[b] Thus, the reader learns at once that this will *not* be a 'Resistance poem'. Almost twenty years later, in the same Mazars interview, Perse insisted upon this point: '*Exil* is not an image of the Resistance. It is a poem concerning the eternal presence of exile in man's condition. A poem born of nothing and composed from nothing.' The acute sense of emptiness the poet suffered in 1941 as a result of being cut off from all things turns out, to the amazement of the poet himself, to be a kind of vortex, the still eye of a cyclone that draws into its spiral all the fragmentary debris carried by the wind: spindrift, sandsmoke, bits of dry bone and feathers, alate seeds and filmy insects. Out of these vain things, miraculously, a poem takes shape. These leftover bits become its premises: 'O vestiges, ô prémisses.' The poet has reached a point of extreme self-denial, but it is a beginning as well as an end. The soul's harshness has taught him many things, 'Une science m'échoit aux sévices de l'âme...' So he can declare that all things are new to him, even the birth of his song:

[a] I know you, O monster!
[b] Others in the temples seize the painted altar-horn.

' "O vestiges, ô prémisses,"
Dit l'Etranger parmi les sables, "toute chose au monde m'est
nouvelle!..." Et la naissance de son chant ne lui est pas moins
étrangère.'[a]
The third canto opens with three parallel strophes that constitute one of the most beautiful passages in all of Perse's poetry.
These strophes 'sing' in a way that is quite rare in French poetry,
and for that reason, the English equivalent is even more unsatis-
factory than usual.

'...Toujours il y eut cette clameur, toujours il y eut cette
fureur,
Et ce très haut ressac au comble de l'accès, toujours, au faîte
du désir, la même mouette sur son aile, la même mouette sur
son aire, à tire-d'aile ralliant les stances de l'exil, et sur toutes
grèves de ce monde, du même souffle proférée, la même plainte
sans mesure
A la poursuite, sur les sables, de mon âme numide...'[b]

So reads the third of these opening strophes. If we rearrange some
of the lines with Procrustean brutality, we get:

'Et ce très haut ressac
au comble de l'accès'

– which forms an alexandrine that has imbedded in it a repetition
of the 'ac'-syllable, which, thanks to the guttural stop [k], forces
a pause. Then there is the 'gull' passage:

'la même mouette sur son aile,
la même mouette sur son aire,
à tire-d'aile ralliant
les stances de l'exil,'

The shift of consonants in 'aile' and 'aire' is obvious, as is also
their recurrence in 'tire-d'aile' and the repetition of 'l's in the last
two phrases. The 'même plainte sans mesure' is a distant but unmistakable echo of the 'longue phrase sans césure' of the second
canto. The reference to Numidia in 'mon âme numide' reinforces

---

[a] 'O vestiges, o premises,' / Says the Foreigner on the sands, 'the whole
world is new to me...' and the birth of his song is no less foreign to him.
[b] '... Always there has been this clamour, always there has been this
furor, / And this towering surf at the pitch of passion, always, at the peak
of desire, the same gull on the wing, the same gull hovering, rallying with
wing-strokes the stanzas of exile, and on all the shores of the world, by the
same breath proffered, the same measureless lamentation / In pursuit, across
the sands, of my Numidian soul...'

the phrase 'sur les sables', since ancient Numidia corresponds roughly to the sandy wastes of present-day Algeria and Tunisia. The reference likewise carries further another image occurring in the second canto, where the poem is said to be assembled 'aux syrtes de l'exil'. The present-day Gulf of Gabès is the classical Syrtis, a name that also had the meaning of 'quicksand'. Finally, the 'souffle' referred to is the same breath as the 'souffle originel' and the 'force errante' that will occur later in the canto. This wandering force, this monster, is no new thing to the poet. He has confronted it repeatedly and not given in. He has travelled too much and seen too much, and most of all, he has become too infected with the obsession of silence: 'Sur trop de grèves visitées furent mes pas lavés avant le jour, sur trop de couches désertées fut mon âme livrée au cancer du silence.'[a] The wayward force is then personified as a wandering prostitute who dogs the steps of the Prodigal Son. But finally even the wind lends its voice, and the message is summed up quite simply: 'Honore, ô Prince, ton exil!' That is the turning point. 'Et soudain tout m'est force et présence, où fume encore le thème du néant.'[b]

The closing portion of this canto is enclosed in quotation-marks, as is the opening series of strophes, and the same images are utilized: the clamour on the shores of the world, and the 'plainte sans mesure' which here becomes 'un ïambe plus farouche à nourrir de mon être'.[c] Resist as he will, the poet knows he cannot hold out. No amount of aloofness will guard him against 'la rive accore de ton seuil'.[d] But he cannot be delivered of this song until he has put off 'all human allegiance', until he is reduced to his essential self.

Each canto overlaps the one before it as waves overtake each other. Canto IV again takes up the doubts and questionings of canto III and then pursues the necessary renunciation even farther. The wandering prostitute is still soliciting, but the poet recognizes her now as a temple-prostitute, sacred in her way. All the usual subjects and all the circumstantial contemporary themes are

---

[a] On too many frequented shores have my footprints been washed away before the day, on too many deserted beds has my soul been delivered up to the cancer of silence.

[b] And all at once all is power and presence for me, here where the theme of nothingness rises still in smoke.

[c] a fiercer iambic to be nourished by my very being

[d] sheer drop of your threshold shore

rejected. Instead, the new poem must utilize only the frailest
winged things and out of them create 'un pur langage sans office'.
This striking phrase baffles all translation. Denis Devlin, perhaps
Perse's best translator, had to 'make do' with 'a language free of
usage and pure'. But that is the merest residue. The French 'office'
may mean a public trust, an official post. But it also designates
the body of prayers and rituals that make up a religious service.
The language that the poet here seeks is one that has never served
for any public function. In that phrase he has stated the essence
of any true poet's task – that is, to create out of the accepted
medium of a speech-community a language that will adequately
express what is yet unexpressed. He must make of the usual language 'un pur langage sans office'.[7]

Again there is the recoil and overlap. Canto v reiterates what
has been said in iv, further enriching it. The fifth canto is full
of purposely exploited ambiguities – 'ambiguïtés voulues' Perse
called them in a letter to MacLeish.[8] First there is an expression
of the feeling of exhilarating release which final acceptance of his
exile has brought the poet. He feels restored to his native shores –
'restitué à ma rive natale'. Surely this is to be taken both in the
sense of Leger's being restored to the Western Hemisphere where
he was born, and, at the same time, restored to his essential self –
the only inalienable thing left to him in his exile. This canto, in
fact, contains a number of reminiscences of the Antillean poems.[9]
As for being restored to one's essential self, that meaning is reinforced by the declaration that there is no history but the soul's
and no ease but the soul's – 'il n'est d'aisance que de l'âme.'[10]
Curiously, the whole canto follows the curve of a single day,
from 'l'enfance de ce jour'[a] through an increasingly melancholy
noon, afternoon, and evening. The sadness becomes especially
intense in the last lines of the poem, where the contemplation of
submerged ruins – or at least submarine formations that suggest
ruins: 'O présides sous l'eau verte!'[b] – makes the poet feel the
full weight of exile and mortality. The huge calcareous sea-fans
that have grown up on these submerged forms appear to the poet
like 'dentelle au masque de la mort'.[c]

If canto v contains echoes from the Antillean poems, canto vi

[a] the childhood of this day
[b] O presidios under the green water!
[c] lace on the mask of death

may be said to reverberate loudly with a clarion-call from *Anabase*, for the longest homologous series of that poem is surpassed in length, richness, and strangeness by the series that makes up the whole of this sixth canto of *Exil*. All persons who, by taste, trade, or calling perform some task that is marginal, that seems to have no immediate role in the gigantic human pattern of supply-and-demand, are declared to be Princes of Exile. When one thinks back over this amazing collection of 'isolates' – these practitioners of queer jobs, these hyper-specialists – one gradually realizes that they are indispensable in assuring the continuance of the human tradition. Their activities appear gratuitous only in a short-sighted view. In the long view, these Princes of Exile often turn out to be the most genuinely human and the most indispensable of men. This is emphasized by Perse in the way he has 'situated' many of their activities in a time of peril. The lens-guardian keeps his vigil 'entre deux guerres', the fountain-cleaner does his job in order to bring great epidemics to an end; the master of the waterworks pursues his tasks 'en temps d'invasion', and so on. The Princes of Exile, unobtrusively and with a wonderful faith, perform tasks that, unknown to the mass of mankind, and perhaps even to themselves, are of vital importance in tiding mankind over. These Princes of Exile have no need of this poem, for they already know first-hand what the poet feels and is trying to do. They are one with him. In fact, he has slipped himself in among these strange specialists in the guise of 'celui qui entre au cirque de son œuvre nouvelle dans une très grande animation de l'être'.[a] This is the same man who appears as the Foreigner who arrived in America with only a negligible sum of money in his pocket and who is an obviously poor insurance risk: 'tu ne franchiras point le seuil des Lloyds.'[b] The only assurance he can give on the immigration questionnaires concerning his dwelling is, 'J'habiterai mon nom.'[c]

The closing seventh canto is even more personal. It begins with a call to the two women closest to the poet in the years before his exile: his mother and his mistress, both far away in occupied France. He can only remind them that, from time immemorial separation has been an essential part of the human lot. After all, what is the poet himself now doing but taking up where he had

[a] he who enters the arena of his new creation, uplifted in his whole being
[b] you will not cross the threshold of the offices of Lloyds
[c] I shall dwell in my name.

left off when he settled in Paris in 1922? 'Je reprendrai ma course de Numide, longeant la mer inaliénable...'[a]

This last canto likewise closes the circle, going back to the lightning image of the first canto. 'Syntaxe de l'éclair! ô pur langage de l'exil!'[b] Those are the first words of this last canto, to be taken up again as the canto proceeds: 'L'éclair m'ouvre le lit de plus vastes desseins.'[c] It is then explained that, during the kind of syncope which exile represents, often the most important acts are prepared: 'aux sables de l'exil sifflent les hautes passions lovées sous le fouet de l'éclair...'[d] The lines that follow this declaration are undoubtedly responsible for the erroneous interpretation of the poem as a 'Resistance poem'.

'Comme celui qui dit à l'émissaire, et c'est là son message: "Voilez la face de nos femmes; levez la face de nos fils; et la consigne est de laver la pierre de vos seuils... Je vous dirai tout bas le nom des sources où, demain, nous baignerons un pur courroux." '[e]

These lines are indeed cryptic; and, considering when the poem was written and published, it was almost inevitable that the part of the passage in quotation marks should be interpreted as a call to arms. But is not the reference to the plunging of a pure wrath into spring-water a figure that carries us beyond the Resistance to a time when the hatred, justifiable as it is, will be quenched and cleansed? I am not sure... But about the very last line of the poem there is no question. It is the celebrated declaration in which Saint-John Perse publicly acknowledges Alexis Leger: 'Et c'est l'heure, ô Poète, de décliner ton nom, ta naissance, et ta race...'[f]

So ends the poem that marks Perse's return to poetry. We have pointed out the images and devices that connect this poem with the earlier ones. From its first lines on, *Exil* is immediately recog-

---

[a] I shall resume my Numidian's wandering, skirting the inalienable sea.

[b] Syntax of lightning! O pure language of exile!

[c] The lightning lays bare to me the bed of vaster designs.

[d] on the sands of exile there hiss high passions coiled beneath the lightning's whip...

[e] Like him who says to the emissary, and this is his message: 'Veiled be the faces of our wives; raised be the faces of our sons; and the order is: wash the stone of your thresholds... I shall whisper low the name of the springs in which tomorrow we shall plunge a pure wrath.

[f] And the time has come, O Poet, to declare your name, your birth, and your race...

nizable as a product of the pen of Saint-John Perse. Yet the poem strikes a very new note. The ceremonious, awed wonder of the Antillean poems and the serene impersonality of the surviving 'diplomatic' poems are gone. *Exil* is a very personal cry of anguish and struggle, the record of a victory over despair – a triumph achieved in part by the very act of transmuting the struggle into song. Moreover, one senses a rhythm that is quite different from anything in *Eloges* or *Anabase*. The periods are longer, the diction more sinuous and less lapidary. The purely formal aspects of this novelty are explained by the poet himself in a letter he sent to MacLeish along with the manuscript of the poem. He speaks of the poem's movement, 'physically, in its alliterations, assonances and incantations (bound by the rhythm of the waves)'.[11] One can extend this even farther: *Exil*, in its content as well as its form, is a sea-poem from beginning to end.

Like all of Perse's poems, *Exil* contains isolated verses that are peculiarly haunting and have about them a magic-spell quality. The most haunting are almost always connected with the sea. There is, for example, in canto II, 'Et la mer à la ronde roule son bruit de crânes sur les grèves',[a] where the 'r' alliteration reinforces the low rumbling quality that is spoken about. And in canto III there is the most quoted line of all: 'la même vague proférant / Une seule et longue phrase sans césure à jamais inintelligible...' The line is completely successful in catching the susurrus of waves that seem to be transmitting some urgent message. Unfortunately, critics – even very favourable ones – have pounced on this forever unintelligible 'one long single phrase without cesura' as a kind of epigraph for the whole of Perse's work. *Exil* and a number of the subsequent poems do indeed have a long, swelling rhythm that hardly permits a real break. There is, though, far more rhythmic variety in Perse than such a comparison implies. But what is most objectionable is the implication of inherent unintelligibility in Perse's poetry. The whole of this study stands as an effort to dispel this misconception. The 'seule et longue phrase' verse is merely a magnificent French version of 'What are the wild waves saying?'

Exil unsealed the springs of poetry and helped bring its author through a dangerous personal crisis. But there was still much bitterness, sadness, and heartbreak to be expressed. *Exil* was fol-

[a] And the rounding sea rolls her noise of skulls on the shore.

lowed by the nostalgic and muted *Poème à l'Etrangère*, a dialogue between two aliens residing in the United States – the poet himself and a foreign lady of Spanish origins. It is also the poem of Washington, D.C. It seems fitting that this city designed by a French military engineer should receive its poetic consecration more than a century later from a French poet. Ironically, though, the poem's epigraph is the stark phrase, 'Alien Registration Act'. That act, passed in 1940, required all foreigners, including Perse and his Spanish friend, to register and report periodically concerning their whereabouts and activities. So here were two Europeans, alone in Washington, D.C., with not much more in the way of possessions than their memories of the Old World.

Though it is not necessary to know many biographical details about the Foreign Lady in order to enjoy the poem written for her, the poem itself does tell us, very discreetly, quite a lot about her. She has already been in Washington three years: 'Et c'est déjà le troisième an que le fruit du mûrier fait aux chaussées de votre rue de si belles taches de vin mûr.'[a] Since the poem was composed in 1942, the lady came to Washington in 1939, the year that marked the end of the Spanish Civil War and the outbreak of World War II. She seems to have known the poet in Europe – perhaps in Paris, or perhaps even at Pau, which is near the Spanish frontier, for the reference in the poem to 'cloches ursulines', the bells ringing in the Ursuline convent, seem a distant echo from the Ursuline convent at Pau where young Alexis Leger's sisters were sent to school. In any case, the lady is high-born, for the 'green blood of the Castiles' throbs at her temples. Now a refugee in Washington, she lives in a frame house submerged in the lush August greenery of the Potomac valley. She has enclosed herself in this house and sought to insulate herself in an artificial world. The house is full of lamps, which are kept burning throughout the day: 'la maison de bois ... mûrit un fruit de lampes à midi'[b]; the lady herself says that she lives 'parmi le peuple de mes lampes'[c]; and in the last section of the poem the poet tells her, 'Sous l'orangerie des lampes à midi mûrit l'abîme le plus vaste'.[d] Behind the locked door and the drawn blinds, she moves among these

[a] And it is already the third year that the mulberry fruit on the pavements of your street makes such beautiful stains of ripe wine.
[b] the wooden house ... ripens its fruit of lamps at noon
[c] among the people of my lamps
[d] Beneath the orangery of the noontide lamps the vastest abyss matures.

lamps and among her huge trunks, still unpacked: 'hautes malles in-
écloses.' Insomniac, she smokes long 'widows' cigars' until dawn.

In the first of the poem's three sections the poet 'situates' the
lady and her house. In the second section the Foreign Lady herself speaks, asking the poet to sing 'un chant du soir à la mesure
de mon mal'.[a] The last section is the poet's response, in the form
of a monologue running through his mind as he once again walks
toward the Foreign Lady's house. Each of the three sections closes
with a brief refrain involving the name of a street in the very
heart of Paris, the Rue Gît-le-Cœur – 'Here-lies-the-heart Street'.

In the first section an atmosphere of strange stagnation is created by means of an extended metaphor in which Washington,
smothered in its August foliage, is seen as a submarine city. In
that summer of 1942 there were still streetcar tracks embedded in
Washington streets, for the complete conversion to motorbuses
had only begun at that date. The end of one of these streetcar-
lines must have been close to the Woodley Road apartment where
the poet lived at the time, and its tracks served him poetically.
The streetcars, now gone, had sung of other days and other
places. With their clicking and sizzling noises they also sang of
'l'Eté boisé des jeunes Capitales infestées de cigales'.[b] But mostly
they sang 'pain at its birth' – the wrong and the pain that are
the source of the Aliens' suffering. Those streetcars, we are told,
have now gone off to fabled Atlantis 'par les chaussées et par les
rampes / et les ronds-points d'Observatoires envahis de sargasses'[c]
– which is simply the Naval Observatory Circle off Massachusetts
Avenue, here imagined glutted with seaweed. The route goes on
past the Zoo, through many of the familiar circular plazas of
Washington, which become 'beaux solstices verts des places rondes comme des attolls'.[d] Even the equestrian statues suggest a
sea-change; where the Federal Cavalry pitched camp one night,
the poet sees 'ô mille têtes d'hippocampes!'[e] Nothing is left now
but the rails at the poet's door, 'laissés pour compte à l'Etrangère'.[f] But even though the streetcars will soon disappear, the

[a] an evensong commensurate with my pain
[b] the wooded Summer of young Capitals infested with cicadas
[c] by the causeways and the ramps / and the Observatory terraces overrun
with sargasso
[d] the beautiful green solstices of plazas round as coral-atolls
[e] O thousand heads of sea-horses!
[f] left on account for the Foreign Lady

rails have still not said their last word of sadness. They have led the poet and the Foreign Lady to this place of exile, and in August, 1942, the war is still far from over.

Then comes the refrain. The Foreign Lady, who, like the poet, had to register under the Alien Registration Act, is here referred to as 'l'Alienne' – a term that will appear strange to the French reader unaware of the special context, since only the form 'aliénée' exists in French, meaning, of course, madwoman. The 'Alienne' sings softly the name of a street, like some faint echo of a streetcar-conductor calling out the next stop. It is the strangely-named 'Rue Gît-le-Cœur', which, as we have said, bespeaks the very heart of the Old World. But the name, we are told, is the result of 'méprises de sa langue d'Etrangère'.[a] As a matter of fact, the original name of the street seems to have been Rue Gilles le Queux, the name of a favoured cook of the royal household in the Middle Ages.[12] But popular pronunciation had transformed the pedestrian name to the homonym 'Gît-le-Cœur' – 'Here Lies the Heart'. Homesickness and sorrow may thus transform the commonplace.

When the Foreign Lady herself speaks in the next section, she begins by explaining that her eyes suffer, not from tears, but from too steady a contemplation of the blade heated white-hot on all the coals of the world – a fairly obvious reference to the violence of the time, underscored by one of Perse's rare purely literary allusions: 'ô sabre de Strogoff à hauteur de nos cils!',[b] which takes us back to the episode of the attempted blinding of the hero by the Mongols in Jules Verne's classic thriller, *Michael Strogoff*. The Foreign Lady admits that this is not the sole cause of her sorrow – there are more personal ones, but this contemplation of violence is the overriding cause. It is here that she openly asks the poet of *Exil*, 'vous qui chantez tous bannissements au monde',[c] to sing her a song commensurate with her sorrow. She addresses him bluntly: 'O vous, homme de France' – the first open reference to Perse's French nationality to be found in his poems.

To the Foreign Lady the daily life of Washington is without history or meaning, so she implores the poet not to point out again all those things that have helped to reconcile him to this foreign city: the song of the bright-red cardinals, the two birds

[a] misapprehensions of her Foreign Lady's tongue
[b] O sabre of Strogoff level with our eyelashes!
[c] you who sing all the banishments of the world

of prey that held Washington spellbound as they hovered above the city (again, an event that actually took place), the squirrel on the veranda, the paperboy, the milkman, the Mendicant sisters. For the Foreign Lady it is all anonymous and nondescript, and her final thrust is a question: 'et qu'est-ce encore, sur mon seuil, / que cet oiseau vert-bronze, d'allure peu catholique, qu'ils appellent Starling?'[a] This is telling irony, for the Foreign Lady does not even realize that this 'uncatholic' bird, the plague of so many American cities, is a 'gift' from the Old World. Europe is not as far away as the lady thinks. But the bells in exile, taking up her plaintive call, likewise mistakenly sing 'Rue Gît-le-Cœur'.

The lady is haunted by the bleeding, mask-faced gods that are invoked in the opening line of the third section, which is an exhortation by the poet. He warns the lady that, try as she will to lock out the mounting green waters of this subaqueous city, through the waterpipes will inevitably rise 'ce goût de l'incréé comme une haleine d'outre-monde, / c'est un parfum d'abîme et de néant parmi les moisissures de la terre...'[b] The poet sympathizes with the lady's sorrow; he sees Europe bleeding through her flanks as the Toril virgin bleeds. She represents a true nobility; the Breda lances, as in the Velasquez painting, still mount guard at the doors of her family. But –

'Mais plus d'un cœur bien né s'en fut à la canaille. Et il y avait aussi bien à redire à cette enseigne du bonheur, sur vos golfes trop bleus,

comme le palmier d'or au fond des boîtes à cigares.'[c 13]

There are other validities, other ideals. But one cannot deny one's heritage, and the two aliens will have to sing many another song of nostalgia and lamentation for 'la splendeur de vivre qui s'exile à perte d'hommes cette année',[d] which involves the transposition of the everyday formula 'à perte de vue', usually translated by 'as far as the eye can see', but literally meaning something like 'to the loss of what-can-be-seen'. Thus, for this one hot summer evening,

---

[a] and what is this again, on my threshold, / this bronze-green bird, of uncatholic bearing, that they call Starling?

[b] this taste of something yet uncreated, like a breath of the other world, a perfume of chasms and nothingness among the musty things of earth...

[c] But many a well-born heart has gone over to the rabble. And there was much to be said against that emblem of happiness, on your too blue gulfs, / like the gold palm-tree under the cigars at the bottom of the box.

[d] the splendour of living that, this year, is exiled beyond the reach of men

the poet will speak again of the old days in an effort to exorcise
in some measure the Foreign Lady's sorrow. As he walks to the
house-of-lamps,[14] he is very much alone, 'très seul', but also free,
'homme libre, sans horde ni tribu', and he is fancifully rewarded,
for he is 'lauré d'abeilles de phosphore'[a] – the fireflies for which
Washington is famous. As he walks along, he whistles, and his
Sibylline, incredulous people come running, along with the beautiful hound-bitch (whose picture still hangs in Leger's study at
Giens), which, in imagination, he pats affectionately, 'ma chienne
d'Europe qui fut blanche et, plus que moi, poète'.[b] Then, for the
third and last time the deformed name of the Paris street is heard,
this time sung softly by the Angel that came to guide and comfort
the biblical exile, Tobias.

The gently ironic sadness of this poem is increased by the poet's
valiant effort to keep the sadness in check. It is a proud but tender
poem, and it is surprising to find so sensitive a commentator as
Father Blanchet saying that Perse really moves us for the first
time only in the much later poem, *Chronique*.[15] But there is also a
note of reconciliation in the poem. The poet now 'feels at home'
in his exile. Igor Stravinsky is quoted as saying of his friend
Saint-John Perse, 'I admire him for the way he has continued to
live, with all of his laurels, in that loneliest of cities [Washington,
D.C.].'[16] Surely it was never lonelier for Perse than in the summer
of 1942. But a lonely place is really the only conceivable natural
habitat for Saint-John Perse...

After the tenderness of *Poème à l'Etrangère* there is a return to
the violence of *Exil*. *Pluies* was composed during a 1943 trip to
Georgia in the company of Mr and Mrs Francis Biddle, to whom
the poem is dedicated. At that time things were going from bad
to worse for France and for most of the rest of Europe. Leger's
anguish was extreme, and it was increased by his profound misgivings over the form that the Free French movement was taking.
He was in a state of profound depression when a sudden downpour of tons of water from the Georgia sky seems to have trig-
gered some sort of release within him. Violent manifestations of
natural forces have, in fact, always fascinated him. Superficially,
the poem that resulted is simply a description of a sudden torrential
downpour of the sort that occurs frequently in the Deep South.

[a] laurelled with phosphorescent bees
[b] my hound bitch in Europe who was white and, more than I, a poet

By the most natural association of ideas, the downpour is presented as a tremendous ceremony of purification and ablution, prior to some major act of fecundation. But just what is being cleansed is not always clear, undoubtedly because what the rains lay bare is a substratum of human consciousness that eludes denotative description and can ultimately be conveyed only in a negative way that says 'It is not this, or that, or this other, but something different, something more fundamental'. Perhaps that explains why *Pluies* is the most enigmatic of all Perse's poems.

Its rhythm is suggested, once more, by the natural phenomenon that provoked the poem. The interlacing crescendos and diminuendos of the wave-rhythms of *Exil* are here replaced by the steady tattoo of onrushing rain. Internal and even end-rhymes are perhaps more frequent in *Pluies* than in any other of Perse's poems, helping to underscore the insistent rhythm. The frequency of vocatives is high, with reiterated apostrophes to the poem itself and to the 'Seigneur terrible de mon rire',[a] and a whole series of addresses to the rain itself, called upon as 'Nourrices', 'Suivantes', 'Guerrières,' 'Danseuses', 'Semeuses', 'Simoniaques', 'Transfuges', 'Mimes', 'Métisses', and even finally, 'Pluies!' The general tone is one of urgent invitation and exhortation. It is the most *stringendo* of all Perse's poems, working up to its climax in the homologous series of canto VII (which, incidentally, is at the same time an extended apostrophe).

The first canto of the poem is an invocation opening with a striking Persean metaphor: 'Le banyan de la pluie prend ses assises sur la Ville.'[b] The huge banyan trees of Southeast Asia send down a coarse fringe of aerial roots from their spreading branches; these aerial roots anchor themselves in a most curious way into the earth and take possession of the surrounding area 'prennent leurs assises'. The whole picture of a streaming downpour suddenly taking over and immobilizing the life of a city is in the metaphor. The submarine imagery of *Poème à l'Etrangère* is, understandably, recalled. 'Un polypier hâtif monte à ses noces de corail dans tout ce lait d'eau vive.'[c] The sea-change is again uncannily appropriate. In the sudden downpours of the South, the famous

[a] Terrible Lord of my laughter
[b] The banyan of the rain takes hold of the City.
[c] A hasty polypary rises to its coral weddings in all this milk of living water.

'white rains', vegetation, especially trees, does seem to rise up like the dendritic forms of a polypary.

All this is straightforward enough, but in the third phrase of the opening strophe there appears a personified abstraction that is not so easy to explain. 'Et l'Idée nue comme un rétiaire peigne aux jardins du peuple sa crinière de fille.'[a] This mysterious woman reappears in the second canto, dancing like a Psylla, that is, like those North African jugglers of classical antiquity who also charmed snakes. She is said to dance at the opening of every sentence of the poem, and her nakedness is again described in terms of the Roman circus – this time she is more naked than a sword-blade in the spectacles of the charioteer-factions. Her function, however, is of the highest importance. She, the living Idea, 'm'enseignera le rite et la mesure contre l'impatience du poème'.[b] This naked Idea at the entrance of each sentence finds an echo in Perse's tribute to his friend Léon-Paul Fargue, of whom he says, 'he was always intelligent enough to keep intellect waiting at the door of the poem'.[17] Here may be the key to one of the major themes of *Pluies*. The onslaught of the rains is a liberation of the captive forces of poetry. The rains are not themselves the substance of poetry; *that* is represented by the fecundated earth. But the rains must come to wash away all the dead debris so that the live poem may emerge, so that the poet may experience as totally as possible the present human instant as it is, undeformed by memories or anticipations, by regrets or distant ideals. Caution, doubt, and propriety must all be washed away; history must be forgotten; the canons of good taste must go by the board. The poet, as a representative of the human species, must accept his humanity without rejecting anything and without disgust. That is the major concern of the climactic seventh canto.

But playing round and about this general theme is a more personal one. In *Poème à l'Etrangère* Leger had called himself an 'homme très seul'. In *Pluies* he goes one step farther, referring openly to his renunciation of any further public action. 'Un homme atteint de telle solitude, qu'il aille et qu'il suspende aux sanctuaires le masque et le bâton de commandement!'[c] Putting

---

[a] And Idea, naked as a net-fighter, combs her girl's mane in the people's gardens.
[b] Will teach me ceremony and measure against the impatience of the poem.
[c] A man stricken with such solitude, let him go and hang up in the sanctuary the mask and baton of command!

aside his symbol of authority, he may also put aside his public *persona*, his diplomatic mask. And here we come across a most arresting strophe: 'Moi je portais l'éponge et le fiel aux blessures d'un vieil arbre chargé des chaînes de la terre.'[a] Association of this with the New Testament image of the bitter wine and the vinegar-soaked sponge raised to the crucified Christ is inevitable. The allusion is striking, for Perse's poems are resolutely un-Christian and contain only a few Biblical references. It seems to me that we are here faced with an image of France in agony and a reference to Leger's role in French political life. France is the old tree, scarred with the grievous injuries of many wars and internal upheavals and enchained geographically and economically in a peculiar way. As Secrétaire Général des Affaires Étrangères, all Leger could do was to furnish palliatives. Now all that is finished, and he has, at least momentarily, the feeling that his whole life among men is over. But then the rains came. 'J'avais, j'avais ce goût de vivre sans douceur, et voici que les Pluies...'[b] Being given back to poetry also involves being reintegrated into mankind. The key-line that is carried over from the end of canto VI to the climactic apostrophe of canto VII is the twice-repeated phrase, with only one word changed: 'Tel s'abreuve au divin dont le masque est d'argile.'..... 'Tel s'abreuve au divin dont la lèvre est d'argile.'[c] The human clay is here a transposition of the freshened clay of the rain-soaked earth. Already in the preceding canto (number V), we were told: 'Et vous nous restituez, ô Pluies! à notre instance humaine, avec ce goût d'argile sous nos masques.'[d] This same human clay crops up again in a very crucial declaration, to wit, the end of Perse's Nobel Acceptance Speech, where he asks and answers a rhetorical question: 'In these days of nuclear energy, can the clay lamp of the poet still suffice? – Yes, if its clay reminds us of our own.'

But all this still leaves various passages in the poem quite obscure. There are, for example, a number of lines in the fifth canto

---

[a] As for me, I raised sponge and gall to the wounds of an old tree laden with the chains of the earth.

[b] Once, once I had a taste for living without sweetness, but now the Rains...

[c] He drinks of divinity whose mask is made of clay. / He drinks of divinity whose lip is made of clay.

[d] And you restore us, O Rains, to our human urgency, with the clay taste under our masks.

that sound curiously like an answer to parts of Eliot's *The Waste Land*, like a rejection of the asceticism proposed in the final section of that poem[18]:

'En de plus hauts parages chercherons-nous mémoire?... ou s'il nous faut chanter l'oubli aux bibles d'or des basses feuillaisons?...

Nos fièvres peintes aux tulipiers du songe, la taie sur l'œil des pièces d'eau et la pierre roulée sur la bouche des puits, voilà-t-il pas beaux thèmes à reprendre,

Comme roses anciennes aux mains de l'invalide de guerre?'[a] The film on the eyes of pools and the stone rolled over the well-mouth seem echoes of the desolation of the Waste Land, while the war-invalid reminds us of Gerontion. The canto continues with other 'Waste Land' images: 'Douceur d'agave, d'aloès... fade saison de l'homme sans méprise! C'est la terre lassée des brûlures de l'esprit.'[b] The vision of Europe falling apart that occurs at the end of *The Waste Land* is echoed in *Pluies* in the passage beginning: 'Dressez, dressez, à bout de caps, les catafalques'[c] etc. And then, to make the whole pattern of images even more tantalizingly reminiscent, there is a reference to 'bedridden Princes' ('Princes grabataires'), of which Eliot's Fisher King might be one. The whole cloudburst is, in a sense, an answer to the prayer for rain in *The Waste Land*.

Another difficult point is the matter of the terrible Lord of the poet's laughter, who is invoked throughout the poem. At moments there is something almost hysterical about this laughter. Is this Leger's mocking rejection of all the overtures that were made to him to resume political life? That seems a possibility, for the last lines of the poem are: '...Car telles sont vos délices, Seigneur, au seuil aride du poème, où mon rire épouvante les paons verts de la gloire.'[d] But again, all this is conjectural, and many other points remain unclear. I do not feel that any commentator

[a] In higher places shall we seek memory?... or must we sing oblivion to the gold bibles of the lower foliage? / Our fevers painted on the tulip-trees of dream, the film on the eyes of pools, and the stone rolled over the well-mouth, are not those fine themes to take up again, / Like old roses in a disabled veteran's hands?

[b] Sweetness of agave and aloe... Insipid season of the unerrant man! It is earth wearied by the mind's searings.

[c] Raise up, raise up, at the ends of promontories, the Hapsburg catafalques

[d] ... For such, O Lord, are thy delights, at the arid threshold of the poem, where my laughter scares off the green peacocks of fame.

has yet seized on the total configuration, the *gestalt* of the poem, that will make all the details fall into place. *Pluies* is certainly one of Perse's most inaccessible texts. One final item of interest must be noted, however – namely, that Perse, in the collective editions of his work, inserts *Pluies* immediately after *Exil*, even though *Pluies* followed *Poème à l'Etrangère* in actual date of composition. Both *Exil* and *Pluies* are stormy poems, though the earlier one is rather like the brooding moments before the downpour that is actually loosed in the later poem. Perhaps a closer reading of the two poems side by side will eventually clear up a number of points.

However that may be, *Pluies* was followed by one of the least baffling and most beautiful of all Perse's poems, namely, *Neiges*. In the collective editions it is inserted ahead of *Poème à l'Etrangère*. Both poems are tender and personal, indeed, intimate in the best sense of the word. *Neiges*, in fact, is as subdued and muffled as *Pluies* is strident. *Neiges* was written in New York in the winter of 1944 and is dedicated to the poet's mother. She had been incidentally mentioned already, with great reverence, in *Eloges* and in *Exil*,[19] but her presence is here felt in every line. The poem is divided into four sections. The first one simply evokes the new-fallen and still-falling snow on the city of New York in the early morning hours. The second section extends this evocation from the immediately visible landscape westward until, in the poet's mind, the far western verge is reached – an extremity that reminds him of distances extending in the other direction, toward France. The third section then openly speaks of the poet's aged mother, praying in captive France, and then returns to New York, where the poet in exile is momentarily living in a corner room of some hotel or apartment house. The fourth section fuses all the material of the three preceding ones in a supremely moving tribute to the poet's mother. The key-metaphor throughout is that of the snows.

First the mere physical presence of the snow is evoked. Every resource of figurative language is utilized to make the sight, feel, and sound of snow vividly present to the reader. A random example:

> 'Et toute la nuit, à notre insu, sous ce haut fait de plume, portant très haut vestige et charge d'âmes, les hautes villes de pierre ponce forées d'insectes lumineux n'avaient cessé de croître et d'exceller, dans l'oubli de leur poids.'[a]

[a] And all night long, unknown to us, under this lofty feat of feathers,

The feathery snow falls slowly down around the skyscrapers of the city, wherein, all through the night, windows suddenly turn bright with electric light and then go dark once more, as if fireflies burrowed through these concrete hives that seem porous as pumicestone. That lightest of stones already suggests weightlessness, but the slow-falling vertical snow completes the illusion. If slow, windless snow is watched intently as it comes down, it may seem to become immobile and impart to the objects in the background an apparent rising movement, as if the objects were suddenly divested of weight. Perse's compounding of imagery to convey this special quality of windless snow around skyscrapers is completely successful. But that is only one of a whole sumptuous series.[20]

In the second section, where the poet extends the vista westward, he speaks of the vast defence plants of the Great Lakes regions, 'où les chantiers illuminés toute la nuit tendent sur l'espalier du ciel une haute treille sidérale: mille lampes choyées des choses grèges de la neige...'[a] The aptness of the metaphors here, even to the one contained in the verb *choyer*, is too obvious for comment; but the beauty of the choice of one crucial word, 'grège', deserves mention. 'Grège' is a loan-word from the Italian, attesting the Italian origins of the silk industry in France, for it is the *greggia* of *seta greggia*, 'raw silk'. But Perse, who had already used the word in its ordinary context in *Exil*,[21] here wrenches it from its textile setting and creates a beautiful metaphor, underscored by the rhyme, 'choses *grèges* de la *neige*'. An English translation makes unavoidable the mention of silk, but that spoils the exquisite discretion of the metaphor in French, where silk is implied but not named, since 'grège', unlike 'raw', can be applied only to silk. Snow, falling in the yellowish light of electric lamps, has something of the purity, coolness, and peculiar texture of raw silk. And then, the whole comparison develops a hint from the first section, where there is reference to 'le premier affleurement de cette heure soyeuse'.[b]

bearing aloft the souls' vestiges, the souls' burden, lofty pumicestone cities bored through by luminous insects had not ceased growing, transcendent, forgetful of their weight.

[a] where the shipyards lit up all night stretch a long sidereal trellis across the espalier of the sky; a thousand lamps fondled by the raw-silk things of snow.

[b] the first breaking-through of this silken hour

Gradually the myriad aspects of the snowfall are related to all the fragile and elusive elements that make up the poet's filial affection. Actually, this relationship is anticipated in the very first line of the poem: 'Et puis vinrent les neiges, les premières neiges de l'absence.'[a] The sense of isolation that newfallen snow can bestow is familiar to anyone who has lived in a cold climate. The separation of the poet from his mother is thus anticipated from the outset, later to be recalled in very similar, but significantly modified terms: 'neiges prodigues de l'absence, neiges cruelles au cœur des femmes où s'épuise l'attente'.[b]

Immediately following this line, which occurs in the first strophe of the third section, the poet's mother is openly mentioned. She was a pious woman, and she is presented in an attitude of prayer. Since she must worship more or less secretly in her bomb-devastated, captive land, references are made to crypts and catacombs 'où la lampe est frugale et l'abeille, divine'[c] – the latter being a reference to the promise of resurrection symbolized by the sacred bee in primitive Christianity. There is considerable elaboration of ecclesiastical imagery in this third section, nowhere more effective than when the poet says to his Mother:

'Car nos années sont terres de mouvance dont nul ne tient le fief, mais comme un grand *Ave* de grâce sur nos pas nous suit au loin le chant de pur lignage; et il y a un si long temps que veille en nous cette affre de douceur...'[d]

This develops 'tout ce plain-chant des neiges'[e] of the opening lines of this section and is taken up again in the closing fourth section, where it becomes, 'et comme un grand *Ave* de grâce sur nos pas, la grande roseraie blanche de toutes neiges à la ronde'.[f]

Plain-song is already a most disembodied form of speech, but it is still a language used in liturgy, it is not 'sans office', and the 'pur langage sans office' mentioned in *Exil* is what the poet seeks more desperately than ever in this fourth section of *Neiges*, which

[a] And then the snows came, the first snows of absence
[b] snows prodigal of absence, snows cruel to the heart of women where hope wastes away
[c] where the lamp is frugal and the bee divine
[d] For our years are lands in tenure which no one holds in fief, but like a great *Ave* of grace on our path, there follows us afar the song of pure lineage; and for so long a time this agony of sweetness has kept vigil in us...
[e] all this plain-chant of the snows
[f] and like a great *Ave* of grace on our path, the great white rose-garden of all the surrounding snows

contains one of the most astonishing *tours de force* to be found anywhere in Perse: I refer to the philological passage. To express the most disembodied veneration he must have the most disembodied language, a primitive parent-language, an *Ursprache* that can only be reconstructed from derived and grossly modified later forms, and for which there are no written texts. It must be 'ce pur délice sans graphie où court l'antique phrase humaine'.[a] This linguistic search is presented in terms of men who go farther and farther from the river mouth, upstream, until they come to the mountain freshets that feed the river's source, only to press on still farther to the glaciers that feed the freshets, and finally to the névé at the glacier's head, where 'ils sont gagnés soudain de cet éclat sévère où toute langue perd ses armes'.[b] The key-metaphor of the snows also serves here, in this evocation of ultimate purity. In one of the 'Eloges' (no. VI) there is mention of gentle things, 'douces comme la honte, qui tremble sur les lèvres, des choses dites de profil'.[c] *Neiges* is such a gentle thing, said with averted face, and finally only silence will do. This 'grande ode du silence' moves inevitably, as the poet tells his mother, into the realm of 'ce langage sans paroles dont vous avez l'usage'.[d] [22]

The strange and almost embarrassing tenderness of this poem is best conveyed by one of its own loveliest lines. Speaking still of the new-fallen snow, the question is asked, 'Et sur la hache du pionnier quelle inquiétante douceur a cette nuit posé la joue?'[e]

[a] a pure delight without script where runs the ancient human phrase
[b] they are caught up suddenly in that harsh glare wherein all language is powerless.
[c] gentle as the shame that trembles on the lips, of things said with averted face
[d] that wordless language of which you are master
[e] And what disquieting gentleness has laid its cheek tonight upon the pioneer's axe?

4

The Poetics

The forty years preceding Perse's 'American period' were a time when poetry about poetry was sedulously cultivated by most French poets and many non-French ones as well. Mallarmé had given the example, and his most faithful disciple, Valéry, had carried the exploitation of this vein to almost obsessive lengths in *La Jeune Parque* and *Charmes*. The results of this 'poetic inbreeding' were sometimes unfortunate; it gave rise, for example, to the nonsensical view that every poem is a record of its own composition. Thus, some critics have felt compelled to see in *Anabase* a kind of allegory of the creative process. There is nothing of the sort in *Anabase*, and in none of the Antillean or 'diplomatic' poems is there any utilization of the poetic act itself as subject-matter for the poems. The theme does appear, however, in *Exil*, where the poet is taken by surprise and forced to contemplate the strange phenomenon of poetic creation that, so to speak, has caught up with him. It is not the dominant theme, however – only an important secondary one – as it was subsequently to be in *Pluies* and even *Neiges*, with its search for the 'pur langage sans office'. It is most fully developed, but still in a very secondary position, in the poem that followed *Neiges*, namely, *Vents*. Here, then, is the appropriate place to stop and look at Perse's poetics.

In 1942 Perse could still write: 'On the subject of literary doctrine I have nothing at all to state. I have never relished scientific cooking.'[1] In the following years, however, the pressure of external circumstances, culminating in the 1960 Nobel award, forced Perse to make a number of marginal declarations in prose that can scarcely escape the qualification of 'literary doctrine'. The initial circumstance that led to explicit formulation of a number of poetic principles was the persistent failure on the part of even very sympathetic critics to grasp certain aspects of his work. The situation turned out to be a fortunate one for Perse's readers, for the prose pieces – letters, notes, articles, transcribed conversations – greatly clarify Perse's intentions as a writer. Actually, there exists a genuine reciprocity between the poetry and the prose pieces. What has been said thus far about the poems themselves will make certain aspects of the poetics more immediately comprehensible, while the poetics, in its turn, will illumine much that we find in all of the poems, but especially in those still to be considered.

There is, however, no doubt at all that Perse was reluctant to talk about poetic principles in the abstract. Any literary discussion is likely to make him feel uncomfortable. As late as 1962 he said to his friend Igor Stravinsky, 'Poetry is a way of life, but I have no literary career, and I hate even to talk about literature.'[2] This instinctive disinclination is abetted by an intellectual conviction to the effect that abstractions, in all domains but the exact sciences, are a source of error and confusion. When Perse wrote to one of his translators in 1949, 'One must, in all things, abhor abstractions',[3] he was simply putting on paper what he had said many times before and has reiterated since. It cannot be too greatly emphasized that, for Perse, in the beginning is the poem, and abstract discussion of principles is merely a detour – perhaps necessary, but surely unfortunate – back to the poem – and to a poem that is never primarily about poetry itself.

A good starting-point for this 'detour' is the sentence just quoted from the conversation with Stravinsky. Poetry, said Perse, is 'a way of life' but *not* a literary career. For him, poetry is a gratuitous and disinterested pursuit, one of a number of activities unconnected with immediate survival-needs or with the accumulation of creature comforts. Perse has a deep reverence for men struggling for the bare necessities of survival, and those wild places on the face of the earth where that struggle becomes immediate and stark have always held a particular fascination for him – witness *Anabase*. In fact, the 'jansénisme du pittoresque' noted by Paul Morand in *Anabase* is really one of several expressions of a fundamental ascetic strain in Perse's makeup. The accumulation of creature comforts has always made him vaguely uneasy, and he refers to the preoccupation with such comforts as 'materialism'. Both the artist and the pure scientist (as opposed to the technologist) stand in opposition to this materialism, because disinterested scientific research and the arts, including poetry, are not motivated by a desire for immediate practical gain or passive contentment. But neither are they simply an elaborate form of play. Both represent a maximum development of our human faculties. Narrowing the field to poetry, it is the art that provides verbal expression of a constant awareness of those 'great forces that create us, use us, and control us'.[4]

This reaffirmation of poetry as a serious undertaking is nowhere more eloquently set forth than in Perse's Nobel Prize acceptance speech of 1960:

> Faithful to its task, which is nothing less than to fathom the human mystery, modern poetry is pursuing an enterprise which is concerned with man in the plenitude of his being. In such a poetry there is no place for anything Pythian, nor for anything purely aesthetic. It is the art neither of the embalmer nor of the decorator. It does not raise cultured pearls, does not traffic in fakes or emblems, nor would it be content to be a mere feast of music. It is intimately related to beauty, supreme alliance, but beauty is neither its goal nor its sole food. Refusing to divorce art from life or love from knowledge, it is action, it is passion, it is power, a perpetual renewal that pushes back frontiers.[5]

This passage is a matter-of-fact summary of negations and affirmations that are more passionately expressed in certain of the poems, especially *Vents*. The rejection of aestheticism, for example, is almost savagely stated in *Vents*: 'Et si l'homme de talent préfère la roseraie et le jeu de clavecin, il sera dévoré par les chiens.'[a] Or, more disdainfully, a little further along: 'O tiédeur, ô faiblesse! O tiédeur et giron où pâlissait le front des jeunes

[a] And if the man of talent prefer the rose-garden and the playing of the harpsichord, he shall be devoured by the dogs. (I, 6)

hommes... Il y aura toujours assez de lait pour les gencives de l'esthète et pour les bulbes du narcisse...'[a]

In the passage of the Nobel speech there is, in connection with this aestheticism, a tantalizing reference that seems very much to point at Valéry. When Perse declared that 'there is no place for anything Pythian' in poetry, he may very well have had in mind Valéry's famous poem, 'La Pythie', wherein the priestess, after the horrors of possession by the god, articulates, as the supreme gift, 'SAINT LANGAGE'. Perse regards the poetry of Valéry as an essentially *verbal* achievement, where the word, as an auditory phenomenon, removed from what it actually stands for, is the point of departure and, ultimately, the very subject, of the poem. Language as such becomes the poet's chief concern. But that is exactly what it is *not* in Perse's poetry.

Another reference that has Valéryan overtones is Perse's rejection of poetry as being exclusively 'a feast of music'. *Poésie pure*, or absolute poetry, so dear to the admirers of Valéry, if not to Valéry himself, reduces poetry to pure incantation (*charme*, to use Valéry's term) and assimilates poetry with music, not merely because poetry addresses itself, like music, to the ear, but above all because poetry must, in this view, affect the reader in much the same way as a piece of music stirs a responsive listener. Certainly all true poetry affects the sensitive reader in this way to some extent, but not wholly or essentially. As Perse puts it, poetry should not 'be content to be a mere feast of music'. After all, music creates beauty by the manipulation of sounds that are devoid of verbal meaning. Poetry, on the other hand, is made up of words, and while every spoken word is a sound, it is also a tool, that is, certain arbitrary meanings have been attached to it which give the word its validity in the speech community. So, at best, poetry has what Perse calls 'a supreme alliance with beauty', but neither can beauty be its ultimate end. Poetry is surely not as pure an art as music; but by that very token, poetry is more immediately involved with the business of day-by-day living. It is not an escape from nor a substitute for life. Its whole function is to make possible for man 'to live better and further' – 'pour mieux vivre, et plus loin', a phrase that Perse has repeatedly used.

[a] O tepid love, O weakness! O tepid love, O lap whereon the brows of young men paled... There will always be sufficient milk for the gums of the aesthete and for the bulb of the narcissus... (IV, 5)

Returning for a moment to the term 'Pythian' as employed by
Perse, there is possibly another allusion in it. When we think of
the Pythian priestess, we think primarily of her oracular utterances, her 'Holy Language'. But we must not forget that these
utterances were induced by inhaling mephitic, trance-inducing
fumes. Could there be a reference to the 'narcotic' view of poetry
which holds that the most direct route to poetic achievement
runs through the artificial paradises that may be conjured up by
stimulants and drugs? Even if that is not the intent in the Pythian
reference, it is clearly the intent of a striking passage in *Vents*:

> 'Homme infesté du songe, homme gagné par l'infection
> divine,
>   Non point de ceux qui cherchent l'ébriété dans les vapeurs
> du chanvre, comme un Scythe,
>   Ni l'intoxication de quelque plante solanée – belladone ou
> jusquiame,
>   De ceux qui prisent la graine ronde d'Ologhi mangée par
> l'homme d'Amazonie,
>   Yaghé, liane du pauvre, qui fait surgir l'envers des choses –
> ou la plante Pî-lu,'[a]

Parenthetically, the accuracy of the botanical references to narcotic plants is attested by any manual on the subject. And there
can be no doubt that here the whole Poe-Baudelaire-Rimbaud
'déréglement systématique de tous les sens' is rejected. It is a particularly important rejection, because it comes from a poet who
has always maintained that active poetic creation must rely on the
subconscious.

In an essay by Archibald MacLeish, the matter is put quite
clearly: 'There is no poetry, Léger insists, no active creation,
without complete reliance upon the subconscious. But the subconscious must be treated rigorously, must be mastered, by reason.
The farther a poet goes into the realm of the mysterious by analogy, by association of ideas, the more he needs the simplest, the
purest of languages.'[6] Thus, the rejection of the 'narcotic' approach would indicate that Perse believes the subconscious must

---

[a] Man infested with dream, man overtaken by the divine infection, / No,
not of those who seek inebriation in the vapours of hemp, like a Scythian, /
Or the intoxication of some solanal plant – belladona or henbane, / Nor of
those who prize the round seed of Ologhi eaten by man in Amazonia, /
Yaghé, liana of the poor, that evokes the reverse of things – or the Pi-lu
plant (III, 6)

'break through' of its own accord – as it did so surprisingly, for example, during those days spent on the barren sands of Long Beach Island, where *Exil* was composed. The subconscious cannot profitably be provoked into eruption by artificial stimulants, and what it provides, even spontaneously, is only the indispensable raw material of poetry. It is up to the poet to turn this raw material into a product that achieves effective communication with other human beings.

The achieving of poetry is, thus, a privilege that imposes an obligation on the poet; and the whole undertaking is, as we have seen, a very serious one that is actually 'a way of life'. Such a view of poetry may strike some persons as unduly exalted and as attributing an almost Magian role to the poet, somewhat as Victor Hugo sought to do. But actually Perse's view is tempered by a fundamentally aristocratic outlook. Poetry can help one to live 'better and further', but only if one is sensitive to it. Perse remarked to Mazars: 'A poet cannot propose his synthesis to the whole world.'[7] That is a tactful way of saying that it can, indeed, be proposed only to a Happy Few. The poet will have impact on mankind only through them. But, in Perse's view, only through the intervention of superior minds is *any* constructive action ultimately achieved. It is this group that is obliquely and beautifully addressed in the last section of Perse's 'poem of old age', *Chronique*: 'Ah! qu'une élite aussi se lève, de très grands arbres sur la terre, comme tribu de grandes âmes et qui nous tiennent en leur conseil...'[a] The poet will be an inciter rather than a leader. A witness, rather than a law-giver and judge – a witness whose function is constantly to remind mankind of all aspects of its condition and of its essential humanity, which are too often and too tragically forgotten. But as a witness, the poet must seek to tell the whole truth, so far as he knows it. In the crucial third section of *Vents* we read: 'Quelqu'un au monde n'élèvera-t-il la voix? Témoignage pour l'homme... / Que le Poète se fasse entendre, et qu'il dirige le jugement!'[b] Or again: 'Et le Poète encore est avec nous, parmi les hommes de son temps, habité de son mal...'[c] And

---

[a] Ah! may an élite also rise, of very tall trees on the earth, like a tribe of great souls that shall hold us of their council...

[b] Will no one in the world raise his voice? Testimony for man... / Let the Poet speak, and let him guide the judgment! (III, 4)

[c] And the Poet is still with us, amongst the men of his time, inhabited by his malady... (III, 6)

most explicitly of all, the closing sentence of the Nobel acceptance speech, 'And it is enough for the poet to be the guilty conscience of his time.'[8]

Thus far we have discussed the function of poetry and of the poet in very general terms. Perse has, however, many more specific things to say about the nature of poetry. These points are largely contained in what Perse has to say about French poetry as opposed to poetry written in English, which he refers to collectively as 'Anglo-Saxon' poetry. The sharp contrast he draws between the two is somewhat misleading, for what he has to say about French poetry really applies only to a certain strain of French poetry that first became explicit in Baudelaire and continues through Rimbaud, up into the present time. His generalizations about 'Anglo-Saxon' poetry are, I feel, far too sweeping and even, when pushed to their limits, quite unfair. But Perse's insistence on the dichotomy will become more understandable when we consider some of the reactions that his own poetry has provoked in Great Britain and the United States.

After characterizing 'Anglo-Saxon' poetry, Perse goes on to say:

> Modern French poetry, on the other hand, feels it is not really poetry unless it merges with its living object in a live embrace, unless it informs the object entirely and even becomes the thing which it 'apprehends', which it evokes or calls forth. Going far beyond any mimetic action, it finally *is* the thing itself, in that thing's own movement and duration. This poetry lives the thing and 'animates' it totally and most scrupulously, and with infinite variation submits to the thing's own measure and rhythm....[9]

Ten years earlier, Perse had already written in the third section of *Vents*: 'Non point l'écrit, mais la chose même. Prise en son vif et dans son tout. / Conservation non des copies, mais des originaux. Et l'écriture du poète suit le procès-verbal.'[a] In the later *Amers* the concept is made even more explicit:

> 'Et mots pour nous ils ne sont plus, n'étant plus signes ni parures,

---

[a] Not the written text, but the thing itself. Seized at the quick and in its entirety. / Preservation, not of copies, but of the originals. And the poet's writing follows the record. (III, 6)

Mais la chose même qu'ils figurent et la chose même qu'ils paraient;

Ou mieux, te récitant toi-même, le récit, voici que nous te devenons toi-même, le récit,

Et toi-même sommes-nous, qui nous étais l'Inconciliable: le texte même et sa substance et son mouvement de mer,

Et la grande robe prosodique dont nous nous revêtons...'*a*

The poetic expression, thus, must be the most *immediate* possible, and the poet must be endowed with, or acquire, the power to identify himself so completely with any phenomenon that he somehow *becomes* that phenomenon. Put in these extreme terms, the concept is rather disquieting. Obviously, it is concretely impossible for the poet to 'become' what he is writing about and, hence, for the poet to 'become' his poem. Perse, writing the most extraordinary poem that has perhaps ever been written about the Sea, wherein the multiple experience of the Sea is communicated with unparalleled force and vividness – Perse, writing that poem, still remains a flesh-and-blood human being, forever physically separate from the Sea. So, one asks in just what sense he means that the poet must 'enter into' and 'become' the phenomenon he apprehends, and in just what sense the poet and the poem become one and the same entity.

Some light may be thrown on the question when we consider a second concept that is dear to Saint-John Perse. For him the essence of life, the very clue to life, is movement. Death is simply complete immobility. Since poetry is to be the most direct possible expression of life, it follows that movement will be the very essence of that expression:

'... to me poetry is, above all else, movement – in its inception as well as in its development and final elaboration. The whole philosophy of the Poet seems to me to be reducible, in its essence, to the old elemental "rheism"[10] of ancient thought – like that, in the West, of our pre-Socratics. And the metric of poetry, which is usually considered as a purely rhetorical matter, strives only for movement and contact with

a 'And words for us they are no longer, being no longer signs or adornments, / But the thing itself which they signify and the thing itself they adorned; / Or better, reciting yourself, who are the recital, behold we become you, the recital, / And we are now you, who were to us the Irreconcilable: the very text and its substance and its sea-movement, / And the very great robe of poetry with which we clothe ourselves...' ('Chœur' IV)

movement – with movement in all its living, most unpredictable forms. Whence the importance for the poet, in all things, of the Sea.'[11]

How this ties in with the 'co-identification' view of poetry becomes clearer when we recall the last sentence of the earlier quotation: '... Going far beyond any mimetic action, [modern French poetry] finally *is* the thing itself, in that thing's own movement and duration. It lives the thing and "animates" it totally and most scrupulously, and with infinite variation submits to the thing's own measure and rhythm.'

This very interesting view takes for granted certain premises that are not self-evident truths. The assumption made in Perse's view is that every phenomenon (*chose* in Perse's sense) has movement and duration and its 'own particular measure' and 'rhythm'. Certainly duration is a property of all phenomena. But *do* all phenomena have movement and a particular, inherent rhythm? The phenomena that Perse actually cites as illustrations are illuminating. He says that the poet and the poem must 'live' and 'activate' a thing totally, in its diversity, 'with its own measure and its own rhythm: spaciously and at length when, for example, the sea or the wind is concerned; tightly and suddenly where the lightning-flash is concerned.'[12] The sea, the winds, and lightning are, all three, natural phenomena, and even more specifically, forces of nature. It may be possible, within certain very definite limits, to translate such phenomena rhythmically into spoken language. But what about those aspects of life that are not palpable, that are not extended in space? What about all our emotions, all our moral configurations? What is the rhythm inherent in courage, haughtiness, contrition, or despair? In all the various kinds of elation? Or what is the rhythm inherent in an inert object: a stone, a book, a blob of colour? Are all these excluded from poetry, and from Perse's poetry in particular? Obviously not.

Is it possible that what Perse is really saying is that the poet must express himself only *through* concrete phenomena? Is this poetics not essentially an extreme extension of his hatred of the abstract? The verbal intercourse of ordinary daily pursuits makes inevitable the constant trafficking in abstractions. But abstractions, Perse seems to say, are Antaean and remain potent and meaningful only when they maintain some point of contact with immediate, undifferentiated reality. It is the poet's job to keep

Antaeus in touch with the earth. Or, put in another way, the poet must not divorce the Dance from the dancer. It is an extreme kind of nominalism that seeks to eliminate the discursive and abstractly intellectual elements that Perse finds characteristic of 'Anglo-Saxon' poetry, but that are even more characteristic of much French poetry, from Chrétien de Troyes to Malherbe, and on down to Hugo and Claudel. It is a poetics that aims at maximum sensory and emotional intensity, both of which Perse achieves. But, in practice, it is impossible to eliminate discursive and expository elements entirely from a poem of any length – and some of Perse's are among the longest in modern literature. One suspects that what Perse would posit as a difference in kind is, after all, a series of differences in degree.

There is a corollary to this poetics that applies particularly to the rhythm of speech and that has a special importance for Perse's own poems; for, with the exception of the one bit of rejected juvenilia, none of his poems obeys standard French prosody. It must be recalled that French prosody is based on the counting of individual syllables (and not of stressed and unstressed syllables forming 'feet' as in English) and that it presents an elaborate set of conventions having to do with mute 'e' endings, hiatuses, alternating of so-called masculine and feminine end-rhymes, prohibitions of grammatically similar rhymes, etc. At the very heart of this prosody is the classical alexandrine, which became dominant in the seventeenth century and remained so until the very end of the nineteenth century. The vaunted poetic revolution of Hugo and the other French Romantics did revitalize the *vocabulary* of poetry, but it left the end-rhyming alexandrine practically untouched. In the long tradition of French poetry, there is nothing really comparable to the unrhymed and infinitely flexible blank verse that is one of the triumphs of the Tudor and Jacobean periods.

Perse, though a genuine admirer of the classical French masters, has always felt that the verse-forms permitted by the rigid standard prosody forced the poet to omit far too much of the rich diversity of human experience. Moreover, that prosody had become too artificial, too far-removed from the original somatic bases of speech-rhythms. Certainly Perse would approve the famous note in which Baudelaire indicated his desire to show 'how poetry resembles music through a prosody that sends its roots down far deeper into the human soul than any classical theory indicates'. And Perse would approve even more heartily Baudelaire's very next note: 'That French poetry possesses a mysterious and as yet unrecognized prosody, just as the Latin and English languages do.'[13]

Perse, of course, was one among many poets who followed Baudelaire's lead in this matter. The strong physiological and psychological bases of rhythm had struck many of Perse's contemporaries. One of the best-known attempts to meet the problem head-on was Paul Claudel's creation of an 'iamb' which sought to restore vitality to the rhythms of French verse by an adherence to the fundamental binary beat of respiration and heart-action. Because of Perse's early association with Claudel, to which we have already referred,[14] and also because of certain superficial similarities in tone and occasional syntactical turn, many critics have seen in Perse's prosody merely an extension of Claudel's versicle. Again, there is actually no significant resemblance. In his technique Perse is far closer to another poet he knew well and admired greatly, namely, Léon-Paul Fargue; and what he has to say of Fargue's poetic technique is equally true of his own: 'Fargue's concealed metric, faithful to human breathing but very flexible and refined in its movement and constantly varying in its articulation, is wholly different from the monodic delivery of the vast *laisses* or *versets* of Claudel.'[15] It should not be forgotten that Perse was born into the teeming world of a tropical island. The strong auditory rhythms of nature – waves, falling water, wind in the trees, insect noises, bird cries – were reinforced by the human noises of drumming and chant, and these in turn by the muscular rhythms of running, swimming, riding, sailing and the visual rhythms of infinitely varied leaf-configurations, rock-forms, sand and wave patterns, cloud formations. Neither the various combinations of classical prosody nor the loose two-beat versicle of Claudel would suffice to embody the diversity of all this. Viewed in this light, Perse's insistence on the appropriate rhythm for the appropriate phenomenon becomes much more understandable. There is a tremendous variety of rhythmic structures in his poems, and painstaking statistical studies (with the help of recording devices and computers, of course) may even reveal intricacies of regularity in them that have escaped the poet himself. But an attentive ear is all that is needed, and in most of Perse's poems, the arrangement on the printed page helps guide the eye and ear, as we shall see.

It would be easy to conclude that Perse's poetics not merely stems from, but is expressly designed for, the expression of out-door Nature – what the French call 'la grande Nature'. We have already noted that the exemplary phenomena Perse cites in illus-trating his rhythmic principles: (the sea, the wind, and lightning) are exclusively natural manifestations. Further, almost all the An-tillean poems are concerned principally with the flora and fauna of Guadeloupe and with its beaches, lava hillocks (*mornes*), and broad sea-vistas. The very titles of most of the poems of the 'American' series clearly indicate a dominant natural phenomenon around which each of these long poems is built: *Rains, Snows, Winds, Sea-marks, Birds.* Yet it is manifestly *not* true that Perse's chief concern is to make us fully aware of outdoor Nature. The rains, snows, birds, and the rest are vehicles for expressing something deeper and more diversified, namely, 'the very movement of Being', a 'mode of life – of life in its totality'.[16] Even in the early poems, the insects, trees, and fishes take their place in a total conscious-ness of the beauty and violence of childhood in the tropics; while in the American series the rains, snows, etc. actually become vast, multiplex metaphors. Indeed, on the purely technical plane, verbal rhythms become the handmaiden of imagery; and Perse is quite rightly thought of as the greatest master of the poetic image modern France has produced.

To divorce rhythm from imagery is, however, to do violence to this poetics, the basis of which, it must not be forgotten, is 'a free play, extremely allusive and mysterious, of hidden ana-logies or correspondences, and even of multiple associations, on the extreme verge of what consciousness can grasp'. That defini-tion was written in 1956.[17] Four years later, in his Nobel accep-tance speech, it was expanded: 'By means of analogical and sym-bolic thinking, by means of the far-reaching light of the mediating image and its play of correspondences, by way of a thousand chains of reactions and unusual associations, by virtue also of a language through which is transmitted the supreme rhythm of Being, the poet clothes himself in a transcendental reality to which the scientist cannot aspire.'[18] The ground is familiar; we think immediately of Baudelaire's insistence on the all-importance of metaphor and 'correspondences'. But Perse goes beyond Baudelaire by conferring such preponderant importance on the image that it is ultimately the image that determines the prosody actually found in Perse's poems.

Since the image must be perfectly congruent with the phenomenon, and since the variety of phenomena is endless, the rhythms adapted to the image must also be infinitely varied. Baudelaire dreamed of something like this when he invented the 'prose poem'. But the very term is self-contradictory, and in writing his 'prose poems' Baudelaire simply wrote prose. Perse himself seems to me to say the definitive word on the matter when he speaks of the 'modulated pages' of Fargue (and by implication, of his own). These pages, he says, differ not only from the purely visual, descriptive prose pieces of Aloysius Bertrand, they differ quite as much 'from Baudelaire's "poems in prose", which are in no way poems, since they pursue only a psychological interest, and in an analytic or discursive key devoid of any melodic concern, properly speaking'.[19] The true poems that have the aspect of prose on the printed page are, according to Perse, Maurice de Guérin's *Centaure* and 'the imperious *Illuminations* of Rimbaud'. These he refers to aptly as *unversified poems* ('poèmes non versifiés').

The great advantage of the unversified poem is that, conscientiously composed, it can dispense with the verbal padding that is inevitable in even the most carefully executed versified poem. Perse quotes Fargue with approval: 'The finest poem in regular verse-form will be the one least stuffed out with padding; but there will always be padding.'[20] The great danger, of course, is that unalloyed prose may easily masquerade as unversified poetry. Distinguishing the genuine poem from the spurious likeness is, however, not as difficult as might be supposed. The most obvious sign of the real thing is the high frequency, complexity, and careful coordination of images. A secondary indicator is the subordination of sonorous devices, which are the dominant feature of conventional prosody, to the imagery. These sonorous devices reinforce the imagery of the poem but do not provide its framework, as they do in standard forms like the sonnet, *terza rima*, alexandrine couplets, etc.

In the case of Perse, there is an extremely high frequency of all sorts of repetitive sonorous devices: alliteration, assonance, internal rhymes, permutations of similar segmentals – they are admirably analysed in Roger Caillois's book on Perse.[21] Yet, on the printed page, Perse's poems often have the aspect of straight prose. But one may legitimately say about all of them what T. S. Eliot said of the one he had just translated: 'But *Anabase* is poetry. Its sequences, its logic of imagery, are those of poetry and not of prose; and in consequence – at least the two matters are very closely allied – the *declamation*, the system of stresses and pauses, which is partially exhibited by the punctuation and spacing, is that of poetry and not of prose.'[22] In fact, in the longer poems, the prosodic unit is sometimes actually brought out by the typographic arrangement. Sometimes the units will be a line or a line-and-a-half long, and these will be grouped together in 'strophes' of three lines (as in *Pluies*) or aligned in longer series, as in the opening portions of *Amers*. More frequently the prosodic unit will be a whole paragraph, and often the length of these 'verse-paragraphs' is astonishingly uniform – a fact that becomes immediately evident to the eye only in the larger format editions of some of the poems, where a great deal of text can appear on a single page. But in all instances, the sonorous devices are subordinated to the imagery.

And there we have the clue to why the poetry of Saint-John Perse translates more satisfactorily into foreign languages than does most other French poetry. Perse himself had serious doubts that his poetry could be at all translated into English, even though Eliot had already done a competent version of *Anabase*. In the unpublished 1941 letter that accompanied the manuscript of *Exil*, Perse wrote to MacLeish:

'I'm not even sure that a work like this can be published in French in the United States. And surely it is untranslatable: not so much in intellectual terms, but in its abstractions, ellipses, and conscious ambiguities, as in physical terms, in its alliterations, assonances and incantations (bound to the rhythm of sea-waves). And in literal terms too, in the etymological resources of certain of its words, the most simple and disembodied ones.'[23]

Parenthetically, besides what this passage tells us about the problem of translating his poetry, it also reinforces much of the rest that we have been saying about Perse's poetics. Note, for example, how the rhythm of the poem is directly attributed to the rhythm of waves, and how Perse explicitly mentions ellipses and consciously-exploited ambiguities, as well as the sonorous devices

of alliteration, assonance, and incantation.[24] These latter, while
they do make for difficulties in translation, are still much easier to
approximate than are the devices of classical French prosody. The
lack of a strong tonic accent in French (which, more than anything else, imposes the syllable as a prosodic unit, rather than the
English 'foot'), the greater importance of pitch, the far greater
abundance of rhymes in French – all these combine to make the
finding of an acceptable English equivalent to any classical French
verse-form a feat of the rarest sort. These features are, however,
not quite so insurmountable where the unversified poem is concerned.

That brings us to the vexed question of the fundamental differences between the English and French languages, as well as
the question of Perse's distinction between 'Anglo-Saxon' and
French poetry. Recalling a conversation he once had with Gide,
Perse writes:

> He told me about the great attraction his increasingly thorough
> study of the English language was beginning to have for him.
> I pointed out to him what I felt to be the opacity of such a
> concrete language, the excessive richness of its vocabulary
> and its too-great facility in wanting to embody the thing
> itself, as in ideographic writing; whereas French, a far more
> abstract language, seeking much more to signify than to
> represent, involved the fiduciary aspect of the word only as
> a sort of monetary exchange value. English, to me, was still
> at the barter level.[25]

This ingenious but, I feel, basically indefensible comparison, was
made during the course of a conversation in 1911. Forty-five
years later, Perse was to use the same comparison, though in a
much milder form:

> Moreover, this difference between two conceptions of poetry
> is further accentuated by the difference between the two
> languages – English being very concrete, substantive, and
> sensorial in nature, and consequently very tangible and spe-
> cific, and thus naturally inclined to exteriorization. By contrast,
> the extreme economy of means of the French language is
> well known, as is also the fact that, having reached the end
> of a long evolution toward the abstract, French today grate-
> fully accepts as a blessing its material impoverishment, which
> is sometimes pushed all the way to ambiguity and multi-

valence in effecting exchanges and long-distance mutations wherein words, having become mere signs, intervene only nominally, in the manner of so-called fiat money.[26]

To what extent is this characterization of the two languages valid? First, the wealth of the English lexicon, as compared with the French, is undeniable. One has only to compare the English-French volume with the French-English volume of any of the great bilingual dictionaries to realize this. But simply because there are more terms – which means, essentially, more synonyms – in English, is the language necessarily 'more opaque' and 'very tangible and specific' as compared with French? I doubt it. First of all, it should be noted that the very concrete everyday English words, usually of Germanic origin – bread, house, heart, tree – are in no way any more discernibly tangible or specific than *pain*, *maison*, *cœur*, *arbre*. As for the abstract and scientific English words, most of them are of Latin origin, many having been transmitted through Old French. Here there is actually a vast common source shared by the two languages. Where there *is* more specificity in English is in the matter of synonymy. French has the one word *bœuf* to express English ox, beef, and steer; a single word *valeur* to express English valour and value; a single word *fléau* for English flail, scourge, and beam (of a balance). This is surely what is uppermost in Perse's mind when he speaks of the French word as a 'fiduciary sign' having only a 'monetary exchange value'. It is perfectly true that a poet can set up richer resonances with a 'multivalent' word like *fléau* than with 'univalences' such as flail, scourge, or scale-beam. What happens is that, when context makes quite clear which of the three meanings of *fléau* is to be primary, the other meanings of the word still lurk in the background and may enrich the primary meaning. In this way a French poet can indeed accept as a blessing the 'material impoverishment' of French, 'which is sometimes pushed all the way to ambiguity and multivalence'. But I cannot see that the greater wealth of synonyms in English puts it at a more primitive stage of linguistic evolution ('English, to me, was still at the barter level'), for the 'fiduciary' quality of some French words, as well as the contrary 'specific' quality of many English words, can be both a help and a hindrance to a writer, especially a poet. Multivalence, if pushed too far, means that communication breaks down entirely. Specificity, on the other hand, if pushed too far, does indeed become cumbersome. But then, there are instances where English is more 'fiduciary' than French – though perhaps not as many. Take, for example, those Protean little words 'do' and 'get'. And French *souci*, *précaution*, *soin* (and even *responsabilité*) may all be adequately rendered by the single English word 'care'. *Oscillement*, *balancement*, *roulis*, *empire*, *domination* may all come out simply 'sway' in English. In short, I think the difference between the two languages in this sector is far less than Perse would have us believe. The phonological differences between the two languages are, to my mind, far more real than the lexical. Both kinds of difference, however, serve as bases for Perse's further and more radical distinction between 'Anglo-Saxon' and modern French poetry. Since the distinction is such an important one for Perse, we are forced to quote at length and even to repeat earlier citations.

The trouble is that the Anglo-Saxon mind has so long been accustomed to the discursive method of English poetry – a poetry of ideas, and thus of definition and elucidation, always explicit and logical, because rational in its origin, and by that very fact given to the formal sequences of an intellectual and moral dialectic. Modern French poetry, on the other hand, feels it is not really poetry unless it merges with its living object in a live embrace, unless it informs the object entirely and even becomes a part of its very substance, to the point of complete identity and unity of subject and object, of poet and poem. Seeking to do much more than point out or designate, it actually becomes the thing which it 'apprehends', which it evokes or calls forth. Going far beyond any mimetic action, it finally *is* the thing itself, in that thing's own movement and duration. This poetry lives the thing and 'animates' it totally and must scrupulously and with infinite variation submit to the thing's own measure and rhythm. . . . .

All this, of course, is far removed from the 'dualism' of English poetry, wherein the expression, from the very outset, strives to be 'exoteric' and always seems to proceed from some 'a priori' – a fact that always renders quite legitimate, no matter what its theme, the preserving of its sobriety, since the elements of which it is made up are already conclusions, its progression a series of affirmations, and its very accentuation a strong reinforcement in the exercise of its prerogatives.

English poetry seems always to be born of meditation and

not of trance, to follow the line of a modulation rather than the inherent complexity of an incantation. Always seriatim or thematic, it shuns ellipse as a nonsequitur and most harmoniously avoids spasm so that there will be no crisis to resolve. What it proffers seems less a revelation than a confirmation; its movement less an insinuation than an intimation. No matter how concise it may be, English poetry still remains commentary and paraphrase. It pays court to and honours the idea with the full homage of song, but not of the dance.[27]

Further along in the same letter Perse praises the continuous vitality of English poetry through the centuries, 'strong in its living continuity', and states that at no point did it have to instigate a violent revolution to reaffirm its identity in the face of a desiccating rationalism. The French poets, on the other hand, had to do just that, had to initiate a violent revolution 'to escape the desiccation of an excessive rationalism'. This latter affirmation is certainly true. The French Romantics tried to revolt against the poetic sterility of that otherwise dazzling period, the Enlightenment. But so strong was the rationalistic hold of the Enlightenment that the great French Romantics – Lamartine, Hugo, Vigny, Musset – still sound like 'reasoners in verse' when compared with the romantic masters of Germany and – Perse's opinion notwithstanding – England and America. In this connection there is almost something symbolic about Hugo's resorting to table-tapping in his later years. He was a great poet, very often a magnificent poet. He had a real poetic awareness and a sensitivity to the mysterious and ill-defined forces of which man is a product and plaything. But the Mystery had to be reduced to some rationally manipulable form, and so, since he was not a great intellect, we find him resorting to the pseudo-simplifications supplied by the direct contact with 'It' through table-tapping. Then, with superb blandness, Hugo published 'It'-inspired verse that is sometimes Hugolian in the very worst sense. But try as he would, his poetry remained adamantly discursive. And it was not long after Hugo's death that the very embodiment of discursive, even forthrightly didactic verse, Sully-Prudhomme, was to become the first recipient of the Nobel Prize that was, over a half century later, to devolve upon Saint-John Perse. In purely poetic terms, the Romantic revolt in France was somewhat *manquée*. Baudelaire, Verlaine, Rimbaud and their followers had the job of making good on the promises that the earlier Romantics failed to keep. It is in this Baudelairean tradition that Saint-John Perse's poetics of 'trance' and 'co-identification' takes its place.

But does not the explanation of Perse's extravagant distinction between English poetry and modern French poetry reside in the very necessity of a violent break in the French tradition? In stating his poetics in such extreme terms, is not Perse still fighting against the pseudo-Cartesian tradition of 'reason' and 'clarity' that lurks everywhere in French art and literature, in spite of the Rimbauds and the Fargues? Once more, is not the distinction one of degree more than of kind? There are plenty of modern French poems that are quite as discursive and exoteric, quite as 'well-tempered', as any poem written in English. And many a British and American poem of the last fifty years is quite as elliptical as anything in Rimbaud's *Illuminations*.

The real interest of Perse's insistence on the contrast between 'Anglo-Saxon' and modern French poetry lies, I think, in the situation that led Perse to dwell at such length on the distinction. It was prompted by a feeling of irritation at the failure of some English-speaking critics to comprehend one very fundamental aspect of his poetry. The only poem of his known to most English-speaking critics before Perse began writing his 'American' series was, of course, *Anabase*. It is already quite a lengthy poem. (Its actual printed text in the 1960 edition of the *Œuvre poétique* runs to about thirty-five pages, albeit generously spaced pages.) But the idiom of that poem is so stenographic, the ellipses so compressed, and the rhythm frequently so staccato (almost as if based on the trampling of horses' hooves) that there was never for a moment any suggestion that this relatively long poem was *too* long or lapsed into verbal complaisance. But then came the 'American' series, culminating in the two vast poems, *Vents* (almost a hundred pages in the 1960 O.P.) and *Amers* (almost a hundred and fifty pages in the same edition).

Because it is next to impossible to read such poems at a single sitting, and because of a deep-seated distrust of long poems ever since Poe and Baudelaire inveighed against them, Perse was accused of 'letting himself go', of indulging in a verbalism that was often repetitive and redundant – in short, of failing to suppress all the extraneous transitional materials with the rigour he had shown in *Anabase*. Perse felt compelled to protest and, at the same time, to try to explain the source of the misunderstanding. Speaking obliquely of his own very long poems, he wrote: '. . . in reality, such elaborations involve more deletions than additions, and are still, when the work is viewed in its totality, simply a sum of contractions, omissions, and ellipses.'[28] To what extent this is true is brought home when we learn that the original manuscript of *Amers* is over twice as long as the published version! The 'units' of the poem may be monolithic, but the basic ellipses are still there – basic because the ellipse is the figure of speech best adapted to 'co-identification', to apprehension with minimum deformation. *All* discursive material, no matter how well put and how intellectually illuminating, is a distraction from the central poetic experience sought by Perse. In *his* poetry, such materials can only be regarded as padding. As for the padding necessitated by the requirements of a Procrustean conventional prosody, Perse would avoid it at all costs.

We are brought back once more to that curious declaration concerning the physical congruity that must exist between the poetic apprehending of a 'thing' and the 'thing' itself. To experience the sea in its plenitude is to experience something vast and overpowering, multiple in its movements and rhythms, yet always conditioned by its special nature. So, quite literally, *Amers*, Perse's poem about the sea, must be vast. I have already pointed out objections to such a view; but, as is so often the case, if such a view is untenable as a universally applicable poetics, it admirably suits Perse's own very special talents. Perse must apprehend things in their *physical* manifestations; it is only through them that he can accede to a mystery that is real and not merely a shifting chaos of illusions. He feels very strongly that, the moment we begin bestowing labels on the very real but elusive forces that hold us in thrall, we create a fictive realm of abstractions with which we may play ingenious and absorbing games, but which will lead us astray into purely illusory realms where the label replaces the reality. He could say, with the pre-Socratic philosopher he seems to like most, 'The things of which there is seeing and hearing and perception, these do I prefer.'[29] But we know that Heraclitus did *not* say that palpable phenomena were the sum of life. Neither does Perse imply any such limitation. But, given his special temperament and gifts, it is through palpable phenomena that he can best 'get at' the fundamental underlying mystery. It is a preference he shares with many, but not all, other poets, and it accounts to a large extent for those points of his poetics that seem untenable in a wide, general application. But there is no doubt that even these moot points help us to arrive at a more immediate comprehension, and hence greater enjoyment, of the astounding *summa* already formed by the published poems of Saint-John Perse.

5

The Last of the Exile Poems

Vents

The prevailing tone of Perse's work is that of the ode and the epic and, less frequently, of the elegy. Yet, latent in this essentially non-dramatic body of poetry is a tense personal drama that becomes involved with the world-wide conflicts of the first half of the twentieth century. The nexus of the personal drama is found in *Vents*. The 'minus-sign' that precedes the four earlier 'exile poems' continues in force through the first three quarters of *Vents*. But the parabola, so to speak, then passes through the origin and, in the last quarter of the poem, swings into the positive quadrant, moving steadily higher throughout the subsequent 'votive poems': *Amers*, *Chronique*, and *Oiseaux*.

Vents is one of the two longest of all Perse's poems – the other being *Amers*. It is also the most complex and varied of all the poems. These circumstances may help explain why it has been rather neglected, Claudel's dithyrambic praise notwithstanding.[1] In addition, *Vents* contains pronouncements on the conduct of nations, especially France, and on the destinies of mankind. That, combined with the frequent tone of imprecation, gives the poem a certain 'Old-Testament-prophet' quality that makes it easy to overlook the very personal, indeed downright autobiographical basis of the poem. But before one can see how intimately the 'prophetic' and the autobiographical elements are intertwined, some understanding of the poem's general theme is necessary.

Put very baldly, *Vents* says that the world has just lived through

SJP H

the end of a great historical epoch and that this fact must be accepted and 'overcome'. The epoch began with the Renaissance and the discovery of the New World. The winds that filled the sails of Columbus's ships, carrying them westward, are the same winds that have pursued Western man across the continents of the New World and beyond the Pacific wastes all the way to those spice islands that were the original goal of the voyages of discovery. These are the same winds that drove Western man to push his intellectual investigations relentlessly forward, concomitant with the conquest of the New World. This intellectual drive culminates in the hurricane fury of atomic explosions, which are at once a promise of fulfilment and of self-destruction. The danger lies, not in the basic daring and restlessness of man, but in mankind's allowing itself to be pushed by these impulses in the wrong direction, namely, into the realm of the inhuman and non-human, where everything becomes mortally predictable.

The development of the poem is not nearly as rectilinear as this summary would make it seem, but it does follow the 'westward course of empire' much more directly than at first appears. What makes the poem particularly fascinating is that, parallel to the exploration and conquest of the New World, we witness the poet's own personal exploration of that same area. Before taking refuge in the United States, Leger already knew those isles of Columbus, the Antilles; and as a boy he had even visited the northern shores of South America. Almost half a century later, from 1940 on, he was to make more and more extensive land and sea trips around the North American continent, which he had already investigated on his return from China in 1921. He has not, so far as I know, actually been in the Andes (which play such an important part in one section of *Vents*), but the poet's insatiable curiosity has thoroughly familiarized him with that area as well. This parallelism of the historical conquest of the New World and the poet's own discovery of that World should be kept in mind as we examine each of the four sections of *Vents*.

SECTION I. The first canto of the first section tells us that over the face of the whole earth, very great winds blew, to toss about and disperse the 'men of straw'. Here the echo of Eliot's 'The Hollow Men' is undeniable, and one recalls that it was a section of that poem which Perse translated for *Commerce* in 1924.[2] The

figure of the straw man dominates this whole first canto but is immediately transformed into something characteristically Persean:
'Car tout un siècle s'ébruitait dans la sécheresse de sa paille,
parmi d'étranges désinences: à bout de cosses, de siliques, à bout de choses frémissantes,
Comme un grand arbre sous ses hardes et ses haillons de l'autre hiver, portant livrée de l'année morte;
Comme un grand arbre tressaillant dans ses crécelles de bois mort et ses corolles de terre cuite –
Très grand arbre mendiant qui a fripé son patrimoine, face brûlée d'amour et de violence où le désir encore va chanter.'[a]
This typically Persean combination of metaphors and similes establishes one of the dominant figures of the poem: the tree. But it is no ordinary tree. In the very next lines we learn that it is a shamanistic tree, 'ce grand arbre de magie sous sa pouillerie d'hiver: vain de son lot d'icônes, de fétiches'.[b] This tree, which remains proud in its destitution and which is oracular – 'très grand arbre du langage peuplé d'oracles, de maximes'[c] – murmurs like a congenital blind person mumbling over his Braille text, which is here a magical text for the initiated – 'murmurant murmure d'aveugle-né dans les quinconces du savoir'.[d] This magic tree, finally despoiled of its last vestige of dry leaves, pods, and icons, will reappear in the very last lines of the entire poem: 'Un très vieil arbre, à sec de feuilles, reprit le fil de ses maximes...'[e] We shall see that another tree appears alongside it, but the old tree remains as a principle of continuity, the essential humanity of man, the tree whose roots are in touch with age-old forces.

The shamanistic tree quite naturally introduces the Shaman himself, who is the poet. The second canto of this first section begins with the Narrator mounting the ramparts 'Comme un

[a] For a whole century rustled in the dry sound of its straw, amid strange desinences: ending in pods and siliqua, in trembling things, / Like a great tree in its last winter's rags and tatters, wearing the livery of the dead year, / Like a great tree shivering in its deadwood rattles and clayware corollas – / A huge beggarly tree that has squandered its patrimony, its countenance seared with love and violence – countenance whereon desire will sing again.

[b] this great magic-tree in its winter threadbareness: vain in its load of icons and fetishes

[c] very great tree of language, peopled with oracles and maxims

[d] murmuring murmur of one born blind among the quincunxes of knowledge

[e] A very old tree, stripped of its leaves, took up once more the thread of its maxims...

Shaman sous ses bracelets de fer'.[a] His costume is immediately
recognizable as the authentic shamanistic garb; and, like the true
Shaman, the Narrator has converse with the Dead; but his word
is for the Living, and his hands are dipped 'aux vasques du futur'.[b]
One cannot help thinking of the Leader in *Anabase* and his inter-
mittent communings with the Dead – an association that is reinforced by the reference, at the very end of this canto, to the
immolation of a black horse. Here in *Vents*, it is the moment for
a great major ceremony, and the horse-sacrifice is a North Asiatic
shamanistic rite. Perse may very well have seen such a sacrifice
during his travels in China, Mongolia, and Korea. In any case, the
listener in *Vents* asks the Shaman to speak as a Master, for the
moment is a crucial one, and there is little time.

In the third canto the rising of the winds is celebrated, the
'grandes forces en croissance sur toutes pistes de ce monde'.[c]
They are the winds of immense historical movements, far-flung
and disconcertingly capricious[3]; but they promise 'murmure et
chant d'hommes vivants, non ce murmure de sécheresse dont
nous avons déjà parlé'.[d] These winds overturn or carry away all
markers of limits and frontiers. They sing a pure song which no
one really is competent to interpret ('où nul n'a connaissance').
They blow away the dead works of literature, leaving the new
writings 'encloses dans les grands schistes à venir'.[e] These forces
set all things at odds, and the poet-shaman feels ever more drun-
ken 'd'habiter / La mésintelligence',[f] from being free in the wind,
unattached to any political group or religious sect or intellectual
movement. For there is, as the first lines of the fourth canto tell
us: 'Tout à reprendre. Tout à redire.'[g]

This fourth canto is one of the most striking in the whole poem.
It is almost a malediction against the pious hoarding of human
knowledge, or rather, of that web of fact, fiction, and superstition
that we call human knowledge. But once again, instead of in-
veighing against human knowledge in the abstract, it is the very

---

[a] Like a Shaman laden with iron bracelets
[b] in the fountain-basins of the future
[c] great forces swelling over the trails of the world
[d] murmur and song of living men, not this dry murmur of which we have
already spoken
[e] inclosed between the great schists of the future
[f] from inhabiting / Disagreement
[g] Everything to be done over. Everything, retold.

concrete Library of Congress that becomes the object of the poet's imprecation. 'Et la faux du regard sur tout l'avoir menée!'[a] first swings with demonic delight through the halls and stacks where Alexis Leger worked at the time he was composing *Vents*. The uncanny rightness of Perse's evocation of the Library of Congress can be attested by anyone who has ever sat at one of the reader's desks in the huge rotunda or climbed the building's stairs to peer down into the main reading room. The sardonyx stairways 'sous les prérogatives du bronze et de l'albâtre',[b] the rooms like 'carrières de marbre jaune'[c] punctuated with lamps, the 'Hauts murs polis par le silence et par la science,'[d] – the whole inner-sanctum atmosphere of the place: 'Prêtres et prêtrises. Sérapéum!'[e], i.e., the priests of Serapis who kept the great library of Alexandria in Hellenistic times – it is all perfectly caught. And what could be better than 'les livres tristes, innombrables, par hautes couches crétacées'[f]? The whole accumulation is frittering away, reverting to dust. Quite appropriately, there follows at this point another of Perse's homologous series, this time a catalogue of all the powders and dusts of botany and zoology, geology and archeology.

The whole vision is swallowed up in a vast yawn. The next (fifth) canto opens with an invocation to the god of the depths of the sea, the chief of the Babylonian trinity: '...Eâ, dieu de l'abîme, ton bâillement n'est pas plus vaste.'[g] Even to name the god properly, one has to yawn. Not only boundary-markers and depots are swept away, even time-markers – holidays and festivals – will be swept away and forgotten. To counteract this choking weight of dust, a primitive ceremony is called for so that 'la source ... d'une plus haute connaissance'[h] shall not run dry: '[que] l'on fasse coucher nue une femme seule sous les combles – '.[i] This is the virgin offered for fecundation by the living god. The arrangement of the rite is given in considerable detail. Thereafter, the Enchanter appears – the poet-shaman, or, even more specifically, Saint-

---

[a] And the scythe of our glance swept across all possessions!
[b] under the prerogatives of bronze and alabaster
[c] quarries of yellow marble
[d] High walls polished by silence and knowledge
[e] Priests and priestly castes. Serapeum!
[f] sad books, innumerable, in high cretaceous layers
[g] ... Eâ, god of the abyss, no vaster is your yawning.
[h] the spring ... of a higher understanding
[i] Let offering be made of a naked woman lying alone under the rooftree –

John Perse himself who 'Va chez les hommes de son temps en habit du commun, / Et qu'il a dépouillé toute charge publique, / Homme très libre et de loisir, dans le sourire et la bonne grâce.'[a] The self-portrait is unmistakable.[4] And this Enchanter, after the ritual aeration and divine copulation, will read the signs in the western sky, and his counsel will again be one 'of force and violence'.

The sixth canto begins with the reiteration of a statement made three cantos earlier to the effect that the poet was all the more drunk for having denied drunkenness: 'Ivre, plus ivre, disais-tu, d'avoir renié l'ivresse...'[b] Complete lucidity is the necessary condition for the greatest intoxication. This lucidity has permitted the poet to sense that this moment – 1945, the year of Hiroshima – is the crest of the age, the Continental Divide in human affairs.

'Ceux qui songeaient les songes dans les chambres se sont couchés hier soir de l'autre côté du Siècle, face aux lunes adverses.

D'autres ont bu le vin nouveau dans les fontaines peintes au minium. Et de ceux-là nous fûmes.'[c]

These lines are followed by a reference to 'la tristesse que nous fûmes'[d] – an open admission of the sadness that pervades the exile poems. Now, sadness and nostalgia are left behind, and there is a terrible sense of urgency. The personal reference here is made even more explicit by the proud, even haughty, passage that follows:

'Qu'on nous cherche aux confins les hommes de grand pouvoir, réduits par l'inaction au métier d'Enchanteurs.

Hommes imprévisibles. Hommes assaillis du dieu. Hommes nourris au vin nouveau et comme percés d'éclairs.

Nous avons mieux à faire de leur force et de leur œil occulte.

Notre salut est avec eux dans la sagesse et dans l'intempérance.'[e]

---

[a] Goes among the men of his time in commoner's garb, / Having laid aside all public office, / A very free man, with leisure, smiling and gracious.

[b] 'Drunk, more drunk,' you were saying, 'for having denied drunkness . . . '

[c] Those who dreamed dreams in the bedrooms went to bed last night on the other side of the Century, facing the adverse moons. / Others have drunk the new wine from the red-lead-painted fountains. We were among these.

[d] the sadness that we were

[e] Seek out for us in the borderlands the men of great power reduced by

It is not hard to recognize Alexis Leger, one-time Secretary General of Foreign Affairs and wielder of great power, reduced to the role of poet and charmer. And the reference to lightning makes one think back to *Exil* and the lightning-spasms that unsealed the springs of song. Then, back beyond *Exil*, one is also reminded, by the language used in this whole sixth canto, of the terms used by the Leader of *Anabase* in his attacks against those who cultivate melancholy and introspection for their own sake: 'Et si un homme auprès de nous vient à manquer à son visage de vivant, qu'on lui tienne de force la face dans le vent!'[a] The very rhythm of this echoes, 'Mais si un homme tient pour agréable sa tristesse, qu'on le produise dans le jour! et mon avis est qu'on le tue'. This recurrent exhortation of *Anabase* is even more insistently repeated in *Vents*. In this same sixth canto there is a kind of prayer beginning: 'Divinités propices à l'éclosion des songes, ce n'est pas vous que j'interpelle, mais les Instigatrices ardentes et court-vêtues de l'action.'[b] These wind-goddesses come cyclonically, causing the strange man ('l'homme étrange') to raise his head. These strange men make one think of the Princes of Exile. They are the man at the wheel-plough, the horseman on the uplands, the seaman. Finally there is the Babouvist philosopher, the revolutionary who steps out to look at the City of foundries, forges, and slag-heaps under the stormy sky. The picture of the Pittsburgh-like city is a particularly arresting one, illuminated three successive times by the lightning: 'illuminée dans ses houillères et dans ses grands établissements portuaires – un golgotha d'ordure et de ferraille, sous le grand arbre vénéneux du ciel, portant son sceptre de ramures comme un vieux renne de Saga.'[c] This spokesman of the industrial proletariat, this follower of the revolutionary Babeuf, appeals to the poet to hasten the destruction of the old order and to be the voice of what is to come. It is this Babouvist who

inaction to the profession of Enchanter. / Unpredictable men. Men assailed by the god. Men nourished on new wine and as if transfixed by lightning. / We have better use for their strength and for their occult eye. / Our salvation is with them in wisdom and intemperance.

[a] And should the face of any man among us betray a lack of trust in the living, let that face be held by force into the wind!

[b] Divinities propitious to the flowering of dreams, it is not you I call up, but rather the brief-clad and passionate goddesses who incite to action.

[c] illuminated in its collieries and huge dock-installations – a golgotha of rubbish and scrap-iron under the great venomous tree of the sky that carries its sceptre of branches like an old reindeer of the Sagas.

tells the poet: 'Et si l'homme de talent préfère la roseraie et le jeu de clavecin, il sera dévoré par les chiens.'[a]

Somewhat more pardonable than such an escape into antiquarian aestheticism is the expression of real doubt. The opening line of canto seven, again invoking Eâ, tells us that 'les tentations du doute seraient promptes / Où vient à défaillir le Vent...'.[b] Here in this last canto of the first section is the most tense expression of Perse's struggle to overcome his own sense of the futility of all things. It is as if he has to shout wildly to drown out the voice of despair. These fateful years of 1944-1945 are referred to as the 'croisement des fiers attelages du malheur'.[c] At such a juncture, in order to sustain the fullness of his song ('pour tenir à son comble la plénitude de ce chant') all this clamour of the soul ('tout ce bruit de l'âme') is not excessive. The poet sings wildly to keep his courage up, and then he openly addresses the younger generations, telling them that their doorway bears the armorial crest of an iron gauntlet. Men in swarms have passed, going where all men go, to their tombs. But the voyage is meaningful if made in the right direction. To symbolize the right direction, the forward-movement of history, the poet says, 'Et c'est au bruit / Des hautes narrations du large, sur ce sillage encore de splendeur vers l'Ouest'.[d] And a little further on, 'Et c'est montée de choses incessantes dans les conseils du ciel en Ouest'.[e] There, a new order of solemnities is being worked out, rites that will give access to the pure source of things ('les purs ferments d'une ombre prénatale') as in the 'grandes cérémonies majeures où coule le sang d'un cheval noir...'[f] – the image, of course, bringing us back to the shamanistic sacrifice mentioned in the first canto.

SECTION 11. The great voyages of discovery and the subsequent migrations into all corners of the New World are now presented as the most telling expression of the wind-driven forces of recent history. The second section is devoted especially to the Canadian

[a] And if the man of talent prefer the rose garden and the harpsichord, he will be devoured by the dogs.

[b] the temptations of doubt would be prompt / Where the Wind suddenly fails...

[c] place where the proud chariot-teams of misfortune cross

[d] And they go to the sound / Of the lofty narrations of the open sea, still in the wake of splendour towards the West.

[e] And there rise unceasing things in the councils of the Western sky.

[f] great major ceremonies wherein flows the blood of a black horse...

wilderness and to the Deep South and Far West of the United States, all areas where Perse had been travelling during the years when *Vents* was taking shape.

The first canto is an ode to the virgin forest of the American Northwest and of Canada, to the tall, outdoor women of the farms and the 'one-way' towns of these regions. The imagery used is too abundant and elaborately imbricated for convenient citation. Consider, as the merest sample, the effectiveness achieved by the telescoping of a whole series of elliptical metaphors in the following passage. The poet has been speaking of the outdoor women, with their free gait and earthy aura: 'Et vos jambes étaient longues et telles qu'elles nous surprennent en songe, sur les sables, dans l'allongement des feux du soir... La nuit qui chante aux lamineries des Villes n'étire pas chiffre plus pur pour les ferronneries d'un très haut style.'[a] This is like an early Dali or Chirico painting, where the shadows are immensely elongated in the horizontal light of the setting sun. Here the long legs of the outdoor women remind the poet of such shadows. But the image is reinforced by another – that of a device or emblem flattened out in rolling-mills and elongated into some elegant flourish as an ornament for fine ironwork.

The second canto of this section continues the ode to the virgin forest, this time in its winter guise. The poet implores the winter to continue teaching 'the iron word' ('Enseigne-nous le mot de fer'). The struggle to fare forward is still a very hard one. Here on the threshold of a vast new country, a reservoir of Power, the poet calls upon the 'plenitude' that is mankind's due. But as yet, there is no answer: 'Je t'interroge, plénitude! – Et c'est un tel mutisme...'.[b] There is nothing to do but press onward.

The exploratory trek this time follows the migrating birds toward the south. Cantos iii, iv, and v present the Mississippi delta and adjacent parts of the Deep South. Perse already knows this South, which furnished the setting of *Pluies*; and the Gulf leads into the Caribbean Sea of Perse's childhood. 'Je te connais, ô Sud', are, in fact, the first words of a description of the Deep South that may well become an anthology piece. We are recog-

---

[a] And your legs were long and like those that surprise us in dreams, on the sands, in the lengthening of the day's last rays... Night, singing among the rolling-mills of the Cities, stretches out no purer figure to adorn wrought-ironwork of a very lofty style.

[b] I question you, O plenitude! – And for answer there is such muteness ...

nizably in the South of Faulkner and Capote, but the accent is unmistakably Persean. Hanging over the area is a sky 'pareil à la colère poétique, dans les délices et l'ordure de la création'.[a] There is New Orleans with its antique shops, the floating alluvial islands, the moss-hung trees of the bayous, with their snakes and water-birds – among them the Anhinga or snakebird curling 'l'absurde paraphe de son col'.[b6] There are the southern belles and the aban-doned plantation-houses, and then a final cryptic image that Saint-John Perse himself has been good enough to explain. Hanging over all this deltal South there is 'un goût de tubéreuse noire et de chapelle ardente'.[c] This pervasive presence of death is summed up thus:

'Et la Mort qui songeait dans la beauté des femmes aux ter-rasses, avivera ce soir d'un singulier éclat l'étoile au front de l'Etrangère, qui descend seule, après minuit, la nuit royale des sous-sols vers la piscine de turquoise illuminée d'azur.'[d]

Once more we are faced with the transcription of a specific event. The Unknown Lady was a guest at the hotel where Perse and his fellow-travellers were staying in the South. The hotel was a very new one, and the construction work was not quite completed. Among other things, there was still no water in the pool, though the illumination was turned on. One of the women guests, wish-ing to take a solitary midnight swim, dived into the empty pool and was killed.

The last portions of canto v then turn away from the South and pursue the exploration once more toward the West. 'Nos routes dures sont en Ouest, où court la pierre à son afflux.'[e] There, in the gorges of the canyon country, the waters that dozed peacefully through the wide valleys awaken, form rapids, and roar: 'Les val-lées mortes, à grands cris, s'éveillent dans les gorges, s'éveillent et fument à nouveau sur leurs lits de shamans!'[f] This last image

---

[a] like the poetic wrath, in the delight and the filth of creation
[b] the absurd paraph of its neck
[c] A flavour of black tuberoses and mortuary chapels
[d] And Death, who has been dreaming deep within the beauty of the women on the terraces, will tonight make glow with a singular radiance the star on the brow of the Unknown Lady who goes down, alone, after mid-night, through the regal darkness of the basements toward the blue-illumin-ated turquoise swimming-pool.
[e] Our rough roads lie in the West, where stone runs to its afflux.
[f] The dead valleys awaken in their gorges, with loud cries awaken and mist once more on their shamans' beds.

reminds us of the shamanistic cast that gives its special character
to the whole poem.

The sixth and last canto of this section is, in fact, a kind of
manifesto of the Poet-as-Shaman. The Shaman, through his ecstatic trances, can traffic with an Otherworld of mysterious forces.
He it is who must bring back the message to ordinary mortals and
interpret it. So here the poet says that he hears the bones of a new
age growing. ('J'entends croître les os d'un nouvel âge de la
terre.') The poet's function is then defined:

'Et vous pouvez me dire: Où avez-vous pris cela? – Textes
reçus en langage clair! versions données sur deux versants!...
Toi-même stèle et pierre d'angle!... Et pour des fourvoiements
nouveaux, je t'appelle en litige sur ta chaise dièdre,

O Poète, ô bilingue, entre toutes choses bisaiguës, et toi-
même litige entre toutes choses litigieuses – homme assailli du
dieu! homme parlant dans l'équivoque!...'[a]

By this time it should have become quite evident why *Vents* is the
source of so many important assertions on poetics and why it
was necessary to draw so heavily upon the poem in the preceding
chapter. In regard to the passage just quoted, two items are note-
worthy: First, the insistence on the clarity of the language, and
second, on the equivocal nature of the actual message. The poet
senses things clearly, but he cannot define them ostensively, by
simply pointing to them; he must use words. These words are
meaningful to others only in terms of already-shared experience.
Therefore, if the poet senses something new, he is obliged to use
words that have already served, that are current in the linguistic
summa of his speech-community. In short, he has to define the
new experience by circumlocution. The words he uses will carry
with them the old meaning, but they must be applied in contexts
and ways that will twist their meaning sufficiently to point toward the 'unedited' experience. So the poet's pronouncements are
bound to be equivocal and bound to vary as effective communication. When the experience he wishes to transmit has been duplicated by others, then the words and figures will lose some of their

[a] And you may say to me: Where did you learn that? – Texts received in
clear language! versions given on two sides!... You, yourself, a stele and a
cornerstone!... And for once more going astray, I summon you in litigation
on your dihedral chair, / O Poet, O bilingual one, amidst all double-edged
things, and you, yourself, litigation amid all things litigious – man assailed
by the god! man speaking in the equivocal!...

ambiguity, and the new meanings he has sought to put into them will be more or less common currency.

One such way of 'twisting' words is to break them down and combine them in various ingenious ways, as James Joyce did in his later works. Perse, however, resolutely avoids the 'synthetic' vocabulary, the specially-created portmanteau words. In his opinion, these creations quite as often obscure the new meaning as reveal it; or worse, they camouflage platitudes and vacuity. Perse prefers the more difficult and more elegant procedure of limiting himself to the use of words that are already part of the common currency. Readers of Perse will protest that his vocabulary is, nevertheless, staggering, and that it swarms with strange words that often look suspiciously 'synthetic'. Perse protests, however, and quite rightly, that his lexicon is the one codified in the great dictionaries.[7] Moreover, none of the rare words is used playfully. Poetry is a serious business. But the poet, by the very nature of language, runs all sorts of risks. The poet may, however, profit from the very 'double-edged' character of language.

An example of profitable use of the ambiguities inherent in language is contained in the very next lines. 'Et toi, Soleil d'en bas, férocité de l'Etre sans paupière, tiens ton œil de puma dans tout ce pain de pierrerie!'[a] The rubble of stone so avidly collected in the American Southwest is precious, for it contains pitchblende, with its radioactive uranium that never ceases its emissions of rays, as if it were without eyelids. That is the dark sun at the heart of matter. But there is also the dark sun of the psychological forces that drive men relentlessly to do what they do. When Perse was asked which he meant, the radioactive nuclear forces or the psychological forces of the unconscious, he replied quite simply, 'Both'.

SECTION III. This section shifts back from the poet to the explorers, conquistadors, and settlers of the New World, all of them men who kept their faces in the wind. Each group is 'fixed' in a separate canto, often unforgettably. The complex of metaphors and similes describing the first sighting of land is centered on the figure of the suspended balance, which Perse has already used in

---

[a] And you, Sun of the lower depths, ferocity of the Being with no eyelids, fix the gaze of your puma's eye on all this conglomerate of precious stones.

Anabase and which he will expand later in the opening section of
Oiseaux:

'Et la terre oscillait sur les hauts plans du large, comme aux
bassins de cuivre d'invisibles balances,
Et c'était de toutes parts, dans une effloraison terrestre, toute
une fraîcheur nouvelle de Grandes ·Indes exondées.'[a]

The helmeted conquistador riding up into the Mexican heartland
is caught in silhouette: 'Les Cavaliers sous le morion, greffés à
leur monture, montaient, au grincement de cuir, parmi les ronces
d'autre race... La barbe sur l'épaule et l'arme de profil.'[b] Their
itineraries still shine 'comme traces de l'ongle au vif des plats
d'argent'.[c]

In canto ii the fortune-seekers follow the conquistadors, then
the traders and missionaries and church officials. Still a little later,
and on shores farther north, come the malcontents, the religious
dissenters of every stripe, some of whom keep intact their strange
sects, snake-worshippers of Georgia or the vestigial groups of
Adamites with their ritual nakedness. Then come those who are
simply curious, followed at last by the men of science, 'physicists,
petrographers, and chemists'. And they, of course, in search of
uranium ore, bring us into the last phase of the westward movement, the nuclear age – which is really the beginning of a new
age, because the onward quest turns inward:

'Car notre quête n'est plus de cuivres ni d'or vierge [...] nous
cherchons, dans l'amande et l'ovule et le noyau d'espèces nouvelles, au foyer de la force l'étincelle même de son cri!...'[d]

The poet says of this sun yet to be born ('Soleil à naître') that he
will be among the first to be present at the irruption of the new
god. The lines that follow bring the canto to a close, tantalizingly:
'Aux porcheries du soir vont s'élancer les torches d'un singulier
destin!'[e] The torches of destiny present no difficulty, but what

---

[a] And the earth oscillated on the high planes of the open sea, as if in the
copper pans of invisible balances, / And from all sides, in earthly efflores-
cence, rose a whole new freshness of great Indies emergent from the sea.

[b] The Horsemen under their morions, grafted to their mounts, climbed,
to the creaking of leather, among the brambles of a new race... Their beards
on their shoulders and their weapons in silhouette.

[c] like fingernail marks on the quick of silver plates.

[d] For our quest is no longer for copper or virgin gold [...] we seek, in
the kernel and the ovule and the nucleus of new species, at the focal point
of force, the very spark of its cry!

[e] In the pigsties of evening will flare the torches of a singular destiny!

about the 'porcheries du soir'? Does it mean that out of the swill and garbage of a declining age, steeped in the bloody filth of war, this new torch will flare?

At least some such interpretation seems justified by the next canto (iii), which is devoted to the atomic scientists. Other new forces wait impatiently 'dans le métal et dans les sels nouvellement nommés'.[a] The research-workers in their protective helmets and masks replace the conquistadors beneath the morion. The radio-active detector is there, 'menant un silencieux tonnerre dans la mémoire brisée des quartz'.[b] Let these scientists be witnesses of 'le pire scandale de l'histoire'[c] – again this word that has occurred at the beginning of *Anabase* ('la plume savante au scandale de l'aile') and that will appear again in *Oiseaux* ('C'est le scandale aussi du peintre et du poète'), with the rather special meaning of 'sudden or brilliant disclosure'. The ultimate promises of atomic energy, its peaceful uses, are duly celebrated: 'la promesse haut tenue d'un infini loisir.'[d] The last strophes picture the atomic scientist as a priest in contemplation as he officiates over a solemn rite.

There is, however, one thing omitted in the projecting of these startling possibilities, namely, Man himself. That is where the poet comes in. (Canto iv.) No longer dare the poet nurse dreams in an aesthete's hideaway. He must identify himself with all the patient workers, all the struggling humanity that tries doggedly to go about its business: 'Avec tous hommes de patience, avec tous hommes de sourire.' 'Avec tous hommes de douceur, avec tous hommes de sourire sur les chemins de la tristesse.'[e] And fin-ally, 'Avec tous hommes de douceur, avec tous hommes de pa-tience aux chantiers de l'erreur'.[e] Examples of each of these are given, forming another homologous series, another list of Princes of Exile. And joining them this time, 'ô sourire, ô douceur', is the poet himself 'à la coupée du Siècle'[f] – 'coupée' here used in the nautical sense. The very notion of Man is in question, and

[a] in the metal and the newly-named salts

[b] rolling a silent thunder in the broken memory of quartz crystals

[c] history's worst scandal

[d] the promise of endless leisure held high

[e] With all men of patience, with all smiling men, / ..... / With all men of gentleness, with all men who smile as they tread the paths of sorrow, / ..... / With all men of gentleness, with all men of patience in the factory-yards of error

[f] O smile, O gentleness, / The Poet himself at the gangway of the Century!

someone must testify on his behalf. 'Que le Poète se fasse entendre, et qu'il dirige le jugement!'[a]

It is, I think, worth noting that this calling into question of the
very concept of man is the major theme of another literary work
produced during the war by another Frenchman, namely, the
fragmentary *Noyers de l'Altenburg* of André Malraux. The real hero
of that book (the narrator's father) is a diplomat-soldier who becomes so obsessed with this question of the validity of the concept
'Man' that he momentarily forsakes his role as a man of action to
attend an intellectual conference at Altenburg (a transposition of
Pontigny), where the main topic of discussion is to be precisely
that question. The parallelism with *Vents* is striking. In both
Perse's poem and Malraux's novel there is no satisfactory *intellectual* resolution of the dilemma. In the novel, affirmation is
achieved only after the most hideous suffering – suffering that
leads the protagonist to the verge of nihilistic despair. In *Vents*,
all the poet can do is brush aside the intellectual arguments and
give voice to the life forces that well up in spite of everything.
In this vein, canto v begins peremptorily: 'Je t'ignore, litige. Et
mon avis est que l'on vive!'[b] The lines that follow are straight out
of *Anabase*, even to the image of the seeled eyes of the falcon. The
poet, speaking of the 'great adventurers of the soul', says of them:

'Qu'ils n'aillent point dire: tristesse..., s'y plaisant – dire:
tristesse..., s'y logeant, comme aux ruelles de l'amour.
Plutôt l'aiguille d'or au grésillement de la rétine!
Brouille-toi, vision, où s'entêtait l'homme de raison...
Le Chasseur en montagne cousait d'épines sauvages les pau-
pières de l'appelant.'[c]

The vehemence of this protest against sadness is a measure of the
terrible sadness Perse himself had to overcome. Few but his very
closest friends will ever know to just what depths of depression
he must have sunk during the fateful war years. But what seems
to have been inexplicably overlooked by almost everyone is the

---

[a] Let the Poet speak out, let him guide the judgment!

[b] Litigation, I have no knowledge of you. And my opinion is that we
should live!

[c] Let them not say: Sadness..., revelling in it. Not say: sadness..., loitering in it as in the alcoves of love. / Injunction against living on it! Injunction
brought against the poet, against the spinners of memory. / Rather the golden
needle at the shrinking of the retina. / Be blurred, oh sight, to which the man
of reason clung... / With wild thorns the Hunter in the mountains sewed up
the eyelids of the decoy.

reiterated expression of this sadness in the exile poems, not to mention the prefiguring of this sadness in the 'contemplative' sections of *Anabase*. Certain tricks of speech (the use of the generic term as a substitute for the specific noun or personal pronoun is one of them) and the unflagging 'high tone' of the language have obscured for many readers the burden of personal suffering that these poems carry, and none more than *Vents*. The desperate groping for a way out is poignantly expressed in the very next lines:

'Et comme un homme frappé d'aphasie en cours de voyage, du fait d'un grand orage, est par la foudre même mis sur la voie des songes véridiques,

Je te chercherai, sourire, qui nous conduise un soir de Mai mieux que l'enfance irréfutable.'[a]

The avowal is modified, though, by characteristically Persean self-restraint. The poet hastens to add a more elaborate simile in which he this time compares himself to the Initiate for whom the door to the mystery is flung open by the storm. In both figures the storm is also the intrusive welling up of unconscious forces, triumphant over all logic. The whole section ends with a bow to the black subterranean sun: 'Et révérence au Soleil noir d'en bas!'

The last canto of this third section sums up the shamanistic and *committed* poetics of which *Vents* itself is a product. The poet is a witness for mankind. He is among us, and his occupation is explicitly stated as 'mise en clair des messages'.[b] The whole section ends in a breathless cry of urgency. The piercing cry of the god, the message of humanity, must be delivered before it is too late.

SECTION IV. The last section is the most personal of all, referring constantly to Perse's own life and to his intentions for the immediate future. It likewise passes judgment on his countrymen and assigns to them their place in the unfolding of the New Age.

After the paroxysm reached at the end of section III there is a sudden and almost despairing let-down. The god of the mysterious and capricious forces that buffet mankind manifests himself

---

[a] And as a man stricken with aphasia in the course of a journey, because of a great storm, is, by the very lightning, led into the pathway of veracious dreams, / So I shall seek you out, O smile, to lead us some May evening more surely than irrefutable childhood.

[b] the clarification of messages.

in disaster but remains mute. Here at the extreme limit he is again suddenly silent: 'O frontière, ô mutisme! Aversion du dieu!'[a] The feeling of emptiness is still present: 'Et les capsules encore du néant dans notre bouche de vivants.'[b] These sedatives or soporifics carry the promise of absorption into nothingness. But the poet overcomes the temptation and continues fighting. If life is like this, then let us live it out in those terms. But the winds must blow again, 'Sinon, c'est tel reflux au désert de l'instant!'[c] This is the isolated moment, cut off from the continuum of time, the hiatus in which we face 'L'emphase immense de la mort comme un grand arbre jaune devant nous'.[d]

If life is this blind forward movement, then, even without the help of the winds, we must push on. In the pattern of the poem, this means pushing farther and farther into the New World and beyond. What else is there to do? The poet disdainfully rejects the usual palliatives. Some men take refuge in laughter; for them life is a huge joke. Others say that escape into illusion is the only way to live life out; one must dissemble ('il faut feindre'). Still others take refuge in woman-as-mother, regressing to the irresponsibility of childhood. None of these recourses is satisfactory. 'Mais quoi! n'est-il rien d'autre, n'est-il rien d'autre que d'humain?'[e] At this point a Claudel or a Pierre Jean Jouve would have answered, 'Yes, there is – God.'[9] Significantly, Perse finds no such answer. The predicament must be resolved in human terms; and, for Perse, all the mysterious forces that flow around and through us are continuous with the sensorium. There is no God separate from his creation, and man can appeal to no higher, yet anthropomorphic, deity. Perse is, thus, in the narrow philosophical sense, a humanist. He can work out his salvation only in human terms. The first hint of reconciliation with mankind and acceptance of human limitation comes, significantly, in the supremely earthy form of a renewal of contact with woman. The specificity of the setting for the actual incident makes one wonder whether this is not another bit of pure autobiography:

'Nous épousions un soir vos membres purs sur les pelleteries brûlantes du sursaut de la flamme,

[a] O frontier, O muteness! Aversion of the god!
[b] And still the capsules of nothingness in our living mouths.
[c] Otherwise, there is such a reflux back to the desert of the instant!
[d] Death's immense overstatement, like a huge yellow tree, there before us.
[e] But then, is there nothing else, nothing but the human thing?

Et le vent en forêt nous était corne d'abondance, mais nos
pensées tenaient leurs feux sur d'arides rivages,'[a]
– so begins this crucial passage. It is only the beginning of a reconciliation with mankind, but a decisive beginning, for the last
lines of this first canto tell us that the women who will read and
understand these pages will know that it was with them that 'nous
reprenions un soir la route des humains'.[b]

The second canto opens with an insistence on the human: the
shadow of a man on the highway, the smoke curling above the
rooftops ('la fumée de l'homme [...] sur les toits' – compare 'et la
fumée des hommes en tous lieux' of *Anabase*, x). The season of
man is a new theme on the poet's lips. There is still doubt, though.
If life is simply the taking of one's place in the family of man, is
there any point in going further, in continuing to the utmost limit
the westward movement? Since there seems nothing else to do,
the poet pushes on in his New World trek. We have mentioned
that Perse has not been to the Andes nor to Easter Island, yet the
description of the Inca sites and of the 'îles solitaires – les îles
rondes et basses, baguées d'un infini d'espace, comme des astres'[c]
is as vivid and *seen* as anything in the poem. The first lines of the
Andean section begin successively with the *introit* 'I remember...'
('Je me souviens de...'). This is an effective literary ruse. There is
no break in the physical presence of the westward pageant. Not
until the middle of this long second canto do we find the explanation: '...Et tout nous est reconnaissance. Et toujours, ô mémoire,
vous nous devancerez, en toutes terres nouvelles où nous n'avions
vécu.'[d] In these Andean portions, the conditional tense of the concluding refrain of each subdivision prepares us for this *jamais vu*
which is really a *déjà vu*: ' – Qu'irais-tu chercher là?' 'Qu'irais-tu
sceller là?' 'Qu'irais-tu clore là?'[e] This 'haut pays sans nom, illu-
miné d'horreur et vide de tout sens'[f] is there before us in all its

---

[a] We espoused your pure limbs one night on the furs that were hot from
the sudden leap of the flames, / And for us the wind in the forest was a horn
of plenty, but our thoughts kept their watch-fires along barren shores.
[b] One night, we took once more the road back through humanity.
[c] solitary islands – the low round islands, ringed with an infinity of space
like stars
[d] ... And everything is recognition for us. And always, O memory, you
will get there before we do, to those new lands where we have never lived.
[e] – What would you go there to seek? / ..... / – What would you go there
to seal? / ..... / – What would you go there to conclude?
[f] high nameless country, illumined with horror and devoid of all meaning

strangeness. To the poet, though, it is bordered by 'cette autre masse d'irréel',[a] the wastes of the Pacific. It is all unreal because it is simply a further projection of what has already been seen: ' – Mais si tout m'est connu, vivre n'est-il que revoir?'[b] or, more concretely, 'et les signes qu'aux murs retrace l'ombre remuée des feuilles en tous lieux, nous les avions déjà tracés'[c] – a melancholy echo of the felicity of leaves that is everywhere in 'Pour fêter une enfance' and that crops up so significantly in *Anabase*. In utter exhaustion and weariness, the trek is pursued farther, to the bitter end, past Easter Island and its 'grandes figures averses aux lippes dédaigneuses',[d] past the ultimate islet where a rare meliacid bush, growing in the lava, became extinct some twenty years previously. Finally there is nothing more. The poet is alone 'comme un gnomon sur la table des eaux'[e] – an apt figure for the triangular sail casting its lone shadow on the vast blue sun-dial of the Pacific. But there is no leaving the self behind. The logical end is an anonymous death at sea. The capsules of nothingness are still under the poet's tongue, now openly referred to as capsules of death that burst in his mouth ('les capsules de la mort éclatent dans sa bouche').

The next canto, which is very brief – much less than a page – is the dramatic climax of the poem and of the whole of Perse's work. It simply records a sudden apparition, a gesture that reverses everything: 'C'est en ce point de ta rêverie que la chose survint: l'éclair soudain.'[f] The shock of this flash is like the shock felt when a sinister and totally unsuspected stranger appears from the roadside ditch in a tale of conspiracy or mystery. 'Et à celui qui chevauchait en Ouest, une invincible main renverse le col de sa monture, et lui remet la tête en Est. "Qu'allais-tu déserter là?..."'[g] This moment the poet must never forget, nor must he forget

[a] that other mass of unreality
[b] – But if all is known to me, is living only seeing again what has been seen?
[c] and the signs the moving shadow of the leaves retraces on the walls everywhere, we have already traced.
[d] great averted figures with full disdainful lips
[e] like a gnomon on the table of the waters
[f] It is at this point in your reverie that the thing occurred: the sudden flash of light
[g] And to him who was riding westward, an invincible hand wrenches the neck of his mount and points its head towards the East. 'What were you about to abandon there?...'

'l'écart où maintenir, avec la bête haut cabrée, / Une âme plus scabreuse'.[a] The primary, but almost forgotten, meaning of 'scabrous' is 'rough, harsh to the touch, beset with difficulties'. Such is the soul of Saint-John Perse, and his aloofness has been preserved in the sense that he has refused to take up political life again. Fortunately for us, his aloofness has not kept him from rejoining the community of man and even, in a marginal way, of writers and artists.

By contrast with this brief, climactic third canto, the two following ones are very long and almost topical in their revelations. Perse completed *Vents* in 1945. He was not to return to France from his self-imposed exile until 1957. In the interim he was solicited by Léon Blum and subsequent French political leaders to resume a diplomatic career, as France's ambassador to the United Nations, as legate to the Vatican, as ambassador to the United States. All these offers were refused. But already here in *Vents* is the formal promise to return one day to France. The opening line of canto iv is: 'Nous reviendrons, un soir d'Automne.'[b] The poet goes on to picture the first glimpse he will have, as the plane is about to land, of 'le pays tendre et claire de nos filles, un couteau d'or au cœur'.[c] Here are the few passages that the future biographer of the diplomat and statesman Alexis Leger cannot neglect, for they speak of the personal affront that Leger suffered in public life, of his unbending pride, of his judgment of pre-World War II France, of his hopes for the future of his own country and the whole world.

First he states his view of history, which is at the same time a defence of his conduct during the years of his Secretaryship of the French Foreign Office. He reiterates that he had an appointment with the end of an age, 'Nous avions rendez-vous avec la fin d'un âge'. For a statesman in the almost impossible position in which Leger found himself, almost but not quite at the top and responsible for the continuity of a foreign policy which he frequently personally disapproved – for a man in such a position there was nothing to do but make the best of a lamentable situ-

---

[a] the aloofness in which to hold, along with the high-rearing beast, / A more scabrous soul.
[b] We shall return, one autumn evening
[c] the bright and tender land of our daughters, a golden knife in its heart!

ation. The end of the age closed in inexorably; all Leger could do was, as he said in *Pluies*, allay the pain of the dying.[10] The principles he stood for in foreign policy – European federation, neutralization of Nazi Germany when Hitler first reoccupied the Rhineland, preservation at all costs of an Anglo-French alliance – all were undercut or made impossible. He was, indeed, as the title of a fascinating essay about him indicates, a fighter for Lost Causes.[11] His final betrayal by Reynaud was of such a character that here in *Vents* he can say bitterly, 'Notre grief est sans accommodement, et l'échéance ne sera point reportée'.[a] His role henceforward will be that of a thorn in the flesh, 'j'irriterai la moelle dans vos os'.[b] In postwar France he will call for new men, 'd'hommes entendus dans la gestion humaine, non dans la précession des équinoxes'[c] – a scathing criticism of the French tendency toward unrelenting pursuit of abstract knowledge, while neglecting the far more difficult challenge of grappling with the ever-changing, crude, cruel but live realities of human affairs.

But this bitterness is followed by a poignant defence of France. Perse tells the rest of the world not to stand in judgment of his people, for 'Ils ont vécu plus haut que vous dans les abîmes de l'opprobre'[d] – a curious and arresting paradoxical statement. France, having collapsed, as much through its own folly as through external pressures, collaborated ignominiously with the enemy. But in the depths of this disgrace the heroism of the Resistance came into being. One may object that this hardly gives the poet the right to place his country above judgment or to say that it lived more loftily in the depths of opprobrium than did some other nations, but as a formulation of France's wartime moral position, Perse's formula is striking.

He goes on to dream of what his return will be like, and then he reiterates his promise. He will return from the ultimate capes of exile one day. Summing up what he has done during that exile, he writes:

'Là nous allions parmi les hommes de toute race. Et nous avions beaucoup vécu. Et nous avions beaucoup erré. Et nous lisions les peuples par nations. Et nous disions les fleuves sur-

[a] Our grievance is beyond redress, its date of maturing will not be renewed.
[b] I shall irritate the marrow of your bones.
[c] men skilled in human affairs, not in the precession of equinoxes.
[d] They have lived more loftily than you in the depths of opprobrium.

volés, et les plaines fuyantes, et les cités entières sur leurs disques qui nous filaient entre les doigts – grands virements de comptes et glissements sur l'aile.'[a]

The summary is completed with an air-traveller's view of New York as it is approached under an electric storm – a view that becomes a sort of momentary prophetic vision.

Canto v is addressed wholly to the French nation. The poet reaffirms the fact that he had an appointment with the end of an epoch and then asks whether he will find himself among the men of a new age. The declaration is a real expression of doubt, as the bitter condemnation immediately following it proves. Public re-cantations will not do; 'l'exigence en nous ne s'est point tue. / Il n'y a plus pour nous d'entente avec cela qui fut.'[b] The rejections are then detailed in a series of jostling synecdoches. The petty bourgeois stability-at-all-costs, the overweening preoccupation with the family nest-egg, the Homais morality – again and again the poet says in one way or another, 'Nous en avions assez, pru-dence, de tes maximes à bout de fil à plomb, de ton épargne à bout d'usure et de reprise'.[c] It is likewise at this point that the ultimate expression of such complacency – namely, antiquarian, ivory-tower aestheticism – is vigorously rejected.[12] This portion of the condemnation is summed up in a condensed image of the gardens of Versailles, stagnant and rank. The refuse-choked basins must be flushed out, by a storm, by rains and winds. Once more a reduced, almost calligraphic figure *fixes* the passage: 'Que l'effar-vate encore entre les joncs nous chante la crue des eaux nou-velles...'.[d]

The canto ends with a call to the future, 'Un monde à naître sous vos pas! hors de coutume et de saison!'[e] The poet has his role in the new enterprise:

[a] There we went among men of every race. And we had lived intensely. And we had wandered far. And we read off the peoples by nations. And we spoke of the rivers flown over and the fleeing plains, and whole towns on their disks that slipped through our fingers – great transferrings of accounts and slidings on the wing.

[b] the demands have not been stilled in our heart. / There is for us no longer any possible coming to terms with what has been.

[c] We have had enough, O prudence, of your maxims weighted to a plumb-line, of your thrift threadbare beyond mending.

[d] Let the reed-warbler amid his reeds sing for us once more the flood-waters rising...

[e] A world to be born under your footsteps! out of custom, out of season!

'Et le poète est avec vous. Ses pensées parmi vous comme des tours de guet. Qu'il tienne jusqu'au soir, qu'il tienne son regard sur la chance de l'homme!

Je peuplerai pour vous l'abîme de ses yeux. Et les songes qu'il osa, vous en ferez des actes.'[a]

The following canto (vi) is the coda of the whole poem, being followed by the very brief seventh canto, which is really only a sustained final chord. The coda begins tellingly with a reference to the great winds 'qui nous chantaient l'horreur de vivre, et nous chantaient l'honneur de vivre'.[b] These winds blew into 'les flûtes sauvages du malheur'[c]; they surprised the poet 'sur la pierre sauvage du malheur'[d] – 'malheur', which is both 'misfortune' and 'unhappiness'. For the depths of Saint-John Perse's anguish and loneliness during these last years of the war was great, far greater than the casual reader could suspect.

The reference to the great winds is followed by a lovely extended figure which compares the man who comes to rest, after being endlessly wind-driven, to the swimmer who suddenly feels the unmoving beach-sands beneath him. (Perse has always been a great swimmer.) This figure is a modulation into the key of utter calm that prevails in the next lines. Here there is a beautiful version of the swords-into-ploughshares figure. But none catches the feeling of supreme calm, which comes as the great winds die down, better than the simile in 'Chante, douceur, à la dernière palpitation du soir et de la brise, comme un apaisement de bêtes exaucées'.[e]

The sustained chord of the last canto reverts to the figure of the shamanistic tree which opened the poem. It is now completely denuded, but already a magnificent new tree is rising alongside it, 'des grandes Indes souterraines, / Avec sa feuille magnétique et son chargement de fruits nouveaux'.[f] [13]

---

[a] And the poet is with you! His thoughts among you like watch-towers. May he keep his sights until nightfall on the fortune of man! / I shall people for you the abyss of his eyes. And the dreams he has dared, you will turn into acts.

[b] That sang to us the horror of living and sang too the honour of living

[c] the wild flutes of misfortune

[d] on the wild stone of misfortune

[e] Sing, sweetness, to the last palpitation of the evening and of the breeze, like the sense of peace of gratified beasts.

[f] from the great subterranean Indies, / With its magnetic leaf and its burden of new fruit.

Those are the last words of the poem that is the dramatic climax of all Perse's work and that is, in itself, the most dramatic of his poems. It is easy to overlook this quality of *Vents* for several reasons. First there is the obvious reason of the unusual length of the poem. It is so long that a complete reading at one sitting is virtually impossible, and piecemeal reading destroys much of the effect of the poem's prolonged dramatic crescendo. Then there is the form of the poem. It is a monologue, but a monologue that in almost no way resembles the 'dramatic monologue' familiar to readers of 'Anglo-Saxon' poetry. The drama in *Vents* is, instead, cast in epic terms, and the tone is primarily that of the epic. Yet there is not even that minimum of individualized conflict that we find in *Anabase*, which is basically a far less dramatic and far more consistently epic poem than *Vents*. The dramatic conflict in *Vents* is unavoidably vague. Drama, of course, means, if not a plot, at least tension and conflict. While both these latter elements are present in *Vents*, what is lacking is a clear-cut pitting of persons and forces against each other or against themselves. In a narrow sense, *Vents* is obviously a drama where the protagonist is in solitary struggle with forces inside himself, but the impossibility of making this struggle into even the most rudimentary sort of 'plot' results from the elusive nature of the forces with which the poet-protagonist is wrestling. Moreover, he wrestles with them both within himself and on the stage of history. The winds, invisible but ever-present and capable of sudden destructiveness, are an excellent metaphor for these forces.

Finally, there is the resolutely depersonalized tone of the poem. That tone, as we have seen, is the 'standard' Persean tone. The point here, though, is that such a tone is not conducive to the immediacy of impact that we associate with drama. Yet, quite beyond the demands of the aristocratic expression that is ever present in Perse, this depersonalization has a much more organic function in *Vents*. The drama of the poem is quite as much a public one as it is a private one. The violent drama of modern history makes itself manifest in and through the protagonist of the poem. Just as Alexis Leger was forced to play a role in some of the most tragic and even ignominious international crises of our time, so he finds that, in *Vents*, his inner conflict and despair are dictated far more by the winds of history than by any incidents in his own domestic and private life. The depersonalized tone effectively underscores the curiously public character of the basic conflict in the poem.

As we have said, all these elements combine to obscure the drama of *Vents*. But it is a real and moving drama. On the personal level, it may be regarded as the thunderous last act of a crisis that began in *Exil* and continued in *Pluies*. In its wider implications this epic drama may turn out to be one of the few really portentous poems of our time. But however that may be, *Vents* marks the end of the crisis, and the calm of its last cantos prepares the way for the great poems of reconciliation: *Amers*, *Chronique*, and *Oiseaux*.

6

The Votive Poems

Amers

Perse actually wrote his next poem, *Amers*, before he kept the promise to return to France which he made in *Vents*. Psychologically, however, Perse's exile was over by the time he began to compose *Amers* (1948). It is Perse's longest poem, and it has been much more extensively commented upon than *Vents*, partly because it is an 'easier' poem, less dependent for its immediate effect on specific historical and autobiographical points of reference. Yet it is surprising how, even here, interpretation often becomes runaway fancy – surprising and downright inexcusable, since Perse himself has supplied an explicit synoptic view of the poem.

Amers is the culminating development of the most persistent theme in all of Perse's work, the very theme mimetically contained in the poem's title, namely, the sea. 'Mimetically' because the French term *amer* is apparently not made up, as the older lexicographers indicate, of *à* plus *mer*, that is 'at sea', but comes from the Dutch *merk*, which is surely the same as English *mark*. The word has the kind of fortuitous ambivalence that Perse loves to exploit, and it must delight him that, to obtain a satisfactory equivalent, English must use a compound word, *Seamarks*. The fact that the first meaning of the word to occur to any Frenchman would be that of 'bitter' (Fr. *amer* from L. *amarus*) only makes things all the better, for the bitter salt waters of the sea differentiate it from the 'sweet' water, which is the French way of designating fresh water (*eau douce*).

The very earliest text of Perse's that we possess, *Images à Crusoé*, is a sea-poem, and a very effective one. 'Pour fêter une enfance' and the 'Eloges' have the sea everywhere present. *Anabase*, mainly concerned with a long overland trek, is more than a third devoted to the establishing of a great seaport on an estuary. *Exil* is as much a sea-poem as *Amers* itself and lists among the Princes of Exile 'celui qui peint l'amer au front des plus hauts caps'.[a] Submarine imagery is the very basis of *Poème à l'Etrangère*, and the fourth section of *Vents* is suffused with the sea; in fact, that section contains a parenthesis that might well serve as an epigraph for *Amers*:

'(Et de toutes parts au loin elle [la Mer] m'est présente et proche, et de toutes parts au loin elle m'est alliance et grâce, et circonlocution – invitée à ma table de plein air et mêlée à mon pain, à l'eau de source dans les verres, avec la nappe bleuissante et l'argent et le sel, et l'eau du jour entre les feuilles)' IV, 2[b]

Small wonder, then, that Perse should have chosen the sea as the most fitting image to express that essential concern for man which came to the fore in *Vents*. In fact, a sea-image is present in the very first declaration of that concern: 'Car c'est de l'homme qu'il s'agit, dans sa présence humaine; et d'un agrandissement de l'œil aux plus hautes mers intérieures.'[c] (III, 4).

This same concern is clearly stated in the answer Perse gave to an inquiry concerning his intentions in *Amers*:

I have striven to exalt, in all its ardour and pride, the drama of that human condition, or rather of that *progression*, that so many persons today take delight in debasing and belittling to the point of depriving it of all meaning, of all supreme connection with the great forces that create us, that use us, and that control us. It is the very integrity of man – of man of all Ages, physical and moral, with his summons to power and his taste for the divine – that I have striven to plant upright on the barest threshold, confronting the splendid night

---

[a] he who paints the seamark on the brow of the highest headlands

[b] (And from everywhere in the distance she [the Sea] is present to me and close, and from everywhere in the distance she is alliance to me and grace, and circumlocution – invited to my table in the open and mingled with my bread, with the spring-water in the glasses, with the bluing tablecloth and the silver and the salt, and the daylight water between the leaves.)

[c] For man is our concern, in all his human presence; and a dilating of the eye to embrace the loftiest inner seas.

of his destiny as it unfolds. And it is the Sea that I chose, symbolically, as the mirror held up to this destiny – as a point of focus and radiation; a genuine 'geometrical locus' and frame of reference, and at the same time a reservoir of the eternal forces that make possible the fulfilment and surpassing of himself by man, the insatiable wanderer.

I chose a march to the Sea as an illustration of that wandering quest of the modern mind, drawn on by the very magnetism of its own insubordination. It is, thus, the working out of the drama of human dissatisfaction, but at the same time it is the drama of human demands at their highest pitch – individual or social, spiritual as well as intellectual. It is likewise an exaltation of life itself, in the stirring mystery of its power and the great unrevealed order of an eternal onward movement.[1]

That declaration is so forthright that any comment on it would be insolent or redundant.

For this 'drama of the human' Perse has chosen the framework of the oldest dramatic representation in the Occidental tradition, the classical Greek drama. As we know, Greek drama was a religious manifestation, and the actual form of the plays was dictated by the requirements of religious rituals. *Amers* is very much more the celebration of a rite than it is the acting out of a drama. In the preceding chapter we tried to show how *Vents* is the most dramatic of Perse's poems in its movement. *Amers*, being a poem of fulfilment, is essentially, and quite appropriately, a choric ode. It is that aspect of the Greek drama, the odes sung by the chorus, that forms the basis of *Amers*. Perse indicates how the central structure of his poem was suggested, not by the drama itself, but by the physical disposition of the Greek theatre:

The sea, our apparent frontier, toward which all our restless yearning and all expansive movements hasten, appeared to me, in the very midst of my song, as the solitary arena and ritual centre, the 'stage-floor' or altar-table of the classical Greek drama around which the action takes place, and around which the supernumeraries and protagonists first take their stations, like fragments of humanity representing the ancient earth of men, forever put to the test.[2]

To understand fully what Perse is referring to, one must recall certain details about the arrangement of the Greek theatre. Its main area was the dancing ground (orchestra), a circular area of beaten earth or paving stones. This is Perse's 'solitary arena'. In its centre was the altar of Dionysus (*thymele*), whence Perse's reference to the orchestra as the 'altar-table' – since it bore the altar at its very centre. Around this altar, the chorus moved in various figures, in one direction for the strophe, back again for the antistrophe, and perhaps standing still for the epode.[3] This dancing and chanting chorus served to comment upon and to highlight the stylized dialogue of the two or three main actors. Chorus and main actors were all men, and all wore elaborate masks and costumes. All these details are worth keeping in mind as one reads *Amers*.

The poem is divided into three main parts: 'Invocation', 'Strophe', and 'Chœur', plus a very brief final section entitled 'Dédicace'. Perse's own explanation of the 'Invocation' is as follows:

The first part of the poem is merely a prologue. It introduces the poet's thought and justifies his liberating theme: recourse to the Sea as the source of all animation and recreation – the urgent and ever-present Sea, lending aid and arbitrating as well as supplying revelation – in the very heart of man.

Having first mentioned everything exceptional that the Sea calls forth in man, the Poet prepares himself for a state of grace wherein he may the better receive such an intercession. He defines the organization and the spiritual stimulus of the poem, the terrestrial evolution around the edge of the Sea, like a solemn procession around the altar. Then, affirming his own special competence in pursuing such an undertaking, and recalling the origin of the poem, he hails the participation of the Sea itself in this work of creation.[4]

This 'Invocation' begins appropriately with a vocative: 'Et vous, Mers'. Whereupon the seas appear immediately as something festive. The rhythm of these opening strophes is excited and eager, underscored by repetitions and internal rhymes, by alliterations and carefully balanced coupled phrases. Unfortunately, almost all these auditory effects are lost in translation. But the imagery remains, and there we are on familiar ground. The 'Greek-theatre' setting of the poem is already suggested in the comparison, 'La Mer en fête sur ses marches comme une ode de pierre'.[a] In the third canto the connection is made entirely explicit:

[a] The Sea festive upon its stairs like an ode in stone.

'Poésie pour assister le chant d'une marche au pourtour de la Mer. / Comme l'entreprise du tour d'autel et la gravitation du chœur au circuit de la strophe.'[a] And in the last canto (6), the Sea actually comes to present itself to the audience 'sur les degrés de pierre du drame'.[b] With that, the chief dramatic types of Greek tragedy are listed, a number of which obliquely refer to specific characters,[5] ending with a reference to the whole recitation advancing 'en marche vers l'Auteur et vers la bouche peinte de son masque'[c] – reminding us that in the earlier days of Greek tragedy, the author was often the chief actor as well.

Returning to the first canto of the 'Invocation', we find roses used, as in *Anabase*,[6] in a funereal context: 'l'odeur funèbre de la rose'[d] and 'l'Océan, de toutes parts, foulant son poids de roses mortes'.[e] There are also subtle variations on synesthetic imagery already encountered in the 'Eloges' and *Anabase*: 'Les tambours du néant cèdent aux fifres de lumière.'[f] In *Anabase* the emptiness of the desert sands is conveyed by 'les tambours de l'exil' which awaken on the ultimate boundaries 'l'éternité qui bâille sur les sables'. And in 'Eloge VII' there is 'un grésillement aux gouffres écarlates, l'abîme piétiné des buffles de la joie (ô joie inexplicable sinon par la lumière!).'[g] *Vents* was concerned chiefly with the struggle against nothingness and emptiness, 'le néant'. That struggle is now won, and *Amers* begins with a forthright declaration of its positive theme: joy, pleasure, the acceptance of life and of death. The sea will be the catalytic agent that will transform sorrow and rebellion into joy and acceptance, for the sea now receives from all sides 'ce ruissellement encore des sources du plaisir...'.[h]

The brief fourth canto is a perfect example of the kind of complex imagery that is developed to its very limit throughout *Amers*. The 'master-metaphor' in this canto is the presentation of a petition by a mandarin (the poet) to an imperial guest (the sea). In the

[a] Poetry to accompany the song of a march around the edge of the Sea. / Like the figure of circling the altar and the gravitation of the chorus within the arc of the strophe.
[b] on the stone steps of the drama
[c] towards the Author and towards the painted mouth of his mask
[d] The funeral smell of the rose
[e] And the Ocean, on all sides, trampling its weight of dead roses
[f] The drums of emptiness yield to the fifes of light.
[g] a sizzling on the scarlet gulfs, the abyss trampled by the buffaloes of joy (O joy inexpressible save by light!)
[h] this continued streaming forth of the springs of pleasure...

preceding canto the poet has asked the sea itself to collaborate in his enterprise. Here in canto iv the poet explains how he will solicit that collaboration. The sea is a royal guest so illustrious that his merit need not be mentioned. That is why 'de la Mer elle-même il ne sera question, mais de son règne au cœur de l'homme'.[a] The poem then will be the gift that accompanies the petition to this visiting prince, for it is well that in such petitions there be interposed 'l'ivoire ou bien le jade / Entre la face suzeraine et la louange courtisane'.[b] The ivory and jade mark this whole passage as a memory of Leger's days in Peiping, as does the description of the perfect bow:

'Moi, m'inclinant en votre honneur d'une inclinaison sans bassesse,

J'épuiserai la révérence et le balancement du corps;

Et la fumée encore du plaisir enfumera la tête du fervent,

Et le délice encore du mieux dire engendrera la grâce du sourire...'[c]

The beauty of the passage increases at each reading. The very movement of the lines with their assonances and repetitions of word-roots (*inclinant – inclinaison, fumée – enfumera*), the rhymes (*inclinant – balancement – fervent, corps – encore, plaisir – mieux dire – sourire*) coalesce with the very gesture described. Here surely one can assent to Perse's declaration that poetry must actually become what it apprehends. The supreme elegance of the diction is likely to make one overlook the almost breath-taking pride and self-assurance that the passage expresses and that is restated in the final line of the canto: 'Et de salutation telle serez-vous saluée, ô Mer, qu'on s'en souvienne pour longtemps comme d'une ré-création du cœur.'[d] Fatuity is completely avoided for the simple reason that the promise is kept. In French literature, not Chateaubriand nor Michelet, not Hugo nor Corbière nor Lautréamont – to cite the great celebrants of the Sea – has come anywhere near *Amers*.

[a] And of the Sea itself there will be no question, but of its reign in the heart of man.

[b] ivory or perhaps jade / Between the suzerain face and the courtier's praise

[c] And I, bowing in your honour in a bow devoid of all servility / Shall fully complete the bow and fully regain the body's poise; / And the smoke of pleasure will once more curl about the adept's head, / And the delight of the perfectly chosen word will once more beget the grace of a smile...

[d] And with such a greeting will you be greeted, O Sea, that it will be long remembered, as one recalls a recreation of the heart.

The essence of the purely literary side of Perse's poetics is like-wise found in the quoted passage. 'Le délice du mieux dire' is certainly his first aim, since that is what will initially assure readers for his poems. The completely patrician pleasure that is expressed in the flowering of a smile (Perse's own luminous and almost childlike smile comes to mind inevitably) is certainly the first re-action that Perse seeks to provoke. The smile... It occurs again in the next canto, where the poet once more refers to his exile and his stay in Washington. He has not been understood, but he can wait, and this sea-poem, which he has carried with him so long that at last he *must* set it down on paper, can also wait.

'Et qui donc m'eût surpris dans mon propos secret? gardé par le sourire et par la courtoisie; parlant, parlant langue d'au-bain parmi les hommes de mon sang – à l'angle peut-être d'un Jardin Public, ou bien aux grilles effilées d'or de quelque Chan-cellerie; la face peut-être de profil et le regard au loin, entre mes phrases, à tel oiseau chantant son lai sur la Capitainerie du Port.

Car il y avait un si long temps que j'avais goût de ce poème, et ce fut tel sourire en moi de lui garder ma prévenance:'[a]

Veiled references are then made to the actual event that deter-mined the setting-down of the poem on paper and to the circum-stances under which it was composed. We are told that it will be a nuptial song, but the bride is referred to as morganatic and the alliance as clandestine. One thinks, of course, of Louis XIV's secret morganatic marriage to Madame de Maintenon. But the reference is surely much nearer home, and the climax of this vast poem will be an epithalamium that is anything but abstract and theoretical. As for the circumstances under which the poem was written, the references to 'un quartier [...] d'équarrisseurs ou de fondeurs – par temps d'émeute populaire – entre les cloches du couvre-feu et les tambours d'une aube militaire'[b] make one think

---

[a] And who then could have surprised me in my secret purpose? guarded by smile and courtesy; speaking, speaking the tongue of an alien among men of my blood – in the corner perhaps of a Public Garden, or else by the grilles, gold-tipped, of some Chancery; face perhaps turned in profile and gaze far off, between my phrases, fastened on some bird singing its lay over the Harbour-Master's roof. / For it had been such a long time that I had nursed a taste for this poem, and with such a smile did I keep my devotion to it.

[b] a district [...] of stone-cutters or smelters – at a time of popular demon-strations – between the curfew bells and the reveille drums of a military dawn

of the section of Washington, D.C. around the Episcopalian cathedral, still in process of being built, with its constant coming and going of stonecutters and welders; while the curfew and the military dawn may well be echoes of the last months of the war in 1945.

The sea then answers the poet's solicitation in canto vi, arriving on 'the stone steps of the drama'. The sea itself dictates the new language, the style to be used:

'Par grands soulèvements d'humeur et grandes intumescences du langage, par grands reliefs d'images et versants d'ombres lumineuses, courant à ses splendeurs massives d'un très beau style périodique...'[a]

And that is exactly the style in which the poem *is* written. As for the poet's qualifications for this undertaking, 'Et qu'il y eût en nous un tel désir de vivre à cet accès, n'est-ce point là, ô dieux! ce qui nous qualifiait?'[b] Then, at the end of the 'Invocation', taking up once more the image of the mandarin, the poet calls for a scribe to whom he may dictate his poem. Then comes the final question: 'Et qui donc, né de l'homme, se tiendrait sans offense aux côtés de ma joie? / – Ceux-là qui, de naissance, tiennent leur connaissance au-dessus du savoir.'[c] This finale is crucial and, unfortunately untranslatable, because of the two words 'connaissance' and 'savoir'. 'Connaissance' means 'knowing', but it also means 'consciousness', that is, immediate, first-hand awareness. While 'savoir' is formal knowledge in the sense of 'learning' or even 'book-learning'. Once more it is a question of those who value the firsthand experience most and who distrust the abstract. 'One must, in all things, hate abstractions...'[7]

The 'Strophe' is by far the longest section of the poem. The Greek meaning of *strophé* is actually cited by Perse in his explanatory letter, namely, 'movement of the chorus around the altar'. Insofar as there is any real 'drama' in *Amers*, it is acted in this 'Strophe'. Citing the letter once more: 'In the implied setting of

---

[a] With great upheavals of humours and great swellings of language, with great reliefs of images and luminous slopes of shade, running to its massive splendours of a very fine periodic style...

[b] that there was in us such a desire to live at that height, is not that, O gods! what qualified us?

[c] And who, then, born of man, would stand without offence, beside my joy? / – Those who, by birth, hold their knowing above knowledge.

SJP K

a hemicycle of maritime cities, harbour establishments and rural communities near the sea-front, [the Strophe] introduces one after the other the eight human representatives (*figurations*) called forth to confront the Sea for questioning, entreaty, imprecation, initiation, appeal or celebration.'[8]

The eight representative human groups or individuals are: 1. port officials and workers, 2. the Navigator, 3. the Actresses ('Tragédiennes'), 4. the patrician matrons, 5. the Poetess, 6. the Prophetess, 7. the young women, 8. the Lovers. Each representative 'figuration' has its own canto, but inserted between groups 7 and 8 there is a canto in which appears a Stranger to whom the young women call. Thus, the seventh 'figuration' is contained in cantos vii and viii, while canto ix, the last and longest of all (longer, in fact, than the others put together) is the part devoted to the Lovers. That canto is usually referred to separately by the opening words 'Etroits sont les vaisseaux...'[a].

But first there is the port-city, the point of departure for voyages into the open sea – the port-city with its dock-works, seawalls, shipyards, its forges and seamen's flophouses. It draws to its wharves and narrow lanes the men from the hinterland who are restless and dream of a different freedom and movement. Land, like a sorceress of Greek legend, holds them in its thrall: 'l'antique Magicienne: la Terre et ses glands fauves, la lourde tresse circéenne, et les rousseurs du soir en marche dans les prunelles domestiques!'[b]

But before the landlubber can set out, the Master of stars and navigation must be consulted. He is one of the masks worn by the poet himself, and through whom the poet speaks directly. His first words are, 'Ils m'ont appelé l'Obscur, et mon propos était de mer.'[c] His last words, 'Ils m'ont appelé l'Obscur et j'habitais l'éclat.'[d] Between these two parentheses the sea is saluted, of and for itself. Not the sea of commerce, but the sea of adventure and mystery, the sea against which a man can test his mettle and which can reveal to him some of the forces that mould him.

Then, in canto iii, the actresses make their appearance. From this point on most of the 'figurations' that confront the sea are

[a] Narrow are the vessels...

[b] the ancient Sorceress: the Earth, her tawny acorns, the heavy Circean braids, and the red evening moving in the pupils of tamed eyes!

[c] They called me the Dark One, and my words were of the sea.

[d] They called me the Dark One and I dwelt in radiance.

feminine: the actresses are followed by the patrician matrons, who then make way for the Poetess and the Prophetess, and they in turn are followed by the young women. Only in the last figuration, that of the lovers, does the male reappear with importance equal to that of women. The fact that the appeal made to the sea is left almost entirely to women surely reflects a fundamental attitude of the poet himself. One senses that this whole interlude is a plea for a restoration of women to their essential femininity, and, in a larger context, for the fulfilment of both man and woman in their natural psychological and biological complementarity – a theme so powerfully celebrated in the last of the eight representative groups, that is, the Lovers.

The actresses in canto iii are referred to exclusively as 'tragédiennes'. They come down through the hemicycle of the seaport to the 'orchestra' or stage formed by the sea around the sea-altar, and they carry with them all the standard equipment of the Greek tragic performers: the elaborate costumes, the tragic masks, the high sandals. But it must again be recalled that in the actual Greek drama, these accoutrements were worn exclusively by *men*, for there were only male actors – no actresses. So, the tragediennes of canto iii have usurped a function reserved for males. More than that, their main roles are those of men. From the very beginning of the canto they declare, 'Ah! nous avions trop présumé de l'homme sous le masque! Et nous qui mimons l'homme...'[a] Or again, 'Elles descendirent, et leurs voix mâles, les escaliers sonores du port.'[b] They are in search of their essential femininity, which has somehow become lost. They have come down to the sea to implore new texts, 'vivaces et très belles',[c] in a new and positive style – 'le vers majeur du plus grand ordre'[d]. In one of those rare specific reminiscences of other poets, Perse has his tragediennes ask for a metre 'qui, sur les granits rouges du drame, nous ouvre l'heure dont on s'éprenne!'[e] – an echo of Rimbaud's 'Chanson de la plus haute tour' with its refrain: 'Qu'il vienne, qu'il vienne, /

[a] Ah! we had presumed too much of man under the mask! And we who mime man...
[b] They descended, along with their male voices, the echoing stairs of the harbour.
[c] full of life and very beautiful
[d] the major verse of the greatest order
[e] which, on the red granite of drama, will open to us the hour with which we can fall in love!

Le temps dont on s'éprenne'. Finally, quite overtly, the tragediennes declare, 'Ah! notre cri fut d'Amantes!'[a] Their cry is for
a new Master. 'Et le Maître, quel est-il, qui nous relèvera de notre
déchéance?'..... 'Ah! qu'il vienne, Celui – nous viendra-t-il de
mer ou bien des Iles? – qui nous tiendra sous sa férule!'[b] Only
from the great primal reservoir of the sea can such a saviour come.

These actresses who have forgotten their femininity and seek
desperately to regain it are followed by the patrician matrons, who
are not much better off. They too appeal to the spasmodic sea
'mimée des femmes en travail, sur leurs hauts lits d'amantes ou
d'épouses'.[c][9]

The canto that follows is brief and puzzling. It is spoken by a
Poetess, or rather, by 'Language which was the Poetess' ('Langage que fut la Poétesse'). She speaks or *is* the language of the
two groups of women who have already spoken, and she foreshadows the declarations of the groups that are to speak in the
two succeeding cantos. In the Greek context of the whole poem,
one inevitably thinks of the poetess par excellence, Sappho, especially since the legends surrounding her have to do with the
islands and with a man of the sea (Phaon) for whom she is supposed finally to have committed suicide by throwing herself into
the sea. Moreover, what few fragments of her poetry we possess
are almost all erotic in nature. The trouble is that there are no
sharply specific allusions discernible in the canto.

Blurred classical allusions also occur in the next canto (vi),
which is considerably longer than the fifth and which is recited
by a girl who is a prophetess. She speaks as the leader of an implied chorus of prophetesses of the sea. The actual presage is
embodied in the image of rain upon the sea. The grey glint of the
rainy sea, limned with sunlight that occasionally breaks through,
provides the setting. What the sea-rains presage is not too clear.
The last line of the canto says: '(Et, là! que voulions-nous dire,
que nous n'avons su dire?)'[d] Fleetingly visible in the background
of this canto, like the gold highlights in the rain it describes, is
the classical legend of the Nereids and Andromeda. Because An-

---

[a] Ah! our cry was that of Lovers!

[b] And who is the Master who will raise us from our abject state? / ..... /
Ah, may he come – will it be from the sea or from the Islands? – who will
keep us under his rod!

[c] simulated by women in labour on their high beds of lovers or wives!

[d] (And now! what did we wish to say, that we were not able to say?)

dromeda's mother dared compare her beauty favourably with one of the fifty ocean-nymphs called Nereids, the land was ravaged by a sea-monster. The monster, it may be remembered, was to be placated only by the sacrifice of Andromeda, chained at the foot of a rocky cape, a prey to the monster. Legend tells us that Andromeda was rescued by Perseus. In the canto we are considering, a host of female victims are offered to the sea: 'Les filles liées au bas des Caps y prennent le message.'[a] Or again: 'De grandes filles liées vives baissent la tête, sous le fardeau de nuée grise orangée d'or.'[b]

The atmosphere is one of expectancy. The canto concludes with a series of strophes on the exquisite pleasure of expectancy. It is like a transposition into Persean terms and rhythms of Valéry's 'Les Pas':

'Et la douceur est dans le chant, non dans l'élocution; est dans l'épuisement du souffle, non dans la diction. Et la félicité de l'être répond à la félicité des eaux...'[c]. . .

'...Nous écoutons, tout bas hélées, la chose en nous très proche et très lointaine – comme ce sifflement très pur de l'Etésienne à la plus haute corne du gréement. Et la douceur est dans l'attente, non dans le souffle ni le chant. Et ce sont là choses peu narrables, et de nous seules mi-perçues... Plutôt nous taire, la bouche rafraîchie de petites coquilles.'[d]

The next canto, in which the young girls join the female chorus, is far less elusive. These are the young athletic girls of our twentieth-century beaches, scarcely nubile as yet. But they too will presently join the ritual drama: 'Demain, nous chausserons les brodequins du drame.'[e] They are enjoying the last irresponsible romps of adolescence. The sea-promise hanging over the preceding canto will be fulfilled. In terms reminiscent of the refrain from the *Pervigilium veneris*[10] these girls declare: 'Qui n'a aimé de

[a] The girls bound at the foot of the Capes take the message there.

[b] Tall girls, bound alive, bend their heads, under the burden of grey cloud oranged with gold.

[c] And the sweetness is in the song, not in the elocution; is in the exhausting of breath, not in the saying. And the felicity of being answers the felicity of the waters...

[d] ... We listen, hailed in a low voice, to the thing in us very near and very distant – like that very pure whistling of the Etesian wind at the highest peak of the rigging. And the sweetness is in the waiting, not in the breath or the song. And these are things not very tellable, and by us alone half-perceived... Better that we keep silent, our mouths refreshed with small shells.

[e] Tomorrow we shall put on the cothurni.

jour, il aimera ce soir.'[a] It is natural to think primarily of the Mediterranean beaches in this passage, especially since there is a reference to the monkeys stuffed with fruit of the prickly-pear and climbing down the rocks – surely a reminiscence of Gibraltar. However that may be, these girls dream of a man of the sea. 'Meilleur des hommes, viens et prends!'[b] In a brief transitional canto (ix) the man of the sea does come – a man foreign to these parts, sailing his boat along the shores. He will take one of the girls, symbolically, into his boat, and the cruise that they make together will be the nuptial voyage of 'Etroits sont les vaisseaux...'.

'Etroits...' is a separate poem in its own right, but it becomes far more meaningful when read in the context of the whole of *Amers*, of which it is the climax. Back in the fifth canto of the 'Invocation' the declaration was made: 'Morganatique au loin l'Epouse, et l'alliance, clandestine!... Chant d'épousailles, ô Mer, sera pour vous le chant: "Mon dernier chant! mon dernier chant! et qui sera d'homme de mer..."'.[c] Fortunately for us, it turned out not to be the poet's last song, but the promise there made in the 'Invocation' is magnificently kept in 'Etroits...'. This single immense canto is divided into seven sub-sections. The first of these ushers in the erotic theme to be celebrated and establishes the 'master-metaphors'. The narrow ships are to become a narrow marriage couch, and later, inevitably, the ship will become the woman's body. The season is 'sea-summer'. And the force that carries the narrow ships is the erotic impulse, here appropriately put in Homeric terms: 'Une même vague par le monde, une même vague depuis Troie / Roule sa hanche jusqu'à nous.'[d] This 're-frain', slightly altered each time, will recur throughout the remaining portions of the canto, enriched each time by what has intervened.

Following this introductory passage comes the ritualistic antiphon of the Female and the Male. In five successive dialogues, the woman offers herself and expresses her misgivings and final reassurance, immediately answered each time by the man, who first

---

[a] Who has not loved by day, will this night love.

[b] Best of men, come and take!

[c] Morganatic is the far-off Bride, and the alliance, clandestine!... A nuptial chant, O Sea, will be for you the chant: 'My last song! my last song! which will be song of a man of the sea...'

[d] One same wave throughout the world, one same wave since Troy / Rolls its haunch towards us.

accepts the offering, is then tempted to abandon the woman once more, and then ultimately finds fulfilment only in a permanent union. This extended antiphon constitutes one of the most sustained celebrations of the physical union of man and woman in any literature known to me. Simply as a *tour de force* it is astonishing, but it is certainly much more than a *tour de force*. The whole complex of sexual union is conveyed in the most minute detail. No physiological phenomenon is omitted and, more important, none of the psychological concomitants is omitted. Yet it would be hard to think of a less clinical description of coitus. The love described is far removed from Platonic love, and even farther removed from any of the Christian derivatives of Platonic and Neo-Platonic love. It likewise has nothing in common with the romantic love-as-annihilation that is given its ultimate expression in *Tristan und Isolde*. The love in *Amers* is anchored in the flesh and restores us to what Auden has felicitously called 'the warm nude ages of instinctive poise'. It is a climactic experience, but it is not the ultimate experience. It is simply one of the most intense expressions of those 'great forces that create us, use us, and control us'.[11] It is not the *only* possible fulfilment, in the romantic manner. Nor does it subsume all other experience. But, accepted in its psycho-physical completeness, it is certainly one of the most intense, most reassuring, and most completely satisfying experiences available to human beings. It is in these terms that this nuptial voyage, which certainly is no imaginary odyssey, is presented.

In spite of the piling on of images – superficially reminiscent of the Song of Songs or of the extravagant imagery we find in translations of Indian erotic poetry – and in spite of the extremely complex technical vocabulary and a good measure of classical (almost all Homeric) allusions, one never has any difficulty in knowing exactly what is going on at any given moment in this protracted love-making. The enrichment of our enjoyment of this antiphon may, however, be enhanced if some note is taken of the way the imagery is put together.

The love-making takes place on a yacht, which is sometimes on the open sea and sometimes anchored in a tropical roadstead or harbour. The sea, then, is always present, and in its most concrete and surprising aspects. In almost all mythologies the sea is present as a female principle. The correspondence between tidal rhythms and menstrual rhythms was noticed early in the development of the human race. So, in 'Etroits...' the sea is Woman. But the sea is so richly varied that it may also serve to express certain male elements. In the first antiphon the woman is undressed by the man and offers herself as the naked sea. But in his response the man says: 'Etrange l'homme, sans rivage, près de la femme, riveraine. Et mer moi-même à ton orient, comme à ton sable d'or mêlé.'[a] Thus, the woman becomes the shoreline, caressed by the male sea. Right on through to the climactic last orgasm and the post-coital sleep, the sea alternately expresses, in its infinite variety, both the male and the female principles, and something that goes beyond both. Any 'one-to-one' set of symbolic analogies that might turn the poem into an allegory is carefully avoided. Instead, a single figurative element will be used in a constantly changing play of multiple analogies.

Besides being identified with the physical presence of both the woman and the man, the sea is also the metaphor of the female yearning for security and, at the same time, of male solitude. The man asks:

'Et qu'est ce corps lui-même, qu'image et forme du navire? nacelle et nave, et nef votive, jusqu'en son ouverture médiane; instruit en forme de carène; et sur ses courbes façonné, ployant le double arceau d'ivoire au vœu des courbes nées de mer...'[b]

But the ship in another context is the man. 'Vierge clouée à mon étrave',[c] he says to the woman at the peak of passion. Or the woman, in the post-coital calm, speaks of herself as an oar, 'A ton côté rangée, comme la rame à fond de barque, à ton côté roulée, comme la voile avec la vergue, au bas du mât liée...'[d], where the ship is specifically the man. But a ship also suggests flight. A sea-side house, where the lovers momentarily reside, seems, as they look up into its rafters, to sail like a trireme, 'et sous l'auvent de bois léger l'alignement des chevrons tient comme un rang de rames égales pour l'envol. Filer! filer, au fil d'ivoire de nos

[a] Strange the man, shoreless, near the woman, herself a shore. And myself a sea at your orient, as if mingled with your golden sand...

[b] And what is this body itself, save image and form of the ship? nacelle and hull, and votive vessel, even to its median opening; formed in the shape of a hull, and fashioned on its curves, bending the double arch of ivory to the will of sea-born curves...

[c] Virgin cleft to my stem

[d] Laid at your side, like the oar in the bottom of the boat; rolled at your side, like the sail with the yard, lashed at the foot of the mast...

lattes...'.[a] Then again it is the place of refuge and security: 'Il n'est sécurité plus grande qu'au vaisseau de l'amour.'[b] Still later it is the wandering principle that drives the male on: 'Ou quel Pilote silencieux monte seul à ton bord, de ce côté de mer où l'on n'aborde?'[c]

And so it is with all the other basic elements of the imagery in this antiphon. The hidden metaphorical resources of each element are sooner or later exploited. But this dizzying flood of images, where metaphors contain subsidiary metaphors and the subsidiary ones in their turn contain still others – this flood of images has only one ultimate purpose, which is wonderfully achieved, namely, the communication to the reader of the complexity, richness, and intensity of the sexual experience in its most fully realized form. Such an experience isolates the lovers from all the rest of the world, just as the sea isolates the ship upon it. And there, in the nakedness of complete realization, all the 'personae', all the masks that the business of daily living – 'land-living' so to speak – requires, are dropped. The lovers are no longer actors, no longer figurations in a ritual, but an ultimate reality. And that is why the antiphon concludes, 'Amour et mer de même lit, amour et mer au même lit... / Hommage, hommage à la véracité divine! Et longue mémoire sur la mer au peuple en armes des Amants!'[d] – which is followed immediately by a last section, a chilly monologue, telling of the anchoring of the ships in their winter port. The memory of the sea-summer is the only earnest against death. The whole canto then ends:

' – Aux portes closes des Amants clouez l'image du Navire!

*

...Une même vague par le monde, une même vague par la Ville... Amants, la mer nous suit! La mort n'est point! Les dieux nous hèlent à l'escale... Et nous tirons de sous nos lits nos plus grands masques de famille!'[e]

[a] and under the roof of light wood the rafters hold their alignment like a row of oars levelled for the flight. To flee, to flee in the path of our ivory laths...
[b] There is no greater security than in the vessel of love.
[c] Or what silent Pilot mounts alone to your deck, from that seaward side whence no one boards?
[d] Love and sea of the same bed, love and sea in the same bed... / Homage, homage to the divine veracity! And long memory on the sea for a nation of Lovers in arms!
[e] – On the Lovers' closed doors, nail the image of the Ship! . . . One same

That is also the end of the 'Strophe', which celebrates the sea as it affects human beings, celebrates 'its reign in the heart of man'.

In the third major portion of *Amers*, the 'Chorus', an attempt is made to dehumanize the celebration, to restore the sea to itself, so to speak. Thus, instead of individual figures confronting the sea in turn, an anonymous collective voice speaks, the voice of the chorus in the ancient Greek tragedies. Perse characterizes it as follows:

> The third part or 'Chorus' gathers together in a single move-ment and a single collective voice all this human exaltation in honour of the Sea. This section finally annexes the Sea as a principle of power as well as a source of knowledge – the Sea identified with the Universal Being, endlessly assimilated by it and assimilating man himself into that Being, on the ulti-mate verge of the human. Fully conscious of the risk involved in such an association and of the extreme audaciousness of such a transgression, the Poet accepts the challenge of the undertaking in order to achieve grander celebrations of the mind and graver spiritual adventures. The collective recitation finally gives way to an ample mass-movement, led by the Poet who has once more taken his place as the Leader of the Chorus: illuminating, sustaining, and guiding the action of this vast human procession all the way to its Sea-causeway – the image of a humanity advancing towards its highest destiny.[12]

The first canto of this last movement invokes the sea in all its aspects. There is the sea of the early Phoenician traders, whose god was Baal; the sea of commerce ('Mer de Mammon'); the sea of Dagon, the fish-god. There is the primeval sea where life first appeared, and the sea of promise to explorers and exploiters; the sea of great maritime empires; the sea of great depths still un-plumbed, for it still has its mysteries, its forbidden chambers. These latter are mentioned in the second canto, and in a striking way: 'Ainsi le Conquérant, sous sa plume de guerre, aux dernières portes du Sanctuaire: "J'habiterai les chambres interdites et je m'y

wave throughout the world, one same wave throughout the City . . . Lovers, the sea follows us! Death is not. The gods hail us in the port. And from under our beds we pull out our largest family masks.

promènerai..." Bitume des morts, vous n'êtes point l'engrais de ces lieux-là.'[a] Again an echo from *Anabase*: first it was the funeral roses, now it is the bitumen of the dead, of the embalmer.[13] In all things, the sea is seen as anti-mortuary. It is declared to be open to a triple living drama: 'Mer de la transe et du délit; Mer de la fête et de l'éclat; et Mer aussi de l'action!'[b] A hymn is devoted to each of these three aspects. The 'Sea of trance and transgression' is that of the swimmer and skin-diver, of the surface-waters through which the sunlight penetrates. The hymn devoted to it should delight any skin-diver, for never has the exhilaration of the sport been more effectively sung. Once more the imagery is intricate in the extreme – a kind of fairy-tale proliferation of the single figure in the opening line of the very early Perse poem, 'Pour fêter une enfance', where we read: 'Alors on te baignait dans l'eau-de-feuilles-vertes; et l'eau encore était du soleil vert.'[c] In *Amers* this becomes:

'... mais là nous vivons, et dévêtus, où la chair même n'est plus chair et le feu même n'est plus flamme – à même la sève rayonnante et la semence très précieuse: dans tout ce limbe d'aube verte, comme une seule et vaste feuille infusée d'aube et lumineuse...

Unité retrouvée, présence recouvrée! O Mer instance lumineuse et chair de grande lunaison. C'est la clarté pour nous faite substance, et le plus clair de l'Etre mis à jour, comme au glissement du glaive hors de sa gaine de soie rouge: l'Etre surpris dans son essence, et le dieu même consommé dans ses espèces les plus saintes, au fond des palmeraies sacrées...'[d]

---

[a] Thus the Conqueror, under his war-plume, at the last gates of the Sanctuary: 'I shall live in the forbidden rooms and loiter through them...' Bitumen of the dead, you are not the fertilizer of these sites!

[b] Sea of the trance and the transgression; Sea of festival and splendour; and Sea also of action!

[c] In those days you were bathed in water-of-green-leaves; water that was also green sunlight.

[d] ... but there we live, and unclothed, where the flesh itself is no longer flesh and the fire itself is no longer flame – in the radiant sap and the very precious seed: in all this edging of green dawn, like a single vast leaf infused with dawn and luminous... / Unity regained! presence recovered! O Sea, shining instance and flesh of great lunations. It is light made substance for us, and the clearest part of Being brought to light, as in the sliding of the sword from its sheath of red silk: Being, caught in its very essence, and the god himself consumed in his holiest species, in the depths of the sacred palm groves...

The 'Sea of festival and splendour' is the all-engulfing ocean into which streams flow and rains fall. It is the sea of storms and water-spouts and gravid skies, or of reflected midday brilliance too dazzling to contemplate. The basic image here is a comparison with the richly caparisoned animals of an Indian durbar.

The 'Sea of action' is the ocean in all its provocative aspects, inviting exploration and voyages of conquest, restless and combative, taking man to the very heart of the mystery, 'la face, soudain du monde révélé dont nous ne lirons plus l'avers'.[a] In the midst of this struggle the Poet reappears, for only with his gift of language is there any possibility of articulating at least something of the mystery.

The opening line of the third canto neatly characterizes the whole style of *Amers*: '...Innombrable l'image, et le mètre, prodigue.'[b] A series of recapitulations follows, saturated, utilizing to the extreme the repetitive devices that are the very texture of the whole poem. Alliteration, for example, is pushed to what would be caricatural lengths in any other context: 'En toi *m*ouvante, nous *m*ouvant, nous te disons *M*er inno*mm*able: *m*uable et *m*euble dans ses *m*ues, im*m*uable et *m*ême dans sa *m*asse.' Adjectival forms with similar suffixes are lined up in relentless files: 'L'incorporelle et très-réelle, imprescriptible: l'irrécusable et l'indéniable et l'inappropriable; inhabitable, fréquentable; immémoriale et mémorable – et quelle et quelle, et quelle encore, inqualifiable? L'insaisissable et l'inaccessible, l'irréprochable irréprouvable.' And naturally, there is the homologous series. Here the common denominator of the series is the sea as dreamed of by men in every strange and anomalous situation.

The next canto (iv) pushes this recapitulation to a climax, continuing the massive repetitive techniques. Having done this, the poet can declare: 'Et maintenant nous t'avons dit ton fait, et maintenant nous t'épierons, et nous nous prévaudrons de toi dans nos affaires humaines.'[c] The sea has been humanly assimilated, so far as that is possible, and humanly expressed, so far as *that* is possible. It is here that the poetics of Perse achieves its most striking expression:

[a] the face, suddenly, of the revealed world whose obverse side we shall no longer read

[b] ... Prolific the image, the metre, prodigal.

[c] And now we have told the world what you really are, and now we shall keep an eye on you and avail ourselves of you in our human affairs.

'...Ah, nous avions des mots pour toi et nous n'avions assez de mots,
Et voici que l'amour nous confond à l'objet même de ces mots,
Et mots pour nous ils ne sont plus, n'étant plus signes ni parures,
Mais la chose même qu'ils figurent et la chose même qu'ils paraient;
Ou mieux, te récitant, toi-même, le récit, voici que nous te devenons toi-même, le récit,
Et toi-même sommes-nous, qui nous étais l'Inconciliable: le texte même et sa substance et son mouvement de mer,
Et la grande robe prosodique dont nous nous revêtons...'*a*

The whole poetics of 'identification with the object' is here, at the very climax of an immense poem that is an attempt at identification with the sea. The poet himself feels he has achieved his end, 'nous t'acclamons enfin dans ton éclat de mer et ton essence propre'.*b* The fundamental reality has been touched.

Then, as a postscript, there is the very brief 'Dédicace' characterized as follows by Perse: 'The final section ("Dedication") frees the Poet and restores him to himself after he has conducted his whole undertaking and his people to the highest point of accession.'[14] Its last line sums up this restoration: 'Et l'homme au masque d'or se dévêt de son or en l'honneur de la Mer.'*c* When, in the ancient Greek theatre, the poet himself was the leader of the Chorus, as such, he wore a mask as did all the other participants in the drama. Now his task is done, and he can 'be himself' once again.

Going back for a moment to the 'skin-diving' passage quoted above,[15] and comparing it with the single germinal line from the much earlier poem, one can immediately understand why *Amers*

---

a ... Ah! we had words for you and we did not have enough words, / And behold, love makes us one with the very object of these words, / And words for us they are no longer, being no longer signs or adornments, / But the thing itself which they signify and the thing itself they adorned; / Or better, reciting yourself, who are the recital, behold we become you, the recital, / And we are now you, who were to us the Irreconcilable: the very text and its substance and its sea movement, / And the very great prosodic robe in which we clothe ourselves...
b we acclaim you at last in your sea-radiance and your unique essence
c And the man with the golden mask divests himself of his gold in honour of the Sea.

is such a long poem – the longest Perse has written to date. The line from 'Pour fêter une enfance' may be regarded as a structural 'unit' in that poem. The equivalent unit in *Amers* is the whole of the page-long 'skin-diving' passage, which in its length is entirely representative of the whole poem. The extreme length of these units in *Amers* tends to obscure the basic similarity in technique of *Amers* and the earlier poems, of which *Anabase* may serve as an example. I choose *Anabase* as a basis for comparison because, with its 'jansénisme du pittoresque', it seems very far removed indeed from the sumptuous brocade-richness of *Amers*. Then too, the framework of the two poems is quite different: *Anabase* has the simple construction of an epic narrative, while *Amers* is a choric ode. Yet the crucial technical device is the same in both poems, namely, the juxtaposition of images and the suppression of connective materials. And the reader of *Amers* has to allow these image-units 'to fall into his memory successively without questioning the reasonableness of each at the moment', as T. S. Eliot said quite rightly of *Anabase*.[16]

Where the units are as massive as they are in *Amers*, it is clear that a reader should try to come to grips with the poem, for the first several readings at least, silently, reading as rapidly as the denseness of the imagery will allow. No time should be lost in the formation of spoken sounds. The multiple analogies and their accompanying rhythms should be felt with all possible immediacy. Only such a procedure finally brings home the organic unity of the poem; only the inner ear can hear each of the very complex units as a single, blending chord in a long melodic progression. Speaking of his various long poems, but surely of *Amers* in particular, Perse wrote, 'such works simply *can not* be recited orally – either publicly or privately – or even be read aloud in the most intimate circumstances, be it by the author himself, and for himself alone.'[17]

Here, though, we come upon a contradiction that has undoubtedly already occurred to any reader even casually familiar with *Amers*, namely, that the sonorous qualities of the poem are often so compelling as to be irresistible – one murmurs certain passages aloud in spite of one's self. Indeed, Perse's poetry is as richly 'musical' as any French verse written during the last sixty years. The great beauty of the auditory effects of *Amers* may indeed be a barrier to the apprehending of the poem's totality, which Perse quite naturally wishes his readers to experience above all else. But I cannot believe that, in the long run, *Amers* will suffer from this situation. Lingering over the 'individual beauties' of the poem, no matter how briefly and intermittently, may also be the way to 'happen upon' the unsuspected door that will give way and let the reader glimpse the poem's total splendour.

This does not mean that *Amers* is ever likely to be a 'popular' poem. Since Poe and Baudelaire, the prejudice against the long poem has become more and more deep-rooted, in spite of sporadic valiant efforts to overcome it. An occasional narrative poem may run on to considerable length and still have a good audience. But a hundred-and-fifty page choric ode!... Curiously enough, though, there are signs that *Amers* is actually becoming the most widely read of Perse's poems, and surely not just for all the wrong reasons. Moreover, any serious reader of Perse has to make the effort to grasp the total configuration of the poem, for it is the fullest expression of Perse's deepest convictions regarding the nature of the universe and man's place in it. We have already pointed out the anti-dualistic, profoundly un-Christian cast of these convictions.[18] The last words of Perse's own commentary on *Amers* are especially revelatory in this regard and make crystal-clear why the sea is the ideal vehicle for the 'poetics of flux' and the wider view of which that poetics is but a small segment.

[In *Amers*] I sought to give the completest possible expression in human terms to man's secret attraction, in the very midst of action, to something in himself that goes beyond the temporal order. A reaffirmation of the great human phrase taken up again, at the highest tide of its sea-movement, in an effort to re-integrate man totally on two complementary planes. For me, it is in that form one must provide an answer to that fragmentation of the human, to that terribly passive nihilism, that real admission of defeat that are supposed to be the sheets with which we are making up the bed of our materialistic age. Were I a physicist, I should be on Einstein's side, for Unity and Continuity, against the 'quantum' philosophy of the random and the discontinuous. Were I a metaphysician, I should gladly accept the task of illustrating the myth of Shiva...[19]

– Shiva, the embodiment of the ultimate generative flux, the Destroyer who destroys only in order to create more fully.

7

The Votive Poems

Chronique and *Oiseaux*

In October, 1959, Saint-John Perse sent a letter to Dag Hammar-skjöld, along with a copy of a poem he had just completed. 'You once told me,' wrote Perse, 'that I would also write a poem to the Earth. Here it is. Bearing the title, *Chronicle* – which is to be taken in its etymological sense – it is a poem to the Earth, to man, and to time, all three merging, as I see it, in the single timeless notion of eternity.'[1] Hammarskjöld was so impressed that, in spite of the crushing weight of his duties as Secretary General of the United Nations, he took time to do the Swedish translation of the poem.

After the sea, the earth. But the sea is still very much present, and the great land-masses are constantly viewed in terms of marine imagery. The great moving mass of sea, however, is the very cradle of life, the reservoir of vitality. The land, on the other hand, keeps the records, is a geological chronicle. The land is, thus, a fitting master-metaphor for this poem of old age – retrospective, looking back over a full and free life, but also projected toward the future, beyond death. The very first words of the poem are 'Grand âge, nous voici', unavoidably translated by the far less resonant 'Great age, behold us', which only partially catches the contextual 'aura' of the French. For 'grand âge' means old age in the sense of 'well along in years', but it also has the meaning of 'grand old age' and, beyond either of these meanings, 'Great Age' in the historical sense, i.e., 'the time of Pericles is the Great Age

of Athens'. Certainly Perse's poem is about his own declining
years, but it is also about the grandeur of those declining years,
and likewise about the Great New Age of mankind hailed in the
last section of *Vents*. Thus, on a much smaller scale and in an
entirely different key, *Chronique* shares the dual 'historico-personal'
structure of *Vents*.

Chronique is divided into eight cantos, and the whole poem is
presented as a single vast quotation. The dominant greens of
Amers give way to the red tints of the sunset and of the bare red
earth, such as one finds in the Arizona-Utah plateau of the American Southwest. In this evening glow, all the essential elements of
a lifetime are summed up. The poem may be compared to one of
those polished metal globes set on pedestals in formal gardens to
capture the whole surrounding panorama in a condensed image
that can be taken in at a single glance. We look at the mirror-
sphere and see an object which we scarcely recognize at first
glance, but which turns out to be the pavilion at the far end of
the garden. The charm of this miniature world is enhanced by our
familiarity with all the objects caught there. So it is with *Chronique*.

First there is a reference to the immediate past, to the composition of *Amers*: 'Et ce n'est point de même mer que nous rêvons
ce soir'.[a] This is followed by an open reference to the poet's own
advancing age: 'Lève la tête, homme du soir.'[b] Then there is mention of the dividing-ridge of the Century that is the subject of
Vents, 'ce grand éclat d'un Siècle vers sa cime'.[c] And as in *Vents*,
here too are references to the poet's many travels and to his ancient
but anonymous race:

'Grand âge, nous venons de toutes rives de la terre. Notre
race est antique, notre face est sans nom. Et le temps en sait
long sur tous les hommes que nous fûmes.

Nous avons marché seuls sur les routes lointaines; et les mers
nous portaient qui nous furent étrangères.'[d]

The Southeast Asian sojourns, trips to Africa, the excursion into
the Gobi – each is referred to in a single figure of speech that

---

[a] And it is not of that sea we dream this evening.
[b] Raise your head, man of evening.
[c] this blinding brightness of a Century toward its crest
[d] Great age, we come from all the shores of the earth. Our race is ancient,
our face is nameless. And time has long known more than it tells of all the
men we were. / We have walked the distant roads alone: and seas have borne
us that to us were foreign.

suggests a whole landscape complex. On the day when the first atomic bomb was exploded, 'quand la louve noire du ciel mordit au cœur le vieil astre de nos pères'[a] – at that moment, 'nous étions peut-être en mer'.[b] Then the reminiscences move on back to the period of *Exil*. 'Eponyme, l'ancêtre, et sa gloire, sans trace. Nos œuvres vivent loin de nous dans leurs vergers d'éclairs. Et nous n'avons de rang parmi les hommes de l'instant.'[c] Then, leaping all the way back to childhood, there is a long passage that is simply another section of 'Pour fêter une enfance' – fifty-two years after. We are told that the ancestral house, with all its fine colonial furnishings, was not the poet's true dwelling-place,

> 'Mais dans l'écale de tortue géante encore malodorante, et dans le linge des servantes, et dans la cire des selleries où s'égare la guêpe; ah! dans la pierre du vieux fusil de noir, et dans l'odeur de copeaux frais des charpentiers de mer, et dans la guibre du voilier sur chantier de famille; mieux, dans la pâte de corail blanc sciée pour les terrasses, et dans la pierre noire et blanche des grands carrelages d'offices, et dans l'enclume du forgeron d'étable, et dans ce bout de chaîne luisante, sous l'orage, qu'élève, corne haute, la lourde bête noire portant bourse de cuir...

> L'algue fétide de minuit nous fut compagne sous les combles.'[d]

After this backward-moving recapitulation, there is the return to the present. The sunset sky, which bathes the whole poem in its crimson light, is, of course, the West. So, just as in *Vents*, the faring-forward is toward the West. The immense distance from childhood to the brink of death is spanned in a series of some five

---

[a] when the black she-wolf of the sky bit to the heart the ancient star of our fathers

[b] we were at sea perhaps

[c] Eponymous was our ancestor, and his glory, without trace. Our works live far from us in their orchards of lightning. And we hold no rank among men of the moment.

[d] But in the shell of the giant tortoise, malodorous still, and in the linens of the serving women, and in the wax of the harness-rooms where the wasp has strayed; ah! in the flint of the black man's old flintlock, and in the fresh wood-chip odour of the ship's carpenter, and in the bow of the sailing craft on the family launching ways; better still, in the block of white coral sawn for the terraces, and in the black and white of the great floor-tiles in the pantry, and in the anvil of the stable forge, and in that length of chain glinting under a thunderstorm when the heavy black beast, swinging his leather pouch, rears with horns tossed high... / The fetid seaweed of midnight was with us under the gables.

strophes that contain some of the most magnificent imagery set
down by this master image-maker. We start out from specific
memories of the childhood of Alexis Leger:

'Balancement de l'heure, entre toutes choses égales – incréées
ou créées... L'arbre illustre sa feuille dans la clarté du soir: le
grand arbre Saman qui berce encore notre enfance; ou cet autre,
en forêt, qui s'ouvrait à la nuit, élevant à son dieu l'ample
charge ouvragée de ses roses géantes.'[a]

Father Düss dutifully records the *Calliandra Saman*, 'a gigantic tree
of Brazilian origin... cultivated on several of the island estates as
a shade tree'. The good father likewise notes the *Brownea*, com-
monly known as the Venezuela Rose,[2] which is the second of the
trees mentioned by Perse. We are back in Guadeloupe. That is
already the West, but there is a West beyond the Antilles. It was,
in fact, many years later in the American Far West that the poet
found the perfect figure for the Olympian, all-embracing glance
of old age:

'Jadis des hommes de haut site, la face peinte d'ocre rouge
sur leurs mesas d'argile, nous ont dansé sans gestes danse immobile de l'aigle. Ici, ce soir, et face à l'Ouest, mimant la vergue
ou le fléau, il n'est que d'étendre les bras en croix pour auner
à son aune l'espace d'un tel an: danse immobile de l'âge sur
l'envergure de son aile.'[b]

The marvellous dignity of the eagle-dance of the American Indian
has never been better caught. And the moveless dance of old age
is the key-figure for the experience that is at the heart of *Chronique*,
and that, for want of a better term, we must call mystical, pro-
viding that we understand that here the word designates simply
an acute awareness, in all domains, of those 'great forces that
create us, use us, and control us'[3] – an awareness that is latent in
all the poems, from the earliest on, but that comes to the fore in

[a] Equipoise of the hour, between all things equal – increate or created... /
The tree burnishes its leaf in the clarity of evening: the great Saman tree
that still cradles our childhood; or that other, in the forest, that spread itself
open at night, raising to its god the ample and finely wrought burden of its
giant roses.
[b] Long ago men of the highland, on their clay mesas, with faces painted
in red ochre, danced for us without gestures the motionless dance of the
eagle. Here, this evening, with face to the West, miming the yard-arm or
the cross-beam, one has only to stretch one's arms to span at one's own span
the space of a year such as that: motionless dance of age on the spread of its
wing.

Vents and is then all-pervasive in *Amers*. It was in connection
with the latter poem that Perse first formulated the phrase we
have just quoted, and it is in the same poem that he speaks openly
of man's 'taste for the divine' ('goût du divin').

Paul Claudel once tried, in what was apparently a very hector-
ing way, to convert young Alexis Leger to Catholicism.[4] He did
not succeed, and certainly the memory of that failure had something to do with Claudel's declaration in connection with *Vents*
made many years later, to the effect that 'God is a word that Saint-
John Perse avoids, shall we say religiously?'[5] In a purely literal
sense, Claudel is wrong. Perse had repeatedly spoken of gods or
of a god long before he composed *Vents*, and here in *Chronique*
one even finds 'God' with a capital letter. But Claudel's contention
is basically right, for the references are quite negative, and the
God referred to by Perse has nothing in common with the God
of orthodox Catholicism or of Christianity in general. 'Mais Dieu
se tait dans le quantième; et notre lit n'est point tiré dans l'étendue
ni la durée.'[a] Wrenched from its context, that declaration might
have won Claudel's approval. But Perse goes on to say in the
same canto (ii): 'Et Dieu l'aveugle luit dans le sel et dans la pierre
noire, obsidienne ou granit.'[b] This God defies abstract formulation. This God is a complex of intractable forces. The awareness
of these forces that surpass us and control us is an intensely personal experience. For Perse, no doctrinaire formulation of it is
possible. At best it can be skirted and pointed to by means of
poetry. It does not involve moral prerogatives, and there is no
possible *credo* to be formulated. So far as his social conduct is
concerned, man must muddle through without moral absolutes.[6]
Yet the awareness is tremendously important to Perse and sufficiently intense for him that he can declare that death, somehow, is
not final. There is some eternal principle in the endless flux, the
dance of Shiva: 'nous vivons d'outre-mort, et de mort même
vivrons-nous.'[c] But this 'mystical' awareness poses more ques-
tions than it answers.

'O vous qui nous meniez à tout ce vif de l'âme, fortune
errante sur les eaux, nous direz-vous un soir sur terre quelle

[a] But God does not dwell in the date or day; and our bed is not laid in
place or time.
[b] And God the blind glitters in the salt and the black rock, obsidian or
granite.
[c] we live on what is beyond death, and on death itself shall we live.

main nous vêt de cette tunique ardente de la fable, et de quels fonds d'abîme nous vint à bien, nous vint à mal, toute cette montée d'aube rougissante, et cette part en nous divine qui fut notre part de ténèbres?'[a]

The awareness itself, however, is described in terms that are deceptively close to those used by Eliot in *Four Quartets*: 'La course est faite et n'est point faite; la chose est dite et n'est point dite. Et nous rentrons chargés de nuit, sachant de naissance et de mort plus que n'enseigne le songe d'homme.'[b] 'Deceptively' because the character of the mystical experience in Perse is so utterly different from the Christian mysticism of *Four Quartets*. Fundamental to all Perse's poetry, even where it is most tense and comes closest to nihilism, is a sort of connivance with the physical world, an acceptance of the world of things and of the flesh, an acceptance of all the pain and ecstasy, all the horror and honour of living. Perse is at home in the world in a way that Eliot had never known, and the acceptance of life and death that Perse expresses in his old age is a voluntary acceptance, not a resignation.

None of the cantos of *Chronique* is more than a page or two long, so the temptation to quote the whole last canto (no. viii) is very strong, for the agèd poet, in a superb expression of great pride tempered with extreme tenderness, offers himself up to the Unknown God, not as a private and especially privileged individual, but as a representative man. We shall rest content with citing only the last half of the canto, which is prepared by the closing line of the first half: ' – fierté de l'âme devant l'âme et fierté d'âme grandissante dans l'épée grande et bleue.'[c] This takes up the image that occurs toward the end of canto v: 'Après l'orgueil, voici l'honneur, et cette clarté de l'âme florissante dans l'épée grande et bleue.'[d] This line, in turn, ties in with a much earlier one that

---

[a] O you who led us to all this quick of the soul, fortune wandering on the waters, will you tell us one evening on earth what hand arrays us in this burning tunic of fable, and from what abyssal depth, for our good, for our ill, came all that welling of reddening dawn, and that divine part in us that was our part of darkness?

[b] The voyage is made and not made; the thing is said and not said. And we come back laden with night, knowing of birth and death more than man's dream can teach.

[c] – pride of the soul before the soul and pride of soul growing to greatness in the great blue sword.

[d] After pride, behold honour, and that clarity of the soul that flourishes in the great blue sword.

is found in the climactic homologous series of *Anabase*, which includes 'celui qui voit son âme au reflet d'une lame'[a] (canto x). Running through all these references is the sword-symbolism that still exists in one form or another in the Far East, for it had its origin in ancient Imperial China. The most obvious present-day survival is the samurai-sword, which is drawn from its sheath only after the most painstaking precautions and only on the most solemn occasions, for the samurai who bares his sword bares his soul. At the coronation of George V in 1910, which was marked by the last great congregation of world royalty, Imperial Japan was greatly embarrassed, for the Mikado could not, by sacred tradition, leave his palace. The dilemma was resolved by sending to London in his place the heir-apparent, who walked in the coronation procession, holding upright in front of him and almost against his face, the Mikado's sword. This was a mark of honour even greater than the mere physical presence of the Mikado would have been, for the sword was his inmost spiritual self.[7]

This confrontation of the soul and the sword-blade prepares the following strophes:

'Et nos pensées déjà se lèvent dans la nuit comme les hommes de grande tente, avant le jour, qui marchent au ciel rouge portant leur selle sur l'épaule gauche.

Voici les lieux que nous laissons. Les fruits du sol sont sous nos murs, les eaux du ciel dans nos citernes, et les grandes meules de porphyre reposent sur le sable.

L'offrande, ô nuit, où la porter? et la louange, la fier?... Nous élevons à bout de bras, sur le plat de nos mains, comme couvée d'ailes naissantes, ce cœur enténébré de l'homme où fut l'avide, et fut l'ardent, et tant d'amour irrévélé...

Ecoute, ô nuit, dans les préaux déserts et sous les arches solitaires, parmi les ruines saintes et l'émiettement des vieilles termitières, le grand pas souverain de l'âme sans tanière,

Comme aux dalles de bronze où rôderait un fauve,

*

Grand âge, nous voici. Prenez mesure du cœur d'homme.'[b]

[a] he who sees his soul in the reflection of a swordblade

[b] Already our thoughts rise in the night like nomad chieftains of the big tent who walk before daybreak toward a red sky, carrying their saddles on their left shoulders. / Behold the places we leave. The fruits of the soil are beneath our walls, the waters of the sky in our cisterns, and the great millstones of porphyry rest on the sand. / The offering, O night, where to

If the typically Persean character of the imagery of these lines and the relationship of that imagery to previous poems are not at once apparent to the reader, then this whole study has been written in vain. And if the supreme beauty of the original is not immediately apparent to the reader who knows French, then too, the effort made in these pages has been fruitless.

The passage has such a final ring that one would scarcely expect the poet to write anything more. But only a slight second-thought will suffice to make apparent how un-Persean such finality would be. As long as there is 'toute cette immensité de l'être et ce foisonnement de l'être, toute cette passion d'être et tout ce pouvoir d'être',[a] as the fifth canto of *Chronique* says, then it behooves the man of pride to live to the full and to the last. So, from the 'hatching of nascent wings' that characterizes the final offering, there takes flight what would have been the most disembodied of all Perse's poems, had it remained exclusively a poem.

Oiseaux was indeed first conceived purely as a poem, but an interesting chain of events resulted in the text finally taking the form of a 'méditation poétique' that is somewhere between the pure poem and the reflective essay. Perse, who had been aware of the paintings of Georges Braque for many years, had never met the painter in person. Only a few years ago, at Braque's initiative, the two men met. Braque had been fascinated by his perusal of *Amers*, and Perse, for his part, was deeply impressed by the human qualities of Braque – his complete abnegation before his art and his attitude of almost religious reverence before the phenomena of life. A real sympathy sprang up between the two men, and when Braque asked if there was some text that Perse might permit him to illustrate, Perse mentioned that he was working on a poem about birds. By sheer coincidence, Braque was working on a series of plates that were to make up *The Avian Order (L'Ordre des Oiseaux)*

bring it? and the praise, to whom entrust it?... We raise, with arms outstretched, on the flat of our hands, like a hatching of nascent wings, this darkened heart of a man where hunger was, and ardour, and so much love unrevealed... / Listen, O night, in the deserted courtyards and under the solitary arches, amid the holy ruins and the crumbling of old termite-hills, hear the great sovereign footfalls of the soul without a lair, / Like a wild beast prowling a pavement of bronze. / Great age, behold us. Take the measure of man's heart.

[a] all this immensity of being and profusion of being, all this passion of being and power of being

and had chosen as an epigraph for his pictures a line from the noontide imagery of the closing 'Dédicace' of *Amers*: 'L'oiseau plus vaste sur son erre voit l'homme libre de son ombre, à la limite de son bien.'[a] Neither man had completed his respective work; so each, in deference to the other, modified his work to suit the requirements of a collaboration. A series of twelve lithographs by Braque was to be published in May of 1962 to celebrate the eightieth birthday of the painter. There was not time enough, however, to bring out the album at that date, and it was not until December of that year that the album was displayed, including the text of *Oiseaux*, by Saint-John Perse.

Writing in January, 1962, to the woman in charge of the publication of the album, Perse had confirmed his willingness to collaborate with Braque in the following terms:

'Dear Madame,

I never dreamt that I would one day have to go back on my promise never to write occasional pieces. Your last letter, though, has completely disarmed me. Apart from my admiration for the work of the Painter whose eightieth birthday you are preparing to celebrate, I find Braque, the man, profoundly congenial. If you think it will make him the least bit happy to have me near at hand at this Festival of Birds, I'll join him there with the greatest willingness. And even with a certain fellow-feeling…'

About the time Perse was finishing his text, he wrote another letter to the same person, and in it he describes his text as 'a poetic meditation on birds in general and on Braque's bird in particular'. And then, when he actually sent off the manuscript, he added: 'I hope my thought may have coincided in some small measure with Braque's: nothing would make me happier.' The 'collaboration' thus left both men a large degree of freedom; and, in a sense, it was a sort of mutual homage, rather than a tight fusion in which each man submerged his will for the sake of a single effect. Speaking about the page-proofs of Braque's illustrations, which had reached Perse at the beginning of March, 1962, Perse wrote: 'I very much liked the proofs. I couldn't get them out of Customs at Washington airport until three days ago. I thought a great deal about Braque while I was writing my text, but I have

---

[a] The bird, more vast in its circling, sees man free of his shadow, at the limit of his weal.

not sought to be literal. I couldn't have done that even if I had
been able to see the selection and order of his plates in time...'[8]

The final result was a large and very expensive *de luxe* edition
that was sold out long before it came off the presses. Fortunately,
Perse's text has since been published separately a number of times,
the first time being in the December, 1962, issue of *La Nouvelle
Revue française*. Braque's lithographs, which are of birds stylized
to the point of utmost simplicity, are probably the kind of illustration best suited to Perse's richly-wrought text. As for the purely
graphic merits of Braque's lithographs, I can only say that they
struck me as very uneven – and then hasten to leave the final
judgment to persons better qualified in these matters than I am.
What is obvious, though, is that certain passages in Perse's text
require the illustrations in order to be entirely intelligible.

That text is really another 'air' poem; but whereas the air in
Vents is in violent motion, and hence a very positive force, in
Oiseaux the air is the passive medium that supports birds in flight.
And it is birds in flight that interest the poet above all else. Perse's
love of birds goes back to his earliest childhood. We have already
had occasion to note the high frequency of birds and bird-imagery
in his poems – not to mention the whole passage devoted to
Audubon in *Vents* (II, i). Birds of prey and water-birds are his
special passion, but by no means exclusively. Moreover, not only
various individual species, but the whole avian phenomenon interests Perse, especially those aspects of it that have to do with
the global migration and distribution of birds.

Oiseaux is preceded by an epigraph from the *Satires* of Persius:
'more than is spanned in the flight of a kite.' This comparison
seems to have been traditional with the Roman poets, for it is
found in Petronius and Juvenal as well, in each instance designating something particularly vast.[9] Thus, the emphasis on flight
is immediately established. The text itself, longer than *Chronique*,
is divided into thirteen parts – it seems inadvisable to refer to
them as 'cantos', in view of the semi-essayistic nature of the text.
It starts off in a matter-of-fact way, stating that birds, of all living
things to which we are allied, pursue the most singular destiny on
the confines of day, for birds alone migrate back and forth, flying
day and night, from the farthest ends of the earth in pursuit of
warmth, of 'l'inflation solaire' – the very phrase used many years
before in *Anabase*.[10] But the matter-of-factness is not long in turn-

ing into pure poetry: 'Au fléau de son aile l'immense libration d'une double saison.'[a] Perse uses the image of the balance and its beam in several different contexts, but already in *Chronique* it is associated with birds, where Perse speaks of the Indian eagle-dancer 'mimant la vergue ou le fléau'.[b] Here, though, the image, condensed in its wording, is greatly expanded in its implication. The outspread wings of the bird are once again the beam of the balance, but the whole arc of the migratory bird's flight is like-wise the beam of a vast balance, the pans of which are the summer at each end of the arc, the northern and southern summers, equi-librating in the rotation of seasons. This search for an uninter-rupted summer ('une seule estivation') is then said to be the bird's heresy, as it is likewise the heresy of the poet and the painter, who also, each in his way, align seasons in unorthodox fashion 'aux plus hauts lieux d'intersection'[c] – which ties in with the figure of the swaying scale-beam.

The matter-of-fact statement followed by a poetic 'fulfilment' is the basic procedure used by Perse in this 'poetic meditation'. Very often the images are second to none in the whole of Perse's work for splendour and rightness. The very next paragraph of this first part states flatly of the bird, considered generically, 'Sa grâce est dans la combustion. Rien là de symbolique; simple fait biologique'.[d] This laconic statement is immediately followed by:

'Et si légère pour nous est la matière oiseau, qu'elle semble, à contre feu du jour, portée jusqu'à l'incandescence. Un homme en mer, flairant midi, lève la tête à cet esclandre: une mouette blanche ouverte sur le ciel, comme une main de femme contre la flamme d'une lampe, élève dans le jour la rose transparence d'une blancheur d'hostie...'[e]

Part II is matter-of-fact in its entirety, being a very precise sum-mary of the bone-structure of the bird, which is so extraordinary in its complete adaptation to flight. This anatomization leads

---

[a] On the scale-beam of its wing the immense libration of a double season
[b] miming the yard-arm or the cross-beam
[c] at the highest points of intersection
[d] Its grace is in combustion. Nothing symbolic here; just a simple bio-logical fact.
[e] And so light for us is the substance 'bird', that it seems, interposed between us and the flaming day, raised to incandescence. A man at sea, sensing noon, raises his head to behold this sudden disclosure: a white gull spread against the sky, like a woman's hand before a lamp-flame, elevating in the broad daylight the pink translucence of the wafer's whiteness...

directly to the painted birds of Braque, which are referred to in part iii, and it is there that the poetic 'fulfilment' occurs. Perse tells us that the bird, caught in the painter's image, 'soustrait à sa troisième dimension',[a] does not, in the case of Braque, really forget that space is its normal habitat.

'Franchissant la distance intérieure du peintre, il le suit vers un monde nouveau sans rien rompre de ses liens avec son milieu originel, son ambiance antérieure et ses affinités profondes. Un même espace poétique continue d'assurer cette continuité.'[b] That statement is then illustrated by a reference to an old legend, from Sir John Mandeville, of a Mongol conqueror who, stealing a bird from its nest, finds he has taken with it all that is essential to it – the tree, its roots, the soil; eventually his whole empire is involved.

Part iv considers quite meticulously the extraordinary optics of the bird of prey, which is then compared to the extraordinary optics of the painter. This, as might be expected, ushers in a consideration of Braque's special achievement. This is the climax of Perse's tribute to Braque, and it occupies most of parts v, vi, and vii. According to Perse, Braque has succeeded in fixing in a visual image the 'asceticism of flight'. There is indeed something ascetic and stripped-down in his bird-engravings.

Part viii is of special interest to anyone interested in Perse's poetics, for it very ingeniously recapitulates that poetics, this time using the bird as an explanatory comparison. Birds, says Perse, are like words, for they are 'noyaux de force et d'action, foyers d'éclairs et d'émissions'.[c]

'Sur la page blanche aux marges infinies, l'espace qu'ils mesurent n'est plus qu'incantation. Ils sont, comme dans le mètre, quantités syllabiques. Et procédant, comme les mots, de lointaine ascendance, ils perdent, comme les mots, leur sens à la limite de la félicité.'[d]

[a] removed from its third dimension
[b] Penetrating the inner expanse of the painter, it follows him toward a new world without in any way severing its ties with its original environment, its former surroundings, and its profoundest affinities. One and the same poetic space continues to assure this continuity.
[c] nuclei of force and action, centres of flashes and emissions
[d] On the white page with infinite margins, the space they measure is nothing now save incantation. They are as in metre, syllabic quantities. And proceeding, as words do, from a distant ancestry, they lose, as words do, their meaning on the limits of felicity.

And, still like words, 'ils sont, comme les mots, portés du rythme universel'[a] – once more the poetics of flux.

Part ix tells of the fascination of birds as weight-defying phenomena, and its last lines refer openly to birds as the inspirers of aviation: 'l'oiseau, à très longs cris, par son incitation au vol, fut seul à doter l'homme d'une audace nouvelle.'[b] The aircraft, which figures very largely in the fourth section of *Vents*, had attracted Leger's attention long before he wrote that poem. In the early days at Pau (1908), he met Wilbur Wright and followed with fascinated interest the experiments Wright was conducting on the *lande* of Pont-Long.[11]

In this same part ix, there is an allusion to 'cette clarté de nacre rose ou verte qui est aussi celle du songe, étant celle des pôles et des perles sous la mer'.[c] This light of the poles is known firsthand to Perse, for not only has he sailed in North Canadian waters and the Straits of Magellan, he has likewise flown over the edges of Antarctica, where he found 'the wind, the ocean, the cold, and the sky and earth empty of the detritus of man'.[12]

Part x is the ultimate elaboration of the image of the balance. It presents the bird as mediator, 'A mi-hauteur entre ciel et mer, entre un amont et un aval d'éternité'.[d]

Parts xi and xii return to the birds of Georges Braque, generalized and unallusive in their 'birdness'. I cannot help thinking that Perse's characterization applies more to what Braque was seeking than to what he actually was able to capture in the lithographs. But there is no doubt that Perse completely grasped the artist's intentions. In part xii, permitting himself the kind of witticism that one never finds in his purely poetic writing, Perse says that, were Braque's birds given a proper scientific name, they would be labelled *Bracchus Avis Avis*, because this repetition is the way naturalists designate the type chosen as archetype ('le type élu comme archétype'). Then, in something very close to a homologous series, Perse lists all the specific birds – actual, legendary, ritual, literary – that Braque's birds are *not*. The catalogue includes

---

[a] they are borne on the universal rhythm
[b] the bird, with insistent cries, calling to flight, was the only one [of the animals] to endow man with a new daring.
[c] that light of pink or green mother-of-pearl, which is also that of dreams, since it is the light of the poles and of pearls under the sea –
[d] Half-way between sky and sea, between the upstream and downstream of eternity

some rare ones, including the problematic Ababil of the Koran, about which Islamic specialists themselves are not sure.[13] The 'literary' birds are interesting, chiefly because they tell us something of Perse's own tastes. The Eagle of Zeus mentioned in Pindar's *Pythian Odes* is the first on the list; and Pindar may well be one of the profoundest purely literary influences in the formation of Perse's own talent, for, at the time he was composing his own first poems in French, he did a translation and study of the *Epinikia* of Pindar, which, unfortunately, were never published.[14] Then there are the 'chilly cranes' that fly through the opening pages of Ducasse's *Chants de Maldoror*, a work in which we find a macabre poetic 'trance' that has, at moments, curious affinities with occasional lines in Perse, especially where animals and the ocean are concerned. The 'Anglo-Saxons' are represented by Poe (the great white bird of Arthur Gordon Pym, not the Raven...) and Coleridge. And even Baudelaire's poor, abused albatross is mentioned. Braque's birds, however, have nothing to do with any of these.

The last (thirteenth) part has no necessary connection at all with Braque. It is no longer a poetic meditation; it is poetry, pure and simple. Birds, who 'gardent parmi nous quelque chose du songe de la création' (the very last words of the text),[a] here take flight toward the far limits of Being that the aging poet approached at the end of *Chronique*. But here the approach is no longer earthbound:

'Avec toutes choses errantes par le monde et qui sont choses au fil de l'heure, ils vont où vont tous les oiseaux du monde, à leur destin d'êtres créés... Où va le mouvement même des choses, sur sa houle, où va le cours même du ciel, sur sa roue – à cette immensité de vivre et de créer dont s'est émue la plus grande nuit de mai, ils vont, et doublant plus de caps que n'en lèvent nos songes, ils passent, nous laissant à l'Océan des choses libres et non libres...'[b][15]

---

[a] keep alive, in our midst, something of the dream of creation
[b] With all wandering things in the world and which are things in the stream of time, they go where all birds of this world go, to their fate of created beings... Where the very movement of things goes, on its surge, where the very course of the heavens goes, on its wheel – to that immensity of living and creating by which the deepest May night was stirred, they go, and rounding more capes than our dreams raise, they pass, leaving us to the Ocean of things free and not free...

Such passages make one wish that Perse had not transformed his poem-in-progress into a 'poetic meditation'. Certainly the essayistic, discursive elements in *Oiseaux* seem to violate Perse's own poetics. Even some of the imagery – and frequently some of the most ingenious – is essentially expository, rather than poetic. Here, though, it is very difficult to draw the line, for Perse is so completely the poet that even his most methodically explanatory comparisons turn into poetry, of their own accord, so to speak. Consider, for example, the critical description and evaluation of the poetry of Léon-Paul Fargue that are implied in the following metaphors:

> Between the basaltic mass of a Claudel and the pure crystalliz-
> ations of a Valéry, one evening in the City, in a feverish and
> fairy-tale spot, there was this unfurling, as of a quivering
> circinate fern-frond; this unfolding, suddenly, as of a neuro-
> ptera drying its fine network wing of green gauze at the lamp-
> flame...

That passage, in the meticulous exactness of its comparisons, tells us more about the essential quality of Fargue (which has, inci-dentally, been so often misunderstood), than a whole critical essay in the academic style. But the passage also has about it an aura of genuine poetry. This highly figured prose, however, is a very touchy thing, and only a consummate master, to whom it has become instinctive, can 'bring it off'. But the passage, even though it comes from a critical essay, really must be read in French, if the poetic aura is to be entirely perceptible:

> 'Entre la masse basaltique d'un Claudel et les pures cristalli-
> sations d'un Valéry, il y eut un soir, et à la Ville, en lieu fiévreux
> et féerique, ce déroulement, soudain, comme d'une crosse de
> fougère ivre; ce dépliement, soudain, comme d'une aile de
> névroptère séchant au feu des lampes son fin lacis de gaze
> verte...'[16]

Unfortunately, numerous critics have sought to characterize Perse's own poetry by adopting his style, and the results have been uniformly disastrous.

If, nevertheless, one cannot help regretting that *Oiseaux* was not completed as the unalloyed poem it started out to be, one can surely appreciate the human warmth of the gesture made by Perse to Braque. The gesture is all the more moving in that Perse has far less interest in the plastic arts than in music.[17] In the long run, the 'compromise' on the literary level is more than compensated by the spontaneity of Perse's homage. I have no doubt that he himself has never for a minute regretted his decision. On the contrary, he must have felt how right his instinct was in this matter, for less than a year after the sumptuous *L'Ordre des Oiseaux* appeared, Georges Braque was dead.[18]

8

The Untimely Poet

If the text of *Oiseaux* is added to the poems contained in the two volumes of the *Œuvre poétique*, the result is an imposing body of poetry that spans a whole lifetime and that, in spite of its incompleteness,[1] forms a genuine *summa*. On the stylistic level, the unity of this poetic sum has been universally recognized. The uniqueness of the style has set this poetry apart *en bloc*, and the block does not readily blend into the general literary landscape of its time. From *Images à Crusoé* to the last line of *Oiseaux*, the vocabulary, the turns of phrase, the choice and organization of images are immediately recognizable as the products of the same unusual sensibility, and it is practically impossible to speak of successive 'manners'. But the style has, nevertheless, evolved, and there is more variety in this uniformity than is usually admitted. Moreover, preoccupation with the stylistic unity has resulted in neglect of the much more important substantive unity of this work. Indeed, some critics have gone so far as to maintain that this poetry is a style – a most remarkable style, perhaps – but not much more, thus reducing it to an essentially rhetorical exercise. In actual fact, there is a cohesion and unity in this work that go far beyond style; and though the published poems do not recount the story of a life, they do express in a 'chemically pure' form the profoundest preoccupations of the poet throughout a lifetime.

In the Antillean poems the chief spur to writing was an awed delight in the sensorium of nature, a nostalgia for the 'warm nude ages of instinctive poise' that Perse had actually known in his early childhood. In the surviving poems of the diplomatic years this initial oneness with physical nature gives way to a restless, speculative concern with human motivations, especially with the hidden springs of action involved in the establishment and exercise of authority. An introspective dialogue is there begun and is continued into the exile poems. But in these latter, the subject of the dialogue is broadened and deepened; the major concern becomes the human condition and the historical forces determining that condition. Finally, in the votive poems the dialogue reverts to monologue; oneness is recaptured. After tragic involvement in the turmoil of his time, the poet accedes to a profound sense of fulfilment.

Throughout these shifts in subject-matter, however, the continuity is unbroken. The transition from one period to the next is never wholly unprepared; there is constant overlapping and interpenetration. The insistence on order and hierarchy that comes to the fore in *Anabase* and *Amitié du Prince* is clearly prefigured in some of the Antillean poems. In their turn, the two 'diplomatic' pieces set the world-stage for the vast exile poems; but the curtain had actually risen on that stage in Perse's very earliest work. Conversely, the wonder at the spectacle of nature that is so effectively expressed in the earlier poems is still entirely present in the exile poems and even gives a special quality to the desperate climax of *Vents*, where one would have expected it to be entirely forgotten. The votive poems go on to complete the circle: they return to the pure delight in the sensorium that was Perse's earliest incentive to write, but the register of that delight is enormously extended, and its tone is one of consummate ripeness.

Preoccupation with style is not the only reason why the vital unity of this work has been overlooked. The fragmentary way in which Perse's poems have been published has been a contributing factor. The blind haste of critics eager to join the chorus (especially when so many of them were taken unawares by the Nobel award of 1960) has likewise contributed to this oversight. If the results had always been simply an incomplete view of Perse that was valid as far as it went, there would be no cause for complaint. But too often the result has been vacuous and irrelevant interpretations, made even more regrettable when, as was frequently the case, they were intended as encomia. That is scarcely the way to

assure Perse's work the place of honour it deserves as one of the
really significant poetic achievements of our time.

There is, of course, no lack of critics who deny that honour to
Perse, precisely because they find that his poetry is not 'of our
time'. And indeed, it is quite untimely in a number of ways. For
one thing, it contains almost no recognizable expression of alien-
ation and metaphysical anguish. I have tried to point up the
anguish that is expressed in *Exil* and *Vents*; but that is clearly
not the 'real thing'. It is far too gentlemanly and never expressed
in visceral terms. But the clearest proof of how far Perse is out of
tune with the times is his open declaration of optimism, made, of
all places, from the podium of the Nobel awards: 'So, by his
absolute adherence to what *is*, the poet keeps us in touch with the
permanence and unity of Being. And his message is one of optimism.'[2] Surely it took more than a little courage to use so universally taboo a term in such a key position. I suspect that Perse,
in so doing, wished to express as flagrantly as possible his deep
conviction that the negative aspects of experience have come to
be over-emphasized, to the detriment of the astringent and cleans-
ing effect that this emphasis originally had. In the light of his
poetry, this optimism, far from being Panglossian and doctrinaire,
appears simply as a declaration that, somehow, the game is worth
the candle. Perse did not come by this optimism easily and did
not use the term until he had lived the greater part of his life and
had produced most of his poetry. This optimism had to be
achieved, had to be wrested from life. The important point is that
it is humanly achievable. Perse's own victory over despair was
not an easy one. A terrible feeling, not of nausea, but of emptiness, pervades *Vents*. The winds of that poem 'nous chantaient
l'horreur de vivre, et nous chantaient l'honneur de vivre'.[a] Perse
has known what the horror of living is, but he has preferred to
accent the honour of living. Other writers, temperamentally better
equipped for the task than Perse, have detailed the myriad horrors
of our time. Those writers merit our praise and thanks, and, by
and large, they have had them. For Perse, however, one of the
most frightening aspects of our time is the denial of the splendour
of living – a splendour which to him is as real as the horror.
In fact, what is really horrible for him is 'la splendeur de
vivre qui s'exile à perte d'hommes' – that splendour of living

[a] sang to us the horror of living and sang too the honour of living

forever exiled beyond the reach of man, which he mentions in connection with World War II in *Poème à l'étrangère*. Even violence and suffering can sometimes be transformed by their grandeur.

What is important here, I believe, is a fundamental, almost physiological difference in basic reactions between the proto-existentialist writers (with Sartre as their most articulate spokesman) and Saint-John Perse. The instinctive revulsion in the face of the *données* of life is so strong in the former that they equate existence with nausea. Even though this nausea is usually overcome sufficiently to allow participation in the normal pursuits of life, it colours everything that is done and felt. Perse, on the other hand, has never experienced this persistent nausea that, for the existentialists, *is* existence. As a child he felt at home in the world in a way that is entirely unknown to many human beings. Robust health and an extraordinarily propitious natural and family environment certainly had much to do with this. However that may be, a tacit accord with his environment at an early age has guaranteed Leger once and for all against the generalized reaction of nausea that is at the base of so much present-day literature. Again, there is no denying the authenticity and validity of some of these expressions of disgust. I am simply pointing out that such a reaction is foreign to Perse and helps explain why he is ostensibly out of tune with the times. As circumstances change, however, Perse may come into his own. We may find that he is already supplying satisfaction for a need that is just as fundamental as the need for exorcism of nausea by vomiting.

But even for many critics who have not espoused existentialist fashions and terminology Perse is something of an anachronism. For one thing, there is at the heart of his world-view a 'cyclism' that can scarcely be regarded as being in the mainstream of twentieth-century thought. In his Nobel address, speaking of the poet, Perse writes:

To him, one law of harmony governs the whole world of things. Nothing can occur there which by its nature is too overwhelming for man to cope with. The worst catastrophes of history are but seasonal rhythms in a vaster cycle of repetitions and renewals. The Furies who cross the stage, torches high, do but throw light upon one brief moment in the development of the immensely long theme. Maturing civiliza-

tions do not perish from the pangs of one autumn; they
merely shed their leaves.[3]

The comparison employed here is simply a slight variation of one
of the master-metaphors of *Vents* – the self-renewing tree which
appears at the beginning of that poem and at its very end as well.[4]
This cyclism is woven into the warp and woof of Perse's work.
The driving force in this cyclic movement can only be guessed at.
The movement itself is manifest, but its causes are hidden. Perse
is careful never to suggest how or why this force operates. He is
especially wary of the least suggestion of anthropomorphism. For
him the universe conforms to no known human norm in its strange
system of forces and counterforces. But it is supreme folly to deny
the existence of these mysterious forces, 'the great unrevealed
order of an eternal onward movement'.[5]

Such a doctrine of cyclical destruction and renewal seems to
cancel out what is for many critics the essence of tragedy, namely,
the finality of each human being's extinction as a sentient, individual entity. The equanimity with which Perse looks toward
death and even beyond death[6] seems to confirm this view. But
'tragedy' and 'tragic' are slippery terms. If by 'tragedy' we designate intense awareness of the inevitability of human suffering and
of the unmitigated loneliness in which each of us must face death,
then we really have no right to deny the term to Perse. It is true,
though, that the essentially non-dramatic character of his poems
never makes them the vehicle for the kind of individual conflict
that is the classical expression of tragedy. Yet the feeling is latent
in almost all of the diplomatic and exile poems. And it is worth
noting that the word is explicitly used in the last of Perse's poems
to date, where it is a qualifier for reality. In *Oiseaux* he speaks of
'the tragic shores of the real' ('rives tragiques du réel'), thus in-
separably wedding tragedy to reality. What is undeniable, however, is that Perse's expression of this tragic sense is totally foreign
to the way it is generally expressed these days.

The efficacy of poetry, however, is only incidentally involved
with the beliefs and tenets that underlie it. Sartre himself has quite
clearly stated: 'The realm of signs is prose: poetry belongs with
painting, sculpture, and music.'[7] Thus, not only existentialist critics, but Marxist critics as well,[8] can and do take pleasure in Perse's
poetry. Nevertheless, the ideas and attitudes that are latent in it
run so counter to prevailing fashions that, for some readers, they

may tend to get in the way of the purely poetic experience. The trouble is that Perse keeps adding injury to insult. The general literary attitude that one can sense determining his poetry is clearly hostile to *littérature engagée*. In that revealing Nobel speech he declared, 'Poet is he who breaks for us the bonds of habit. And that is how, in spite of himself, the poet also is tied to historical events. Nothing in the drama of his times is alien to him.'[9] This may seem at least a first step toward some sort of doctrine of 'committed' literature, but it is not. The little phrase 'in spite of himself' must not be overlooked. The poet is inevitably of his time, but as an artist, he participates in his time in a very special way. Alexis Leger, who spent the major part of his life plunged in national and international politics, can scarcely be accused of a Pontius Pilate attitude toward the dirty-work of living. But political or social action as an end and justification of artistic literature is unthinkable to Perse. In his 1951 tribute to Larbaud he wrote:

My dear Larbaud, our Age lets itself be drawn into strange literary defections, so that the literary work as such is slighted, even looked upon with suspicion, and language itself is scoffed at. And sterility comes to be a matter of pride, now that literary action is replacing literary creation, the manifesto, the literary work of art, the idea of social behaviour the idea of man.[10]

Although the attitude here expressed is decidedly not fashionable, it is still shared, and will continue to be shared, by many writers. It is a perennial attitude and goes back a long way. An anecdote attributed directly to Perse is most apposite here. Recalling his friendship with Conrad, which began over half a century ago, Perse is quoted as saying:

Conrad once told me about a dinner he had had somewhere in the country with Shaw, Wells, Bennett. When these *savants cyniques* of the literary industry talked about writing as 'action', poor Conrad, horrified, left the table, pretending he had to catch an earlier train. He told me later, in *épouvantable* French, except for one English word I will never forget, 'Writing, for me, is an act of faith. They all made me feel so *dowdy*.'[11]

It does not take a master-psychologist to sense which side Perse was on, and such an attitude probably does little for his popularity at the present time.

In reality, most of these 'anachronistic' aspects of Perse simply reflect a supreme indifference to literary fashions rather than a genuine 'being out of tune' with the times. Even in some very obvious ways, this poetry very much belongs to the twentieth century. Its encyclopedic character, which has been so often noted, is wholly contemporary and might be more accurately described as 'global', if one could forget how that word has been abused during the last few decades. This global approach is animated by a conviction that a meaningful synthesis must include not only the data of the physical and natural sciences, but all manifestations of the human spirit as well, throughout history and in every part of the globe. It is, in short, the same conviction that animates modern anthropology. In keeping with this attitude, Perse's poetry admits no accepted religious creed or political dogma as a frame of reference. Instead, it seeks to embrace all manifestations of the human phenomenon, and, having done that, to view the human as a part of the total phenomenon of the natural world. Many of the best minds of our time are engaged in this same attempt in one way or another.

And then, in spite of his expressed optimism, Perse is haunted by some of the besetting fears of our time. I think it is fair to say that the two dominant fears of modern times are what may be designated as the 'apocalyptic' fear and the 'utopian' fear. Both, of course, are tied in with technological progress. The first of these two fears is foreign to Perse. He does not believe in the possibility of the total self-destruction of mankind, even though he was so deeply involved in World War II, which seemed well along the road to Apocalypse. An eloquent proof of the strength of Perse's conviction in this regard was his refusal to collaborate in the book to which so many outstanding artists were contributing when he found out that its subject was to be the Apocalypse.[12] Perse does, however, very much fear the 'utopian' danger of total mechanization. That fear informs much of his poetry from *Vents* on, even though it is never overtly expressed. Instead of writing allegorical horror-tales or nightmare visions of insect-societies – two *genres* in which our period excels – Perse has sought to celebrate those forces which, according to him, can most effectively be mobilized against the undoing of the human spirit through mechanistic manipulation. The technological progress that makes the successful satisfaction of all material human needs a very real possibility may also bring about the extinction of the spark of discontent. Dead and predictable habit may become universalized. 'Inertia,' writes Perse, 'is the only mortal danger. Poet is he who breaks for us the bonds of habit.'[13] In this way Perse restores its widest meaning to the word *poet* (from the Greek *poiein*, to create). The dehumanizing effects of modern industrialism have led Perse to make the one public declaration of alarm that he has permitted himself – a hasty but frightened allusion to 'the growing perils of our industrial civilization'.[14] In his Nobel speech this fear is placed in a larger context:

> ... The real drama of this century lies in the growing estrangement between the temporal and the untemporal man. Is man, enlightened on one side, to sink into darkness on the other? And his forced growth in a community without communion, what would that be but a false maturity?[15]

A 'forced growth in a community without communion' neatly characterizes the horror-utopias that have been described by so many modern writers. For Perse, however, there is no question of cancelling out or reversing technological advances. The problem resolves itself into restoring the primacy of that creative human curiosity without which these advances would never have been made and which is now actually threatened by those very advances. For Perse, that curiosity is kept alive by man's constant confrontation of the forces that surround, limit, and transcend him. Before the triumph of mechanization, man was so constantly threatened by these forces, and likewise so dependent upon them, that there was little possibility of eluding the confrontation. That is no longer necessarily so.[16] The insistence upon this confrontation is celebrated in *Amers* and is Perse's way of working against this 'growing estrangement between the temporal and the untemporal man'. One may dispute the 'timeliness' of this formulation of the problem, but surely no one will deny the contemporaneity of the problem itself.

But the very style of Perse's poems, which has elicited more comment that any other aspect of his work, has contributed greatly to the illusion of untimeliness. Even in the days when it was taking shape and being perfected, this style very little resembled that of other French poets of the time. It is quite alien to the neo-symbolist manner of the last years of the *belle époque*. But it was equally far from the casual and 'spontaneous' styles of the

Apollinaire-Cendrars group that came to the fore during and immediately after World War I. And if the tension of some of Perse's
images seems at times to justify André Breton's declaration that
Perse is 'surrealist at a distance', one can only say that the distance
is so great as to put surrealism out of sight. As for the various
'beat' styles of our own time, they represent the very antithesis of
everything we find in Perse. The pace of his poems is slow and
ceremonious, the language is a self-consciously literary one quite
apart from the language of everyday intercourse. There is ever
present the 'délice encore du mieux dire'[17] – not merely the delight
in what is well said, but in what is *better* said. Such a taste is
suspect in many quarters today.

But even readers who have no care for the timeliness or untimeliness of Perse's work sometimes find its ceremonial aloofness
and highly wrought verbal texture a barrier to enjoyment. The
abundance and strangeness of the imagery are constant; great
demands are made on the reader's attention, and the leaven of wit
is not there to make the effort easier. We are no longer used to
such a sustained elevated tone, and we are likely to feel a little
uncomfortable in the presence of a writer who takes his poetry
seriously in so bland and unquestioning a way. Clearly, this work
is, in Conrad's words, an act of faith. But here unarguable matters
of taste come into play, as well as the caprices of fashion. It is
quite conceivable that this style may not only cease to be a barrier
to readers – it may supply a welcome change. But even should that
happen, the recalcitrance of many readers of good-will may remain
because of the much-discussed obscurity of this poetry.

In the introduction to this study I sought to distinguish between an obscure poet and a difficult one.[18] In the chapters that
followed I sought to demonstrate that, while Perse is difficult, he
is not very often downright obscure. We are now in a position to
sum up our arguments.

Little more need be said about Perse's unusual vocabulary. We
have repeatedly seen how he simply adds a great number of scientific and technical terms to the standard vocabulary of carefully
spoken French. These terms, recondite though they may be, are
almost all in the *Petit Larousse*. Furthermore, the 'standard' vocabulary of our time is becoming daily more heavily laden with such
terms, and I risk the prediction that this aspect of Perse's vocabulary will become less and less problematic. But the doubt may still

linger that the use of such a vast quantity of unusual terms is not wholly necessary, that there must be some equally effective and much simpler method of 'getting the job done'. I, for one, do not think so. I see Perse's extensive but careful use of such terms as one ingenious solution to the dilemma posed by his poetics. Here it is necessary to recall what Perse said about the 'poverty' of the French language:

> ... the extreme economy of means of the French language is well known, as is also the fact that, having reached the end of a long evolution toward the abstract, French today gratefully accepts the blessing of its material impoverishment, which is sometimes carried all the way to ambiguity and multivalence in effecting exchanges and long-distance mutations wherein words, having become mere signs, intervene only as a token, in the manner of so-called 'fiat' money.[19]

This joyous acceptance of a linguistic currency that is reduced to a fiduciary token, so to speak, seems in direct contradiction to what I have called the extreme 'nominalism' of Perse's poetics, wherein an almost physical congruence between the 'thing' expressed and the words used to express it is required. The introduction of technical and scientific terms tends to reduce this discrepancy. Such terms are meaningful only in relation to a whole craft-context or a whole taxonomic picture. They are, thus, about as univalent as it is possible for words to be; and because of this, they limit and polarize the 'multivalence' of the everyday 'abstract' vocabulary of French.[20] Ordinary human communication takes place most often in concrete contexts where the verbal fiduciary token may become totally superfluous – a finger placed over the lips may suffice to make someone understand he is to stop talking. More often, though, words do intervene, but the immediately present reality-situation makes possible the ostensive definition of smooth-worn, abstract terms that might otherwise be confusing or even incomprehensible. What a writer of any sort of literature must decide is to what extent he can take reality-contexts for granted. The poet is in the most difficult position of all, for he is constantly dealing with a reality-context made up of feelings and impulses, non-physical entities that are ineluctably subjective and, very often, elusive and unstable. Perse, in resorting to craft-terms, refers the reader to a context that is eminently palpable and precise, while the scientific nomenclature implies a vast taxonomic picture that is the common property of students of the natural sciences the world over. Together, these two domains furnish a rich, clearly established, and unusually stable frame of reference, readily available to anyone willing to take the trouble to familiarize himself with it. Alongside the technical and scientific terms, Perse uses an unusually large quantity of words such as *grand*, *vaste*, *pur*, *vide*, *beau*. These are his 'materially impoverished' words, and any device that will 'validate' them as acceptable currency is legitimate. The exploitation of the contexts furnished by the crafts and natural sciences is one such device.

At any rate, Perse's vocabulary alone is not a real obstacle to a reader's determining what is going on in his poems. There are other, more serious, obstacles that must be considered. For one thing, the reader who is not very familiar with his work may often feel that the events and feelings described by Perse are so private that it is simply impossible to determine what they are. This effect is sometimes the result of the 'radical suppression of transitional material' that Eliot pointed out in his first preface to *Anabase*. Greater poetic intensity, and consequently, greater durability for the poem, is what the poet seeks by means of this process of suppression. The question is, how far can the poet go in this direction and still communicate effectively with his reader? The answer, of course, depends on a number of variables. First, what degree of patience does a poet have the right to expect from a reader of good-will? And second, what fund of acquired knowledge and experience on the part of the reader has he the right to expect?

Eliot made a much-quoted statement in regard to the first question. In that same introduction to *Anabase*, speaking of the arrangement of imagery in the poem, he wrote: 'And if, as I suggest, such an arrangement of imagery requires just as much "fundamental brainwork" as the arrangement of an argument, it is to be expected that the reader of a poem should take at least as much trouble as a barrister reading an important decision on a complicated case.'[21] The contention, I think, is basically sound, but the comparison is not too felicitous. The barrister is always assured that, no matter how futile the arguments he finally comes to understand, there still remains the reward of his fee. The reader of a poem has no such assurance. In many instances the only reward for his efforts will be fatigue and the persuasion, usually justified, that final comprehension was really not worth the effort. I do not quarrel with Eliot's argument, I would simply prefer to shift the comparison to another sphere. I have always found that a difficult piece of music that I have finally come to like, and even to be deeply attached to, always had something in it that made an immediate appeal on first hearing, no matter how generally irritating and incomprehensible the first total impression was. And that *something* is always an earnest of pleasures not yet perceived, an assurance that final comprehension will very probably be worth the trouble of repeated and even painful listening. The *something* may be a particular modulation, a snatch of melody, a particular blend of instruments, an arresting sequence of chords – almost anything. Applying this analogy to Perse, what is most likely to make a reader feel that the effort may be worth making is the striking quality of certain isolated images.[22] There is also an immediate appeal in the pervasive tone, to which Fabre was the first to refer. But in spite of everything, such immediately appealing elements are still no certain guarantee that the whole poem will coalesce into a meaningful and satisfying whole.

Part of the coalescing process is, of course, dependent on the answer to the second question: What fund of acquired knowledge does the reader bring to the poem? To appreciate Perse, the reader's purely literary equipment can be far lighter than any plunge into Eliot or Pound or, to stay within the realm of French poetry, Valéry or Apollinaire, would require. Some acquaintance with the literature of classical antiquity, especially Greek legend, is indispensable. But Perse's poetry is seldom crucially dependent on literary sources for its effectiveness. A direct experience of the outdoors, especially the sea, will be of more help in understanding Perse than any literary source. To such direct experience must be added a familiarity with the fundamental concepts of geology and biology. But this latter sort of knowledge is taken more and more for granted in the modern world and should present no major problem to the reader. The same may be said for the notions of history and anthropology that Perse's poetry takes for granted. Naturally, over and beyond these specific informational items, a familiarity with the sonorities of French poetry is ultimately the only thing that can make the full flavour of Perse come through. But the relative independence of Perse's poetry from any traditional sources, other than the most generalized fund of classical legend, is one more reason why a fairly large measure of the essence of his poetry remains intact in translation. As for the historical and scientific knowledge required, I do not feel that the demands on a reader of Perse are at all unreasonable.

One has less right to demand a familiarity with the technicalities of trades and professions that are highly specialized and far-flung. Extending this, one can say that it is unfair for a writer to take for granted the same wide-ranging experience he himself has been fortunate enough to have. Surely some readers must feel that there is a certain cavalier condescension in the way Perse draws on all the recondite and little-known phenomena that he has been privileged to witness. Here is where the critic can be genuinely helpful, can fill in the gaps.

There remains, however, one more possible objection, and it is a serious one: namely, that there are too many private allusions in Perse that no amount of patience and acquired knowledge can possibly make clear. This is a point on which I feel particularly strongly, for I deplore the condescension and laziness that a high frequency of such private allusions betokens in a writer. It is this sort of allusion that makes so much of the poetry of our time the happy-hunting ground of pedantic 'initiates'. With reference to Perse, the first thing to note is that such private allusions, while they do occur, are not numerous and almost never crucial. Or even more often, the private aspect of such allusions is really a matter of indifference in the total picture. Simple human curiosity makes one wonder just who the Spanish lady, the foreigner of the *Poème à l'Etrangère*, might be. But even if we knew her identity, that would not greatly change our comprehension of the poem. Knowing of Perse's connections with the Library of Congress leads us to situate very specifically a whole section of *Vents*, but even a reader unaware of the exact identity of the library described can understand the deeper concern here expressed, which has to do with the crushing dead weight of accumulated knowledge. Both these examples, moreover, illustrate another characteristic of private allusions in Perse – their discretion. Not only would it be unbecoming to insist on the identity of the Spanish lady; the important thing is not the poet's personal relationship with a specific person, but the attitudes toward exile that are 'concretized' in that relationship. Again, the Library of Congress is no more or less at fault than the Bibliothèque Nationale or the

Vatican Library, or still further back, the Alexandrian library with which the Library of Congress is assimilated in *Vents* ('Prêtres et prêtrise, Sérapéum!'). This discretion is even more important where personal relationships and inner crises are concerned, as in *Neiges*, *Amers*, and above all, in the 'return-to-France' sections of *Vents*, where the affront to the statesman Alexis Leger lends vehemence to the poem. Strangely, though, that personal affront is made important only insofar as it is symptomatic of something much more far-reaching. There will be those who say that, actually, far from being discretion, the whole device is simply a mode of self-aggrandizement through lending an aura of mystery and importance to small personal matters. There is no doubt that Saint-John Perse is a proud man, but a pride that led to the self-denial of the long years of exile and to dignified silence under provocation is hardly the kind that lends itself to factitious mysteriousness. And then, many of the allusions turn out to be quite forthright when they are placed in the overall context of his works.

Some, it is true, can be cleared up only by Perse himself or persons very close to him – the swimming-pool allusion in *Vents* is such a one.[23] But those are the exception and not the rule. There are instances, however, which do not involve such personal allusions, where the term 'obscurity' may be justified. When ellipse is carried too far, communication breaks down. By a kind of psychological myopia, the poet assumes that the conscientious reader will be able to fill in the gaps, when, as a matter of fact, there are too few clues for even an enthusiastic reader to divine the poet's intent. *Anabase* in particular suffers from this sort of obscurity. How many readers, for example, would be likely to come up with the correct interpretation of the 'cancers du camphre et de la corne' (*Anabase*, vii) without explicit help from the poet himself? Again, however, familiarity with the total configuration of Perse's work will dispel more and more of these apparent obscurities, and since a great poet usually anticipates changes in modes of perception, the readers of future generations may find many an 'obscure' image quite comprehensible. In my own experience over the years, I have been constantly surprised at myself for not having grasped the intent of this figure or that, which suddenly springs into place and becomes lucid; I wonder why it did not occur to me sooner.

All this has to do with determining 'what is going on' in the poems. It is a truism, unfortunately abused, that a genuine poem is ultimately ineffable; that is, it would not be a real poem if it could be quite as satisfactorily expressed in a prose paraphrase or summary. What makes the poem a poem is not 'what is going on' in it, but what the poet expresses *through* what is going on. That is what is ultimately ineffable. I say that this basic truth is abused simply because vacuity and muddle-headedness are constantly masquerading as something ineffable, and because far too often it is not even possible to state what is going on in a poem – because really nothing is going on. But the validity of the principle is not affected by these abuses.

I have tried to circumscribe what is going on in Perse's poems by fixing whenever possible the circumstances, persons, and events that are actually talked about in each poem and by considering the poet's own expressed intent. Even though much remains to be done along these lines, my hope is that at least enough has been accomplished to show how irrelevant so many interpretations are – such interpretations, for example, as those that explain *Anabase* as a record of poetic creation, or the one that equates *Neiges* with a mystical Beatrice-and-Dante experience.[24] But this puts the matter too negatively. My chief concern has been to win for the poetry of Saint-John Perse a larger audience than it has thus far had, and I have thought, perhaps rather naïvely, that the best way of doing this was to insist first on what the poetry is really talking about. I can only hope this has helped to persuade the reader that this poetry is real nourishment, not pap or *ersatz*. But even if that has been accomplished, I am only too well aware that whether the food will be eaten depends on the appetite and the tastes of the guest.

The poetry of Saint-John Perse is real food. The full flavour of this food, however, can be tasted only in the original French. The finest translation is still a processed or cold-storage product. I have tried to indicate why Perse is more rewarding in translation than are most other great poets, but I have also tried to show, by sometimes unavoidably pedantic analyses of isolated lines, how inextricably enmeshed in the French language this poetry is. The whole body of Perse's work is a splendid tribute to, and illustration of, 'the French language, whose magic power is too often obscured by its genius for precise analysis'.[25] The way Perse has turned this French language to the expression of scenes and feel-

ings and impulses it had never before expressed is still best conveyed in one of the earliest characterizations of that achievement:
'In his hands,' wrote Larbaud in 1925, 'the language of French
poetry is like some splendid thoroughbred he is riding; he uses
its qualities but forces it to move at a gait new to it and contrary
to its habits.'[26]

The performance is worth beholding.

Notes

Introduction

1 *Œuvres Complètes de Valery Larbaud | Tome dixième | Journal inédit* (Paris: Gallimard, 1954), pp. 170-171.
2 Though I have not hesitated to consult the available English translations of both the poetry and prose of Saint-John Perse, I alone am responsible for the form in which all English versions appear in the present study. (A. J. Knodel)
3 'Commentaries on *Charmes*' in *The Art of Poetry* (Random House, 1958). Vintage paperback. Translation by Denise Folliot. Page 155. [Original French text, 'Commentaires de *Charmes*' published in 1929.]
4 *Ibid.*, pp. 157-158.

I

1 See R. P. Düss, *Flore phanérogamique des Antilles françaises* (Mâcon: Protat frères, 1897). For the Aniba, p. 304. For the Abutilon, p. 68. Other plant descriptions drawn on by Perse are to be found on pp. 35 (Gomphrena), 162 (Pilea), 229 (Guilandina).
2 From a letter quoted by André Gide in 'Don d'un arbre' in *Les Cahiers de la Pléiade*, été-automne 1950, p. 25. In this text the name of the tree Oreodoxa is misprinted Orcodoxa.
3 'Préface pour une traduction russe d'*Anabase*' *La Nouvelle Revue française*, 1er janvier 1926, p. 65.
4 'Face aux Lettres françaises / 1909' *La Nouvelle Revue française*, 29 mai 1951, pp. 79, 80. The reference is, of course, to the group

of French Renaissance poets of whom Ronsard and DuBellay were the leaders. DuBellay wrote its 'manifeste' entitled 'Défense et Illustration de la Langue Française.'

5 At least at the present date of publication, 1965.
6 *La Nouvelle Revue française*, novembre 1962, p. 773.
7 'A Note on Alexis Saint Léger Léger' *Poetry: A Magazine of Verse*, March 1942, p. 330.
8 See *St-John Perse, poète de gloire* (Paris: Mercure de France, 1952), p. 121 *passim*.
9 *Poétique de St.-John Perse* (Paris: Gallimard, 1954), p. 194.
10 In *La Nouvelle Revue française*, avril 1910, p. 443.
11 *Op. cit.*, p. 330.
12 Gabriel Frizeau writing to Claudel from Bordeaux, December 18, 1906: 'Je lisais hier au jeune Léger votre ode les *Muses*.' Claudel, Jammes, Frizeau *Correspondance 1897-1938*, éd. André Blanchet (Paris: Gallimard, 1952), p. 96.
13 See note 1, above.
14 Review of *Eloges* in *La Phalange*, 20 décembre 1911, pp. 499-502.

2

1 Francis Jammes, Arthur Fontaine, *Correspondance 1898-1930*, Jean Labbé, éd. (Gallimard, 1959), p. 163.
2 Since 1944, date of the parallel French-English edition of *Eloges and Other Poems* (W. W. Norton and Co.), *Amitié du Prince* has always been printed as part of the group entitled *La Gloire des Rois*. The widely varying dates of composition of the five poems making up that group have already been pointed out (p. 7), one of them, *Récitation à l'éloge d'une reine*, having been composed in 1907. This circumstance has led commentators – even such well-informed ones as Bosquet (*op. cit.*, p. 43) and Charpier (*op. cit.*, p. 120) – to assume that *Amitié du Prince* was composed prior to, or at least simultaneously with, *Anabase*. Judged by its style alone, it would be difficult to imagine *Amitié* coming before *Anabase*. Monsieur Leger himself has assured the present writer that, as a matter of fact, *Amitié du Prince* was composed considerably later than *Anabase*.
3 The English words here attributed to Larbaud differ slightly from the version reported in the Mazars interview. (See note 7, below.) The biographical data in this and the three preceding paragraphs are taken largely from the Bosquet and Charpier works already referred to, supplemented by information generously furnished by Monsieur Leger himself.

4 Indeed, the original idea for the review seems to have been suggested by Leger. See Iris Origo, 'Marguerite Caetani' [i.e. Princess Bassiano] in *Atlantic*, February 1965, p. 82. This extremely informative article is rich in details about Leger's literary associates. Concerning his role in the actual editorial work of *Commerce*, there is this interesting statement: '. . . although his name was not permitted to appear, it was the taste and judgment of Alexis Léger that was the supreme court of appeal.'

5 The 'Lettre sur Jacques Rivière' which appeared in the April 1925 issue of *La Nouvelle Revue française*, is really the last publication before the long silence; but it is a prose piece, not poetry.

6 The 'pence pour Haendel', for example, is an oblique reference to Larbaud's great favourite, Samuel Butler. Butler had a passion for the music of Handel and wrote much about him. The 'pence' undoubtedly refer to a specific incident in Handel's life.

7 Lest the reader suspect that my English translation may be completely at fault, here is the original French text: '. . . *Anabase* a pour objet le poème de la solitude dans l'action. Aussi bien l'action parmi les hommes que l'action de l'esprit envers soi-même. J'ai voulu rassembler la synthèse non pas passive mais active de la ressource humaine. Mais on ne traite pas de thèmes psychologiques par des moyens abstraits. Il a fallu "illustrer": c'est le poème le plus chargé de concret; aussi on y a vu de l'orientalisme.' (*Le Figaro littéraire*, 5 novembre 1960.)

8 The few place-names that actually occur, and in a most incidental way, are all Asiatic (Jabal, Ilion, Saba), except for the indirect reference to Egyptian Thebes implied in the mention of the singing statue of Memnon.

9 Paul Morand, *Papiers d'identité* (Paris: Grasset, 1931), p. 165.

10 For detailed explication of the entire poem, see Knodel, 'Towards an Understanding of *Anabase*' in *PMLA* (June 1964), pp. 329-343. Much of the material in the present chapter is taken from that article.

11 'Hommage à la mémoire de Rabindranath Tagore' in *La Nouvelle Revue française* (octobre 1961), p. 868.

12 *Poétique de St.-John Perse* (Paris: Gallimard, 1954), p. 92.

13 Information in this paragraph was largely supplied by Monsieur Leger himself.

14 Quoted in André Gide, 'Don d'un arbre' in *op. cit.*, p. 26. See Chap. 1, note 2, of the present study.

15 See Chap. 1, p. 28.

16 In regard to Rilke: In a date-book of Adrienne Monnier's under 'Mai, 1940', one finds the following entries:

Mardi 14. – . . . Pour remercier Hoppenot, Benjamin va lui faire présent d'*Anabase*, l'édition originale que Rilke lui avait envoyée

tout près de mourir en lui demandant de traduire ce poème qu'il
n'avait plus le temps de traduire lui-même....
Jeudi 16. – . . . Vu l'*Anabase* de Benjamin. Porte en trois endroits
des essais de traduction écrits par Rilke au crayon.
(*Trois Agendas d'Adrienne Monnier*. Texte établi et annoté par
Maurice Saillet. Firmin Didot, 1960, hors commerce, p. 27.)
It should be recalled that Rilke died in 1926.

17 See note 2 above.

18 'A Letter from Saint-John Perse' in *The Berkeley Review* (Winter
1956), p. 41.

19 Quoted in MacLeish, 'A Note on Alexis Saint Léger Léger' in
Poetry: A Magazine of Verse (March 1942), p. 334.

20 See p. 39 of present chapter.

3

1 *La Nouvelle Revue française*, avril 1925, p. 455.

2 'Le Temps de la louange' in *Cahiers de la Pléiade*, été-automne 1950,
pp. 117-118.

3 See Alexis Léger, *A Selection of Works for an Understanding of World
Affairs since 1914* (Library of Congress, 1944). Select List of References, No. 1588.

4 *Loc. cit.*, note 2 above.

5 The Old World orioles (Oriolidae), which figure in Chinese bird-
paintings and which are noted for their song, are quite unrelated to
the New World 'orioles' (Icteridae).

   Perse, instead of using the familiar French name for the oriole,
namely, *loriot*, uses *oriole* throughout this poem – a form that may
be regarded either as a derivative from the scientific *Oriolus* or the
Old French *oriol*.

6 See Chap. 2, note 7.

7 Igor Stravinsky, explaining the use of Ciceronian Latin for the
libretto of his *Œdipus Rex*, uses this Persean formula to indicate
what he was after. See Stravinsky and Craft, *Dialogues and a Diary*
(New York: Doubleday & Co., 1963), p. 4.

8 Holograph letter accompanying manuscript and typescript of *Exil*.
Letter is dated '9 Sept. 1941'. Library of Congress Rare Book Collection PQ 2623.E386E9.

9 The whole passage beginning 'Sur des squelettes d'oiseaux nains',
and the day 'traversé d'un os vert comme un poisson des îles'.

10 It is interesting to note that this verse ('il n'est d'histoire que de
l'âme, il n'est d'aisance que de l'âme'.) is quoted by Dag Hammarskjöld in his journal, in the original French – a detail not mentioned

in the Sjöberg-Auden translation of that journal. The quotation is part of the entry dated April 28, 1957. See Dag Hammarskjöld *Vägmärken* (Stockholm: Albert Bonniers Förlag, 1963), p. 121.

11　See note 8 above.

12　Or even 'Gui-le-Queux'. See Jacques Hillairet *Connaissance du Vieux Paris* (Paris: Club Français du livre, 1959), p. 219.

13　Among the few things Leger says he remembers from visits to museums all over the world is, 'à Brême, une collection historique d'images irréelles pour fonds de boîtes à cigares'. ('Fragments d'une lettre privée de Saint-John Perse à Archibald MacLeish [1942]', *Cahiers de la Pléiade*, été-automne 1950, p. 155.)

14　The poet's route may be almost exactly retraced by anyone strolling through the northwest sections of Washington, D.C., with the text of the poem in hand. Across from Dumbarton Oaks is the School for the Blind, and a little further east are the gullies where cemeteries are enclosed by steel-rod fences, and nearby are a few of the finest old mansions in Washington. Compare 'ce haut quartier de Fondations d'aveugles, de Réservoirs mis au linceul et de vallons en cage pour les morts, . . . les grilles et les lawns et tous ces beaux jardins à l'italienne dont les maîtres un soir s'en furent épouvantés d'un parfum de sépulcre . . .'.

15　André Blanchet, S.J., 'Le Masque d'or de Saint-John Perse' in *La Littérature et le Spirituel III: Classiques d'hier et d'aujourd'hui* (Paris: Aubier, 1961), p. 176.

16　*Op. cit.*, p. 45.

17　'Léon-Paul Fargue, Poète' *La Nouvelle Revue française*, août 1963, p. 198.

18　Perse knew Eliot's poetry at least as early as 1925, for he contributed a not-too-accurate translation of part of Eliot's 'The Hollow Men' to the Summer 1924 issue of *Commerce*. Perse admires Eliot's poetry but regards Eliot's idiom as far removed from his own. This fact may account for the three successive revisions of Eliot's original translation of *Anabase*. Eliot, on the other hand, shows clear traces of Persean imagery in a number of his poems: see, for example, the 'Journey of the Magi'.

19　See 'Pour fêter une enfance', 'Eloge viii', 'Eloge xv', and *Exil* iv.

20　For detailed explication of *Neiges*, see A. J. Knodel, 'The Imagery of Saint-John Perse's *Neiges*', *PMLA*, March 1955, pp. 9-18.

21　'L'Officiant chaussé de feutre et ganté de soie grège', *Exil* iv, and also 'soies grèges de tribut' in *Chronique*, II.

22　This pushing of language to the verge of silence is certainly reminiscent of Mallarmé; and, in fact, there are Mallarméan overtones throughout *Neiges*. The whole evocation of the snowy heights of the fourth section reminds one of the snowscape of 'Le vierge, le vivace, et le bel aujourd'hui', although the respective contexts are very different. The 'pur délice sans graphie' seems to echo Mallarmé's 'pur délice sans chemin' of 'Autre Eventail', while the very last words of *Neiges*, 'Désormais cette page où plus rien ne s'inscrit', recalls 'le vide papier que la blancheur défend', of 'Brise marine'.

4

1 Quoted in MacLeish, *op. cit.*, p. 336.
2 Stravinsky and Craft, *op. cit.*, p. 196.
3 Letter to Octavio Barreda, dated October 6, 1949. Reproduced in facsimile in *Et Cætera* (enero-marzo 1961) four unnumbered pages between pp. 16 and 17 of printed text.
4 Saint-John Perse, 'La Thématique d'*Amers*' reproduced in appendix of *See-Marken* (*Amers*), translation into German by Friedhelm Kemp (Berlin: Hermann Luchterband Verlag, 1959), p. 246. Text originally published in the January 1959 issue of *Bonniers Litterära Magasin*.
5 *Poésie* (Paris: Gallimard, 1961), unpaginated [p. 3].
6 'A Note on Alexis Saint Léger Léger' in *Poetry: A Magazine of Verse* (March 1942), p. 33.
7 Mazars, *op. cit.* See Chap. 2, note 7.
8 *Poésie*, [p. 5].
9 'A Letter from Saint-John Perse' in *op. cit.*, p. 36. See Chap. 2, note 18.
10 Greek *rheos*: current, flow.
11 Fragment of a letter written in 1953 and quoted in Caillois, *op. cit.*, p. 181.
12 *Loc. cit.* See note 9 above.
13 *Œuvres complètes* (Bibliothèque de la Pléiade), p. 186.
14 See Chap. 1, pp. 26ff.
15 'Léon-Paul Fargue, Poète' in *La Nouvelle Revue française* (I [première partie] in août 1963; II [fin] in septembre 1963), p. 407.
16 *Poésie*, [p. 3].
17 See note 9 above.
18 *Loc. cit.*, note 16 above.
19 'Léon-Paul Fargue, Poète' in *op. cit.*, p. 407.
20 *Sous la Lampe* (Paris: Gallimard, 1937), pp. 58-59.
21 *Op. cit.* (See Chap. 1, note 9, of present work.)
22 *Anabasis / a poem by / St.-John Perse*, translated by T. S. Eliot (London: Faber & Faber, 1959). Quotation is from the 1930 'Preface', p. 11.
23 From an unpublished letter. See Chap. 3, note 8.
24 Cf. Chap. 3, p. 70.

25 'Face aux Lettres françaises / 1909' in *op. cit.*, p. 10. (See Chap. 1, note 4 of present work.)

26 'A Letter from Saint-John Perse' in *op. cit.*, p. 40.

27 *Ibid.*, pp. 36, 38.

28 *Ibid.*, p. 36.

29 Heraclitus, fragment 200 in G. S. Kirk and J. E. Raven, *The Presocratic Philosophers* (Cambridge Univ. Press, 1957), p. 189.

5

1 'Un Poème de Saint-John Perse: *Vents*' in *Les Cahiers de La Pléiade* (été-automne 1950), pp. 58-67. (First published in the *Revue de Paris*, novembre 1949.)

2 See Chap. 3, note 18.

3 The age-old and universal character of the winds is brought out in a number of references. These winds made themselves felt back in classical antiquity 'at the doors of the Curiae' ('Elles sifflaient aux portes des Curies.') – the Curiae being the staunch plebian family that was the very type of Roman republican virtue. But they blew around the world, overturning stone-gods and baptismal fonts, and even whole temples: 'under the jungle the Bayon' ('sous la jungle le Bayon') being a reference to the Bayon temple of Angkor-Thom in Cambodia. They also carry off a huge circus-tent pitched in the suburbs of some modern city – more than likely a reference to another specific happening.

4 Cf. Chap. 3, p. 75.

5 See Chap. 4, p. 86.

6 See Chap. 1, p. 23.

7 See Chap. 1, pp. 12, 13.

8 Cf. Chap. 4, p. 89.

9 In the Claudel article referred to in note 1, above, we find the following declaration: 'But God is a word that Saint-John Perse avoids – shall we say, religiously? And which he would, even were he promised an empire, not let escape from his lips', p. 67.

10 See Chap. 3, p. 78.

11 Elizabeth R. Cameron, 'Fighters for Lost Causes: Alexis Saint-Léger Léger', Chap. 12 of *The Diplomats / 1919-1939*, edited by Gordon A. Craig and Felix Gilbert (Princeton University Press, 1953), pp. 378-405.

12 See note 5 above.

13 This brief last canto of *Vents* was surreptitiously included in Gide's *Anthologie de la Poésie française*, in violation of the adopted principle of including no living poets in the collection. Gide circumvented

the principle by quoting these lines from *Vents* as the conclusion to his own introduction to the anthology.

6

1 *Op. cit.* in Chap. 4, note 4.
2 *Ibid.*
3 See Gilbert Norwood, *Greek Tragedy* (New York: Hill and Wang, [n.d.]). See especially Chapter II of Norwood's book.
4 *Op. cit.* in note 1, above.
5 Among others: Œdipus ('grands Acteurs aux yeux crêvés'), Medea ('Magiciennes trépignant sur leurs socques de bois'), Andromache ('grandes Veuves silencieuses sous des cendres illustres').
6 See Chap. 2, p. 44 and *passim*.
7 See Chap. 4, note 3.
8 *Op. cit.* in note 1, above.
9 Curiously, in the middle of this canto the figure of the hieratic tree, recalling the shamanistic tree of *Vents*, reappears. The sea is compared to a 'grand arbre d'expiation'.
10 Cras amet qui nunquam amavit, quique amavit cras amet. (Love tomorrow, you who have never loved; you who have loved, love also tomorrow.)
11 See quotation on p. 131 of present chapter.
12 *Ibid.*
13 See note 6, above.
14 *Op. cit.* in note 1, above.
15 Page 147.
16 *Op. cit.* in Chap. 4, pp. 45, 52.
17 *Op. cit.* in Chap. 2, note 18.
18 See Chap. 5, p. 121.
19 *Op. cit.* in note 1, above.

7

1 Passage reproduced in French on p. 8 of Hammarskjöld's translation of Saint-John Perse *Chronique: Krönika* (Stockholm: Alb. Bonniers, 1960). The passage is an extract from a letter dated '24 octobre 1959'.
2 R. P. Düss, *op. cit.*, pp. 240, 254.
3 See Chap. 4, note 4.
4 See Jacques Rivière / Alain Fournier, *Correspondance / 1905-1914* (Paris: Gallimard, 1926), tome II, p. 12, Rivière's letter dated '1er janvier 1907'.

5 *Loc. cit.*, Chap. 5, note 9.

6 See Chap. 5, p. 121.

7 Cf. *Amers*: 'et le plus clair de l'Etre mis à jour, comme au glissement du glaive hors de sa gaine de soie rouge' ('Chœur' 2). See
Chap. 6, p. 147.

8 All quotations in this paragraph are taken from longer quotations
that appear in the brochure published by the Bibliothèque Nationale
for the 'Exposition des Manuscrits et Eaux-Fortes / 17 décembre
1962 – 17 janvier 1963' under the title *L'Ordre des Oiseaux / Saint-
John Perse / Georges Braque*. Eight unnumbered pages, no author
indicated.

9 Perse, who is an excellent Latinist, justifies the variant he uses:
'Quantum non milvus oberret' – the more usual version has *errat*
instead of the subjunctive *oberret* – on the grounds that the Human-
ists of the French Renaissance, in whose texts he found his version,
are more reliable and had a surer instinct in these matters than subsequent Latinists. His version is found in Henri Estienne's *The-
saurus linguae latinae*.

10 See Chap. 2, p. 50.

11 See Charpier, *op. cit.*, p. 34.

12 Quoted in English in Stravinsky and Craft, *op. cit.*, p. 196.

13 See notes on Surah 105 in *The Qur'ān*, translated by Richard Bell
(Edinburgh: T. & T. Clark, 1939), Vol. II, p. 678.

14 See Charpier, *op. cit.*, p. 31.

15 'cette immensité de vivre et de créer dont s'est émue la plus grande
nuit de mai', inevitably makes one think of Alfred de Musset's 'Nuit
de Mai', where one reads that: 'le vin de la jeunesse / Fermente cette
nuit dans les veines de Dieu'.

16 *Op. cit.*, p. 200. See Chap. 4, note 15, of present work.

17 A very close friend of Leger in Washington has written: 'For a
man who has so much feeling for color in words he is not particularly interested in painting or the plastic arts as such.' (Katherine
Garrison Chapin, 'Saint-John Perse: An American View' in the
Washington, D.C. *Sunday Star*, February 26, 1961, p. B-3.)

18 Perse, in fact, is the author of a moving commemorative tribute to
Braque. See 'Pierre levée' in *Derrière le Miroir*, mai 1964, unpaginated.

8

1 Missing from the published poems are: a) the five poems in manuscript confiscated by the Gestapo (see 'Introduction', p. 5), b) those
portions of the original versions of the longer poems eliminated by

the poet himself (see Chap. 4, p. 103), c) the poems in progress or still to be written.

2 *Poésie*, [p. 4].

3 *Ibid.* (Perse actually wrote: 'elles ne font que muer', that is, 'they merely moult'.)

4 See above, Chap. 5, pp. 107, 127.

5 *Op. cit.* in Chap. 4, note 4.

6 Cf. *Chronique*, ii: 'Et ceci reste à dire: nous vivons d'outre-mort, et de mort même vivrons-nous'.

7 'Qu'est-ce que la littérature?' in *Situations*, II (Paris: Gallimard, 1948), p. 63.

8 For favourable Marxist criticism, see Roger Garaudy, *D'Un Réalisme sans Rivages: Picasso, Saint-John Perse, Kafka* (Paris: Plon, 1963), pp. 117-149.

9 *Poésie*, [p. 4].

10 'Message pour Valery Larbaud', *Cahiers de la Pléiade*, automne 1951-printemps 1952, p. 13.

11 Stravinsky and Craft, *op. cit.*, p. 196.

12 See Guillaume Hanoteau, 'Monsieur, vous avez le Nobel' in *Paris Match*, 5 novembre 1960, p. 102.

13 *Loc. cit.* in note 9 above.

14 'Réponse à une allocution américaine (1950)' in *Cahiers de la Pléiade*, automne 1951-printemps 1952, p. 157.

15 *Poésie*, [p. 5].

16 The insistence on a renewal of this confrontation by replacing man in a natural (i.e. non-mechanized) setting is undoubtedly one of the reasons why Perse is so admired by Black African authors writing in French. See the fervent tribute by Léopold Sédar Senghor, 'Saint-John Perse ou Poésie du royaume d'enfance', in *La Table ronde*, mai 1962, pp. 16-36.

17 *Amers*, I, 4. See above, Chap. 6, p. 135.

18 See 'Introduction', pp. 7, 8.

19 'A letter from Saint-John Perse' in *The Berkeley Review*, winter, 1956, pp. 39, 41. Cf. Chap. 4, p. 98.

20 I have already indicated how I feel that this is not really in contrast to English, but rather a situation common to all highly developed languages. See Chap. 4, pp. 99, 100.

21 'Preface' to the 1930 edition, reproduced in *Anabasis, a poem by St.-John Perse*, translated by T. S. Eliot (London: Faber and Faber, 1959), p. 10.

22 Alain Bosquet was, I feel, on the right track when he preceded the lengthier excerpts quoted in his Saint-John Perse volume by a series of such isolated images picked at random. Charpier used a similar device in 'Phrases' of his Perse compilation.

23 See above, Chap. 5, p. 114.

24 Concerning the misinterpretations of *Anabase*, see A. J. Knodel, 'Towards an Understanding of *Anabase*' in *PMLA* June, 1964, pp. 341-342.

    The painstakingly irrelevant 'mystical' interpretation of *Neiges* is developed at length in Cécile Koerber, 'Saint-John Perse: *Neiges*', in *The French Review*, October 1963, pp. 22-30.

25 Quoted from a personal letter in MacLeish, 'A Note on Alexis Saint Léger Léger', *op. cit.*, p. 335.

26 'Préface pour une traduction d'*Anabase*' in *La Nouvelle Revue française*, janvier 1926, p. 67. An English translation of this article is reproduced in the 1938, 1949, and 1959 editions of T. S. Eliot's translation of *Anabase*.

Bibliography

I. THE POETIC WORKS OF SAINT-JOHN PERSE[1]

Unless otherwise indicated, quotations from the poems are based on:
Saint-John Perse *Œuvre Poétique* I / Eloges. La Gloire des Rois /
Anabase. Exil / Edition revue et corrigée (Paris: Gallimard, 1960)
250 pp.

—— *Œuvre Poétique* II / Vents. Amers / Chronique / Edition revue
et corrigée (Paris: Gallimard, 1960) 359 pp.
These two volumes include all the published poetic texts by Perse to
date, with the exception of the one major and three small items noted
below. A meticulous bibliography of the original and all subsequent
printings of each poem is given in the 'Index Bibliographique' of this
edition (I, 237-244; II, 347-352). In addition, all translations of the
poems into various foreign languages, including English, are listed.
The poetic texts not included in the edition are:

1. *Oiseaux*. Saint-John Perse *Oiseaux* (Paris: Gallimard, 1963) 34 pp.
Quotations in the present study are taken from this edition.

This *méditation poétique* was first published in a limited *de luxe* edition,
with twelve original lithographs by Braque, by the art publishers, Au
Vent d'Arles, Paris, 1962, under the title: Georges Braque – Saint-
John Perse *L'Ordre des Oiseaux*, unpaginated. Perse's text was then

---

[1] An asterisk (*) before any listing indicates that the piece in question is
reproduced in *Honneur à Saint-John Perse*, an important compilation that appeared too late for inclusion in the present bibliography. See special note at
the end of the bibliography (pp. 202ff.) for a fuller description of *Honneur à
Saint-John Perse*.

published separately under the title 'Oiseaux' in *La Nouvelle Revue française*, décembre 1962, pp. 969-987.

2. Three 'fugitive' pieces:

(a) 'Des villes sur trois modes' in *Pan*: Revue libre paraissant tous les deux mois. (Montpellier) juillet-août 1908, pp. 189-191.

* (b) 'Poème' (Pour M. Valery Larbaud) in *Intentions*, novembre 1922, pp. 52-53. Reproduced in the special Saint-John Perse number of *Les Cahiers de la Pléiade*, été-automne 1950, pp. 153-154.

(c) An untitled text bearing the epigraph 'Aumône aux hommes de peu de poids' in *Commerce*, hiver 1924, unpaginated. This is a French translation of the opening section of T. S. Eliot's 'The Hollow Men'. The English original, without title, but bearing the epigraph 'A Penny for the Old Guy', and dated 'Nov. 1924', is printed opposite the French text, which is signed, '(Adaptation de St.-J. P.)'.

II. PROSE TEXTS BY SAINT-JOHN PERSE

The published prose pieces are in the main tributes to various literary people but also comprise a few personal letters – usually fragmentary, a few speeches, a few 'diplomatic' texts, and miscellaneous pieces. All the items are here listed together chronologically, by date of publication, except where a specific date of composition is available, in which case the item is listed under that date.

1925

'Lettre sur Jacques Rivière' in *La Nouvelle Revue française*, avril 1925, pp. 455-462. Signed 'A. Saint-Léger Léger'.

1930

*'Mémorandum sur l'organisation d'un régime d'union fédérale européenne par Alexis Léger' dated 'Paris, le 1er mai 1930'. First published in *Les Cahiers de la Pléiade*, été-automne 1950, pp. 166-177.

1942

*'Fragments d'une lettre privée de Saint-John Perse à Archibald MacLeish (1942)' in *Les Cahiers de la Pléiade*, été-automne 1950, pp. 155-156. This text first appeared in English translation on pp. 334-336 of *Poetry: A Magazine of Verse*, March 1942, where it forms part of MacLeish's 'A Note on Alexis Saint Léger Léger'.

*'Briand' dated '28 mars 1942'. Speech delivered at New York University. First published in brochure *Briand* par Alexis Léger (Aurora, New York: Wells College Press, 1943) 20 pp. Reproduced in *Les Cahiers de la Pléiade*, été-automne 1950, pp. 158-165.

1944
Alexis Leger, *A Selection of Works for an Understanding of World Affairs since 1914* (Washington, D.C.: Library of Congress, 1944) Select List of References No. 1588. 87 pp.

1949
Personal letter to Octavio Barreda, dated '6 novembre 1949', unpaginated facsimile reproduction in *Et Cætera*, enero-marzo 1961, four pages inserted between pp. 16 & 17 of printed text. This letter is included as an 'illustration' to a Spanish translation of *Anabase* by by Octavio Barreda, with introductory notes.

1950
*'Réponse à une allocution américaine (1950)' in *Les Cahiers de la Pléiade*, été-automne 1950, p. 157. Text of acceptance speech upon receipt of the American Academy of Arts and Letters' Award of Merit Medal.

1951
'Face aux lettres françaises / 1909' in *La Nouvelle Revue française*, mai 1951, pp. 75-86. This text is a tribute to André Gide, to whom the whole issue of the N.R.F. is devoted. An English translation by Mina Curtiss entitled 'André Gide: 1909' appeared in *The Sewanee Review*, Autumn 1952, pp. 593-604.
'Message pour Valery Larbaud' dated 'Boston, 10 août 1951' in *Les Cahiers de la Pléiade*, automne 1951-printemps 1952, pp. 11-14.

1953
*Fragment of a personal letter to Roger Caillois, dated '26 janvier 1953' published in an appendix to Roger Caillois *Poétique de St.-John Perse* (Paris: Gallimard, 1954), pp. 180-181.
'Poète, Schehadé' dated 'Washington, décembre 1953' in *Le Petit Théâtre, Cahiers de la Compagnie Madeleine Renaud—Jean-Louis Barrault*, 2e année, 4e cahier, 1954, p. 23.

1955
'Silence pour Claudel' dated 'Mer Caraïbe au large de Saba, 4 mars 1955', in *La Nouvelle Revue française*, septembre 1955, pp. 387-391.

1956
'Pour Adrienne Monnier' in *Le Mercure de France*, janvier 1956, pp. 11, 12. Reproduced in Adrienne Monnier *Rue de l'Odéon* (Paris: Albin Michel, 1960), pp. 9-10.
*'Une lettre de Saint-John Perse' to George Huppert, dated 'Tenant's Harbor, Maine, 10 août 1956' in *The Berkeley Review*, Winter 1956, pp. 34, 36, 38, 40. English translation by A. J. Knodel on facing pages 35, 37, 39, 41. Reproduced under the title 'Une lettre de Saint-

John Perse sur l'expression poétique française' in *Livres de France*, janvier 1959, pp. 7, 8.

1957

'Larbaud ou l'honneur littéraire' in *La Nouvelle Revue française*, septembre 1957, pp. 387-400. Reproduced in separate plaquette *Valery Larbaud; ou l'Honneur littéraire* (Liège: Editions Dynamo, 1962) 20 pp. Collection 'Brimborions', No. 95.

1958

'Message pour Giuseppe Ungaretti' dated 'Washington, 10 février 1958', in Ungaretti *Il Taccuino del vecchio*, con testimonianze di amici stranieri del poeta raccolte a cura di Leone Piccioni e uno scritto introduttivo di Jean Paulhan (Milano: Mondadori, 1960) p. 103.

1959

*'La Thématique d'*Amers*' in *Bonniers Litterära Magasin* ('BLM'), January 1959, pp. 26 and 28. Swedish translation by Erik Lindegren on facing pages. Reproduced as 'Les Thèmes d'*Amers*' in *La Nouvelle Revue française*, avril 1959, pp. 734-736.

**Poésie | Allocution au Banquet Nobel du 10 décembre 1960* (Paris: Gallimard, 1961) unpaginated (text covers five pages). Nobel Acceptance speech that was printed previously in several reviews and newspapers including *Cahiers du Sud*, décembre 1960 – janvier 1961, pp. 375-380 and *La Nouvelle Revue française*, janvier 1961, pp. 79-84. English translation: St.-John Perse *On Poetry | Speech of Acceptance upon the Award of the Nobel Prize for Literature | Delivered in Stockholm | December 10, 1960 | Translated by W. H. Auden | with the French Text* (New York: Bollingen Foundation, 1961) 23 pp. English text, pp. 7-12, followed by French text, pp. 13-18. This brochure contains a concise bibliography of 'Works of St.-John Perse published, with English translations, in the United States of America' on pp. 19-22.

1961

'Hommage à la Mémoire de Rabindranath Tagore' in *La Nouvelle Revue française*, octobre 1961, pp. 868-871.

1962

Fragments of letters written in 1962 concerning the publication of *Oiseaux*. Quoted in the unpaginated eight-page brochure of the *Oiseaux* exhibit at the Bibliothèque Nationale entitled 'L'Ordre des Oiseaux | Saint-John Perse | Georges Braque | Exposition des Manuscrits et eaux-fortes, 17 décembre 1962 – 17 janvier 1963'.

1963

'Léon-Paul Fargue, Poète' in *La Nouvelle Revue française*, août 1963, pp. 197-210, septembre 1963, pp. 406-422. Reproduced as a preface,

under the same title, to Léon-Paul Fargue *Poésies* (Paris: Gallimard, 1963), pp. 7-31.
'A Ceux des "Cahiers du Sud" ' dated 'septembre 1963' in *Cahiers du Sud*, Sept.-Oct.-Nov. 1963, pp. 3-5. Tribute written for the fiftieth anniversary of *Cahiers du Sud*.
'Grandeur de Kennedy' in *Le Monde*, 20 novembre 1963. Tribute to President John F. Kennedy. English translation, unsigned, appears in *A Tribute to John F. Kennedy* Edited by Pierre Salinger and Sander Vanocur (Chicago: Encyclopaedia Britannica, Inc., 1964) pp. 78-79.

1964
'Sacre d'un deuil' in *Vogue*, February 1964, pp. 144-145. Tribute to Mrs Jacqueline Kennedy.
'Pierre levée' in *Derrière le Miroir*, mai 1964, two pages, unnumbered. Contribution to a special 'Hommages à Georges Braque' issue.

III. ENGLISH TRANSLATIONS OF THE POETRY OF SAINT-JOHN PERSE

All the poems included in the two volumes of the 1960 *Œuvre poétique*, as well as *Oiseaux*, have been translated into English and published along with the original French text. Listings follow the chronological order of composition of the original poems, so far as that is possible.

ELOGES ET AL.
*Eloges / and other poems / By St.-John Perse / The French text with English translation by Louise Varèse / and an introduction by Archibald MacLeish (New York: W. W. Norton, 1944) 179 pp. Includes 'Ecrit sur la porte' (I), 'Pour fêter une enfance', 'Eloges', 'La Gloire des Rois', 'Images à Crusoé' and 'Ecrit sur la porte' (II) in the order indicated. French and English *en regard*.
*Eloges / and other poems / St.-John Perse / Bilingual edition / translation by / Louise Varèse (New York: Pantheon Books, 1956) 103 pp. Bollingen Series LV. A revision of the 1944 Norton edition, with one additional poem: 'Berceuse' ('Lullaby'). French and English *en regard*.

ANABASE
*Anabasis / a poem by / St.-J. Perse / with a / translation into English / by / T. S. Eliot (London: Faber and Faber, 1930) 75 pp. Preface by T. S. Eliot, pp. 7-11. French and English *en regard*.
*Anabasis / A poem by St.-J. Perse / with a translation into English by / T. S. Eliot (New York: Harcourt, Brace and Co., 1938) 75 pp. Reproduces 1930 edition, with minor revision. Preface by T. S. Eliot reproduced. French and English *en regard*.

Anabasis | A poem by St.-John Perse | translated by T. S. Eliot (New York: Harcourt, Brace and Co., 1949) 109 pp. Considerably revis version of 1938 text. Preface by T. S. Eliot reproduced. French and English *en regard*, followed by a Bibliography and the English translations of three Prefaces, by Valery Larbaud, Hugo von Hofmannsthal, and Giuseppe Ungaretti, respectively.

Anabasis | a poem by | St.-John Perse | translated by | T. S. Eliot (London: Faber and Faber, 1959) 96 pp. Radically revised translation. Preface by T. S. Eliot reproduced. French and English *en regard*, followed by a Bibliography, the Prefaces by Larbaud, von Hofmannsthal, and Ungaretti, plus an English translation of the 1924 review of *Anabase* by Lucien Fabre.

The following note is printed separately on p. 15, preceding the poem itself: 'The alterations to the English text of this edition have been made by the author himself, and tend to make the translation more literal than in previous editions. (signed) T. S. Eliot, 1958'.

EXIL, POÈME À L'ÉTRANGÈRE, PLUIES, NEIGES

Exile | *and other poems* | by | St.-John Perse | Bilingual edition | Translation by Denis Devlin (New York: Pantheon Books, The Bollingen Series XV, 1949) 166 pp. French text of *Exil, Poème à l'Etrangère, Pluies, Neiges* pp. 9-74, English on pp. 75-140, followed by the note of Archibald MacLeish and English translations of notes by Roger Caillois, Alain Bosquet, and a Bibliography.

Second edition published in 1953, with French and English texts of poem *en regard*, without notes and in smaller format. 93 pp.

VENTS

Winds | by | St.-John Perse | Bilingual Edition | Translation by | Hugh Chisholm (New York: Pantheon Books, The Bollingen Series XXXIV, 1953) 252 pp. French text pp. 13-113, followed by English text pp. 119-220, followed by English translation of four articles by Paul Claudel, Gaëtan Picon, Albert Béguin, Gabriel Bounoure, respectively, and a Bibliography.

Second edition published in 1961, with French and English texts of poem *en regard*, without the four additional articles and in a smaller format. 193 pp.

AMERS

Seamarks | by | St.-John Perse | Bilingual edition | Translation by | Wallace Fowlie (New York: Pantheon Books, 1958) 363 pp. The Bollingen Series LXVII. French text pp. 13-180, followed by English text pp. 187-356, and a Bibliography.

Second edition published in 1958, with French and English texts *en regard*, smaller format. 239 pp.

Seamarks | St.-John Perse | Bilingual edition | Translation by | Wallace

Fowlie (New York: Harper & Brothers, Harper Torchbooks / The Bollingen Library, 1961) 240 pp. French and English texts *en regard*, followed by Bibliographical Note. Paperback.

CHRONIQUE

Chronique / by / St.-John Perse / Translation by / Robert Fitzgerald / Bilingual edition (New York: Pantheon Books, The Bollingen Series LXIX, 1961) 60 pp. French and English texts *en regard*, followed by a Bibliography.

OISEAUX

'Birds' in *Portfolio*, no. 7, winter 1963, pp. 24-31, 117-120. Translation by Wallace Fowlie. French and English texts in parallel columns, preceded by brief introductory note and interspersed with reproductions of four of Braque's lithographs.

IV. BOOKS ABOUT SAINT-JOHN PERSE

Only the books entirely devoted to the work of Saint-John Perse are listed. Separate essays in books and periodicals are already too numerous for detailed listing here. A fair sampling of such items, up to 1962, is given in the Charpier book listed below. For essays and articles published since 1962, consult the 'French VIII: Twentieth Century' section (listings under 'Perse') of the 'MLA International Bibliography' published yearly in the May issue of *PMLA* (Publications of the Modern Language Association of America).

Alain BOSQUET *Saint-John Perse* / Présentation par Alain Bosquet / Choix de textes, bibliographie, dessins, portraits, fac-similés (Paris: Pierre Seghers, 1956) 197 pp. Series 'Poètes d'aujourd'hui' no. 35.

——Les Cahiers de la Pléiade, x, été-automne 1950, 188 pp. Issue entirely devoted to Saint-John Perse, including short tributes and articles by the following writers: André Gide, T. S. Eliot, Léon-Paul Fargue, Herbert Steiner, René Char, Jules Supervielle, Jorge Guillen, Georges Schehadé, J. G. Cruchaga, Valery Larbaud, Blaise Allan, Pierre Jean Jouve, Paul Claudel, André Breton, Gaëtan Picon, A. Rolland de Renéville, Albert Béguin, G. Ungaretti, Denis Devlin, Jorge Zalamea, Roger Caillois, Gabriel Bounoure, M. J. Lefebvre, A. MacLeish, Stephen Spender, Renato Poggioli, L.-M. Raymond, Friedhelm Kemp, Denis de Rougemont, Max-Pol Fouchet, Allen Tate.

Roger CAILLOIS *Poétique de St.-John Perse* (Paris: Gallimard, 1954) 212 pp.

Jacques CHARPIER *Saint-John Perse* (Paris: Gallimard, 1962) 299 pp. Series 'La Bibliothèque Idéale'.

Pierre GUERRE *Saint-John Perse et l'Homme* (Paris: Gallimard, 1955) 92 pp.

Albert HENRY *'Amers' de Saint-John Perse / Une Poésie du Mouvement* (Neuchâtel: Editions de la Baconnière, 1963) 181 pp. Series 'Langages'.

Albert LORANQUIN *Saint-John Perse* (Paris: Gallimard, 1963) 203 pp.

Christian MURCIAUX *Saint-John Perse* (Paris: Editions universitaires, 1960) 129 pp. Series 'Classiques du XXᵉ Siècle'.

Maurice SAILLET *Saint-John Perse, Poète de Gloire*, suivi d'un essai de biographie d'Alexis Léger (Paris: Mercure de France, 1952) 190 pp.

Charpier's *Saint-John Perse* is a very handy compilation, including a detailed biographical chronology (pp. 23-58, 'Les Jours') and an extensive bibliography (pp. 261-292, 'Documents'). 'Documents', in fact, includes, besides a 'Bibliographie', an 'Iconographie', 'Musicographie', 'Cinématographie', 'Phonographie', and 'Discographie'. Charpier's listing of secondary materials is useful but does not pretend to be complete. Some of the more interesting items he has omitted are cited in notes to the present study.

Perse, usually under the name 'Léger', figures incidentally in a number of novels including Proust's *A la Recherche du Temps perdu*, Louis Chadourne's *Le Maître du navire*, Romains's *Les Hommes de bonne volonté*, Aragon's *Les Communistes*, Sartre's *Le Sursis*, several novels by Roger Peyrefitte, and a number of others. Finally, almost every book concerning the history of Western Europe during the years 1930-40 mentions, and frequently discusses at length, the role of Alexis Leger.

Special Note on *Honneur à Saint-John Perse*

This omnibus work would logically have had to be included in all four categories of the preceding bibliography. The full reference is:

Honneur à Saint-John Perse / Hommages et Témoignages littéraires / suivis / d'une documentation / sur Alexis Leger / diplomate (Paris: Gallimard, 1965) 817 pp.

The collection is introduced by Jean Paulhan (pp. 7, 8) and divided into five parts, as follows:

I.   Hommages collectifs (pp. 11-377)
II.   Témoignages individuels (pp. 383-628)
III. Témoignages officiels (pp. 631-647)
IV.   Textes et documents (pp. 651-667)
[V.] Annexe: Alexis Leger diplomate (pp. 675-807)

It will be noted that parts I and II together fill over six hundred pages and constitute, thus, the most extensive collection of articles about Saint-John Perse ever published. All texts are in French, the numerous articles by foreign critics having been translated especially for this collection. Parts III and IV and the 'Annexe' contain reproductions of many of the pieces listed above in Section II: 'Prose texts by Saint-John Perse', but they also include over a dozen hitherto unpublished items, some of very great interest. These 'new' items are here listed chronologically, in keeping with the arrangement of Section II of the preceding bibliography.

1917
'Une lettre privée d'Alexis Leger à son Ministre en Chine, Alexandre Conty'. Dated 'Pékin, juillet 1917', pp. 687-690. A highly humorous account of the transporting of the wife, concubines, and children of deposed Chinese president Li Yuan Hong to the French Legation.

1927
'Discours aux représentants de trente-sept parlements nationaux', pp. 753-758. Speech written for Aristide Briand by Alexis Leger and delivered by Briand before the Congrès de l'Union Interparlementaire in Paris on April 27, 1927.

1928
'Discours pour la signature du Pacte Briand-Kellogg', pp. 695-697. Presentation speech delivered in Paris on April 27, 1928 by Aristide Briand, written for him by Alexis Leger.

1935
'Une enquête sur l'optimisme', p. 783. Brief reply to a journalist of the Paris daily, *Excelsior*, on Feb. 27, 1935.

1940
'Lettre au Président Edouard Herriot'. Dated 'Arcachon, 28 mai 1940', pp. 713-714. Important letter explaining circumstances of Leger's dismissal by Paul Reynaud from the post of Secrétaire Général des Affaires Etrangères.

1942
'Réponse d'Alexis Leger au Général de Gaulle'. Dated 'Washington, 25 mai 1942', pp. 727-728. Reply to a letter from de Gaulle dated 'Londres, le 18 mai 1942.'
'Réponse de M. Alexis Leger'. Dated '26 juillet 1942', p. 729. Reply to a telegram from Winston Churchill which had been transmitted through the British Embassy in Washington on June 17, 1942.

1943
'Lettre au Président Roosevelt'. Dated 'Washington, 3 nov. 1943', p. 730.

1945
'Lettre à Léon Blum'. Dated 'Washington, 28 sept. 1945', p. 731.

1948
'Extrait d'une lettre à Max-Pol Fouchet (1948)'', p. 654. Brief fragment.

1951
'Réponse de Saint-John Perse', personal letter to Francis de Mio-
    mandre, dated '7 juin 1951', pp. 636-637. Letter declining candidacy
    for membership in the Académie Mallarmé.

1955
'Réponse à un historien allemand'. Dated 'Washington, 15 sept. 1955'
    pp. 725-726. Letter to Dr. Klaus-Jürgen Müller concerning Leger's
    conduct in London during the month of June, 1940.

1959
'Réponse de Saint-John Perse', a brief acceptance speech delivered in
    Paris on November 9, 1959, p. 640. Reply to the presentation of the
    Grand Prix National des Lettres to Leger by André Malraux.
    Previously published in part in the Parisian daily press.

1960
'Lettre à M. Pierre Béarn'. Dated '9 octobre 1960', p. 667. Brief note
    refusing title of 'Prince des Poètes'.

All but four of the pieces listed above are found in the 'Annexe' of
Honneur à Saint-John Perse. The 'Annexe' is, in many ways, the most
fascinating portion of the book, for, besides the letters and speeches
by Leger himself, the letters *to* him are also included, along with other
relevant explanatory materials.

Finally, there is one 'new' poetic text in *Honneur à Saint-John Perse*:
a quatrain that is an adaptation by Saint-John Perse of a Japanese text
included in a Zen painting of the seventeenth century. A photograph
of the painting and of Perse's handwritten text, along with a printed
transcription of the text, is found on the page facing p. 807. The text
is undated.

Vents (cont.)
  Section III, 116-20
  Section IV, 120-6
  Shaman, 107-8, 109, 114-15, 120
  shamanistic tree, 107, 127, 191
  theme of, 105-6, 134, 170, 174
  theme of poetic creation, 84, 90
  the sea in, 131
  tone of, 128-9
  vocabulary of, 23
  writing of, 15, 124
Verlaine, Paul, 101
Verne, Jules, *Michael Strogoff*, 73
verse forms, 17-18
Veuillot, Louis, 14
Vigny, Alfred de, 101
vocabulary
  difficulties of translating, 7
  flamboyance of, 20
  of *Amitié*, 56-8

vocabulary *(cont.)*
  of *Exil*, 81
  of *Vents*, 23
  revolution of, in French poetry, 93
  sureness of, 18
  use of foreign words, 81
  use of scientific and technical terms, 12-13, 21, 176-8, 180
  use of words, 115-16
  width of, 12-13, 23-4, 168, 176-8
votive poems, 62, 105, 130-67, 169

Washington D.C., 37, 71, 72, 73, 74, 75, 136-7, 188
Webster's Dictionary, 13
Whitman, Walt, 46
Wright, Wilbur, 164